Through the Eye of the Needle

Through the Eye of the Needle:
Immigrants and Enterprise
in New York's Garment Trades

Roger D. Waldinger

New York University Press
New York *and* London
1986

Burgess

HD
9940
.U5
N78
1986
c.3

Library of Congress Cataloging-in-Publication Data

Waldinger, Roger David.
  Through the eye of the needle.

  Bibliography: p.
  Includes index.
  1. Clothing trade—New York (N.Y.) 2. Clothing
workers—New York (N.Y.) 3. New York (N.Y.)—Emigration
and immigration. I. Title.
HD9940.U5N78 1986   331.6′2′097471   86-12451
ISBN 0-8147-9212-X

Copyright © 1986 by New York University
All rights reserved
Manufactured in the United States of America

Book design by Ken Venezio

For Hilary

RSH 119721 PKi 8019724

Contents

Preface

This book is a completely revised version of my doctoral dissertation. I have chosen to treat the dissertation as an exercise in hypothesis formulation and to use this book as an occasion to elaborate those initial hypotheses and then subject them to a more rigorous assessment with new data. Chapters 1–4 and Chapter 6 draw on the dissertation, although they contain much new material, and the presentation and many of the ideas have been extensively reworked. Chapters 5, 7, and 8 are entirely new and are based upon the data collected expressly for this book. Chapter 9, also new, sums up and reviews the argument developed in the book.

Any book as long in the writing as this one normally accumulates manifold obligations. In my case, the debts to those who have provided me with support are particularly great. This book owes its inception to Michael Piore, and it is he whom I would like to thank first. Michael first suggested that I explore the issues pursued here, helped to get funding, and constantly encouraged me to see the project through. Michael's research has also been a source of great insight; I hope that some of what I learned from him is reflected in the pages that follow.

I am also grateful to faculty, friends, and colleagues who read my work and heard out my arguments. My graduate advisors, Lee Rainwater and Orlando Patterson, were helpful and encouraging throughout. Emmanuel Tobier gave freely of his time, interest, and expert knowledge of the economic development of New York. He carefully read several chapters, and they greatly benefited from his critical remarks. Peter Doeringer's careful reading of a proposal was also of great benefit in formulating the research problem; he was also helpful in obtaining funding, for which I remain most grateful. Lisa Peattie encouraged me at a crucial stage to take the idea of small-scale enterprise seriously; her continuing interest in this research has been much valued. I also wish to thank my colleagues in the Department of

Sociology at the City College of New York and, in particular, my chairman, William Helmreich, for providing a congenial and stimulating environment. My friend Tom Bailey deserves particular mention, and I am especially indebted to him. Tom has shared freely of his own closely related research, which has been a source of considerable insight. My thinking on the subject owes much to his thoughtful reactions to my ideas and to the interest stirred by our many exchanges.

Assistance from my many friends and asssociates in the field has also been of inestimable importance. Jay Mazur, General Secretary-Treasurer of the International Ladies' Garment Workers' Union (ILGWU), an unusual and gifted trade union leader, showed a constant interest in this research and graciously made many of the union's resources available to me. Walter Mankoff, Associate Director of the ILGWU's Research Department, helped instruct me in various aspects of international trade in clothing and also provided much valuable statistical material. My friend Muzaffar Chishti, Research Director of Local 23–25, ILGWU, has been a source of support and wise counsel since the day this research began. Of course, none of the above-mentioned are responsible for the conclusions drawn in this book; nor do my findings reflect their views.

There would be no conclusions to draw, however, had I not succeeded in finding people willing to answer my many, often inconvenient, and sometimes inexplicable questions. Looking back, I find it difficult to believe that so many people—workers, factory owners, union officers, government officials—were willing to give so freely of their time. I am deeply grateful to them all.

Financial assistance has been most helpful as well. A small summer grant from the Sloan Foundation to Michael Piore got this research going longer ago than I care to remember. As a graduate student, I was the beneficiary of generous assistance from the Employment and Training Administration of the U.S. Department of Labor, from the Joint Center for Urban Studies of MIT and Harvard University, and from the International Labor Organization's Program in International Labor Studies. The Joint Center for Urban Studies also provided a congenial and pleasant home during much of the dissertation-writing stage, and I would like to express my appreciation to the Joint Center's staff and directors for their help. A grant from the City University Research Foundation made it possible to undertake the new research on which this book is based. In a time of diminishing financial assistance for social science research I feel very fortunate to have been supported so well. The responsibility for the conclusions reported here, again, is all mine.

Thanks are also due to the research assistants who helped at various stages. Narciso Cruz, Rene Eng, Stephen Finegold, Sandy Kark, Victor Mui, Daniel Paulino, and Helen Wong conducted many of the interviews with factory owners, activities that went quite beyond the usual confines of normal research assistantship. Tony Bernard programmed the tabulations from the 1970 and 1980 censuses of population. Stephen Finegold also scrounged through government documents and union records, put tables together, and hunted down books; I am particularly grateful for his efficiency and the interest that he took in the project.

In a sense, this study is testimony to the strength and depth of my parents' own scholarly bent. Their example set me along this track very early on and has been a source of continuing inspiration. Of course, their support and encouragement have been essential. Much the same could be said for my grandmother, who also took good care of me when I was shuttling between Cambridge and New York.

This project would never have seen the light of day without my wife, Hilary. Hilary expressed unswerving confidence, urged me on when my spirits flagged, tolerated my interminable succession of drafts and revisions, and finally took on the arduous and unenviable task of editing the final manuscript. I hope that she will take this book as my best, if barely adequate form of thanks. In any case, I'll gladly give it to her with love.

Through the Eye of the Needle

[1]

Introduction

Over the past twenty-five years, the industrial societies of the West have again gained a large immigrant population. Though not always welcomed, the immigrants came because they were needed, sought after as replacements for native workers lifted out of menial jobs by economic growth or newly upgraded skills. Just where the labor market absorbed immigrants varied from country to country: in France and Germany, metal manufacturing and construction took on the bulk of the foreign arrivals; in Britain, the newcomers were more likely to work in textiles and engineering; in the United States, immigrants mainly gravitated into light manufacturing or services, apart from the borderlands, where agriculture still attracted a large migrant flow. Regardless of these industrial variations, there was much that the new immigrants held in common: their jobs were generally low in status; their work was poorly paid; and few had the skills, schooling, or linguistic facility that would allow them to assimilate into the native working class. Thus, whether a construction worker in Paris or a foundryman in Birmingham, a waiter in New York, or a coal miner in the Ruhr, the immigrant's prospects for advancement were poor. In all likelihood, what the newcomer landed was a job that promised no chance of ever becoming a career, a dead-end mobility trap with no outlet into the paths that natives used in the race to get ahead.[1]

Such was the scenario in the heyday of economic growth more than a decade ago. Since then the western economies have run into hard times, which seem to presage further trouble for the immigrants. The root of the problem is that the new immigrants have been hit with a double whammy. They are heavily overrepresented in those industries most affected by economic stagnation, shrinking markets, and international competition; at the same time, they are largely shut out of sectors, such as high technology manufacturing and advanced business services, that have been the main

source of recent economic growth. Moreover, the restructuring of the western economies appears to be widening the mismatch between job requirements and the immigrants' skills: the dynamic industries demand technical proficiency and emphasize interpersonal communication—precisely those qualities that most immigrants lack.

But before declaring immigrants a new underclass, it is important to note that there is something new under the sun. Not that immigrants are moving into large corporations, with their structured mobility ladders, promise of stable employment, and standards of high pay. Rather, immigrants are setting up businesses of their own. Of course, like other small business owners, immigrant capitalists are prone to failure. Yet a sizable percentage of those who start out on their own succeed; that success seems to motivate others; thus, there is a burgeoning ethnic economy, strong enough to give native business owners a run for their money.

The capital of new immigrant enterprise in the United States is probably Miami, owing to the success of the Cubans, who started arriving there as refugees in the late 1950s and have since built up a flourishing economy of Cuban-owned businesses that includes more than 150 manufacturing firms, 230 restaurants, 30 furniture factories, a shoe factory employing 3,000 people, and 30 transplanted cigar factories.[2] While the Cubans can boast of their success, it is also the case that many began with the advantages of transplanted capital and ample technical expertise; what is more impressive, perhaps, is that other immigrants, less favored with either resource, have encountered considerable business success. In Los Angeles almost one third of the Korean adult population is self-employed; Jewish refugees from Russia have made steep inroads into the taxi business; and newcomers from India are a growing presence in the import-export trade.[3] In New York City, once again a mecca for immigrants, Koreans have virtually taken over the retail produce business, much to the consternation of the native-owned supermarkets with which they compete. In addition to the 950 or so Korean-owned greengroceries, Koreans operate some 1,000 dry-cleaning establishments and roughly 350 fish retail stores, not to speak of the many businesses specializing in Korean-American trade. Greek, Chinese, and other newcomers are so heavily involved in the restaurant business that over 60 percent of the city's eating places are immigrant-owned. Indians and Pakistanis dominate the city's newsstand business, with an estimated 70 percent of New York's 5,000 kiosks under their control.[4] Elsewhere in the nation signs of immigrant businesses abound, as evidenced by the nation-

wide proliferation of Indian-owned motels (even in states like Georgia, traditionally considered inhospitable to new immigrants); the success of Vietnamese shrimpers on Texas' Gulf Coast; and the burgeoning of small, Arab-owned retail outlets in San Francisco, Detroit, Toledo, and Chicago, to cite just a few examples.[5]

No less than the United States, the immigrant-receiving countries of Europe have seen a similar mushrooming of immigrant-owned firms. Chinese immigrants in Manchester, for example, now dominate the traditional fish-and-chips trade, having driven native English owners out of business. Indian and Pakistani storekeepers in London have taken over the shops abandoned by small retailers who could no longer withstand competition from much larger chains. In Amsterdam, Surinamese immigrants started out in business selling tropical products to other immigrants but have since branched out into travel agencies, restaurants, driving schools, and even video shops.[6]

Wherever they have settled, immigrant entrepreneurs have consistently gravitated into the clothing trade. In Holland, Turks have reintroduced garment manufacture to Amsterdam. In Britain, Cypriots and Asians have revived London's dying East End clothing trade, while Pakistanis and Indians have given birth to a burgeoning clothing trade in the depressed West Midlands, where clothing production had never previously existed. Chinese-owned garment firms have proliferated in both San Francisco and Los Angeles; in the latter case, 350 Korean-owned garment firms have joined the competition. In Miami the Cubans have principally contributed to an expanding garment industry and, according to industry sources, virtually all the smaller garment firms are Cuban-owned.[7] But the greatest flourishing of the immigrant garment industry has taken place in New York City, where nearly all new garment factories are established by immigrant entrepreneurs. In New York's Chinatown the number of Chinese firms grew from 30 in 1965 to 480 in early 1985, with increasing spillover to newer Chinese neighborhoods. By 1985, 20,000 Chinese workers—more than one sixth of the city's entire apparel labor force—were employed in Chinese-owned concerns. Though the evidence for other groups is more fragmentary, Greeks, Koreans, and especially Hispanics have clearly penetrated into entrepreneurial positions in large numbers.

This book is a study of New York's latest immigrant garment capitalists, the businesses they have founded, and the industrial environment in which they have grown up. The garment industry is the paradigmatic case of

immigrant enterprise. Where else if not in clothing—an industry that is risk-laden, supportive of small concerns, and still dependent on traditional sewing skills—will immigrants find business success? But if the basic conditions of business success in this industry apply to the other fields in which immigrant entrepreneurs are active, then so do the questions raised by the growth of immigrant garment capitalists. In the first place, the independent small business owner has long been in decline; and if ours is a world where most organizations are bigger, and bigger usually means better, whence do the opportunities for small firms, such as those that immigrants run, arise? Perhaps there are inherent limits to the techniques of mass production and distribution; and therefore small immigrant firms will thrive in those parts of the economic world where these methods do not apply. But even if we assume that opportunities for petty enterprise do exist and that the prevailing wisdom about the inevitable disappearance of small business is incorrect, why is it that immigrants—and not natives—exploit these opportunities for petty proprietorships? And how is it that newcomers to American society find themselves overrepresented in business positions? One possibility is that immigrants succeed because they are disciplined, while others have grown soft; hardworking, while others seek leisure; willing to take risks, while others look for security. Indeed that image of the immigrant—independent, self-sufficient, sacrificing, justly rewarded—is already enshrined in American culture. But, lest we forget, the immigrant business has also been home to the sweatshop. In 1900 a garment shop was a place where Jewish immigrants to New York sought refuge in a familiar environment run by a fellow *landsman* who promptly set about exploiting them to the full. Perhaps, it is the same with today's immigrant garment capitalists: They may be disciplined and risk taking, but doesn't the key to their success lie in a special ability to get other immigrants to work hard? Then again, there may be a measure of self-exploitation in the newcomer's willingness to work long and hard for his or her immigrant boss: what is learned at low wages today might be what is needed to go into business on one's own tomorrow. These are the issues posed by the growth of business activity among the immigrants of the 1980s. They are the questions to which this book is addressed.

The rest of this chapter is mainly devoted to a reconnaissance of the terrain. In the next section, we shall see how other scholars have sought to understand the phenomenon of immigrant enterprise and why their answers, though often quite insightful, remain incomplete. The following section outlines a new framework for analyzing immigrant business; the final section then describes how the material for this book was gathered.

Explaining Immigrant Enterprise

In the prevailing models of modern society, there is little room and precious little time left for the small firm and the independent entrepreneur. Karl Marx argued that the lower strata of the middle class would gradually sink into the proletariat; whatever has been the reception of his other views on the development of capitalist society, these prognostications have been seconded by most subsequent observers. The conventional view is that working for oneself has been reduced to a marginal phenomenon. Small businesses persist, either because market size has not *yet* permitted sufficient economies of scale, or because some residual need for specialization or a hankering after personalized services has postponed the advent of mass production or distribution.

If the prevalence of self-employment and the importance of small business have declined in the population at large, they continue to be poles of attraction for immigrants, as we have just seen. Historically, newcomers flocked into small business in disproportionate numbers. In turn-of-the-century New York, immigrants were overrepresented, not only in the petty trades of peddling and huckstering, but also among "manufacturers and officials," "merchants and dealers," and other occupations linked to business activity.[8] Small enterprise played an important role in the economic progress of a variety of immigrant groups that implanted themselves in business then—Jews, Italians, Greeks, and others—and their proportionally higher involvement in entrepreneurial activities continues to differentiate these groups from much of the native population. That small business remains a concentration of immigrants is shown by data from the 1980 Census of Population, which confirms that the latest wave of immigration has brought an infusion of new immigrant owners into the ranks of petty proprietors. In New York, 12.2 percent of employed foreign-born males were self-employed in 1980 as opposed to 9.2 percent for the native-born. For these immigrants, self-employment appears to be an important part of the settlement process. Only the most recent newcomers are self-employed at a rate below that of the native-born; after ten years in the United States, self-employment rates exceed those for the native-born and continue to climb with length of stay.[9]

Cultural Theories of Immigrant Enterprise. How, then, does one account for the persistent overrepresentation of immigrants among the ranks of the self-employed? One possibility is that immigrants share unique group

attributes that create a cultural or psychological propensity toward entrepreneurship. The starting point for this argument is Max Weber's famous study, *The Protestant Ethic and the Spirit of Capitalism*.[10] Of course, Weber's concern was with the effects of religion, not ethnicity, and in part his book can be read as a riposte to Werner Sombart, who argued that the Jews were responsible for injecting the drive for accumulation into otherwise stagnant western economies. Weber's contribution stems from his argument about the affinity of a particular mentality or psychology for the development of economic activity. Somewhat modified, this same line of thinking can be extended to explain immigrants' success in business; to wit, that immigrants advance through business because their culture favors those attributes needed for entrepreneurial success—discipline, hard work, risk taking, and so on. Just such an argument was offered by Nathan Glazer, who contended that the historical experience of being a "stranger" combined with the traditions of "Jewish Puritanism" to give Jewish immigrants a strong entrepreneurial bent.[11] Similarly, William Petersen argued that the Japanese succeeded in business because they brought with them the "Protestant" values of hard work, diligence, and frugality, values albeit inspired not by Calvinism but by Confucianism.[12]

These interpretations apply Weber's thesis about Calvinism to ethnic cultures in a fairly straightforward way. There is also a particularly imaginative variant of this argument, developed by Ivan Light in his now classic *Ethnic Enterprise in America*. Here the contention is that collective ethnic resources, not individualism, furnish the source of immigrants' elective affinity with business. Analyzing Chinese, Japanese, and West Indian immigrants in the first half of the twentieth century, Light documented the role that kinship and place-of-origin groups played in organizing and capitalizing ethnic concerns. All three groups used rotating credit associations to pool funds and generate capital. The Chinese and Japanese belonged to family associations that evolved into trade guilds that set prices and wages and that regulated competition among ethnic firms. For example, the Chinese laundrymen's guild effectively restricted access to those immigrants who had passed through an apprenticeship, paid their fees, and had been admitted to the guild; and it further limited the number of new laundries by specifying that laundries be separated by at least ten doorways.[13] More recently, Bonnett and Laguerre have shown how rotating credit associations continue to funnel start-up capital to West Indian and Haitian businesses in New York City. Similarly, Kim's and Hurh's research on Korean business owners in

Chicago showed that many were *kye* (Korean rotating credit association) participants.[14]

Although cultural explanations such as these are suggestive for the importance that they attribute to predisposing factors, they are open to criticism on several counts. The entrepreneurial-values approach can be thought of in a "hard" and a "soft" form; the hard form would ascribe those values to a belief system independent of a group's economic role; the soft form would see entrepreneurial values as an adaptation to the original conditions in which a group lived. One strike against the hard form is simply that groups noted for their entrepreneurial bent also seem remarkably adaptive. Their tendency is to become more like the native labor force, shifting from self-employment to salaried employment over the course of two to three generations (discussed at greater length in the next chapter). A more important criticism of the hard form is that its conditions are difficult to meet, since what one needs is evidence of business-relevant values that are not ultimately reducible to a group's premigration experience. Some groups do indeed seem inclined toward entrepreneurship, thanks to the influence of a particular belief system. Such is the case of Koreans immigrating to the United States, many of whom are Protestants but still maintain Confucian values; the value systems common to both religions emphasize self-abnegation and self-control, thereby reinforcing the qualities needed for small business gain. But, as Illsoo Kim has shown, the character structure of Korean immigrants also has its source in the after effects of state centralism and in the fluid class structure of preindustrial Korea—both of which bred marginality and individualism. Thus, whatever the origins of the initial thrust toward competitiveness, Koreans' entrepreneurial values were thoroughly reinforced by the character of their original society and consequently were internalized prior to immigration to the United States, which lends support to the soft rather than to the hard form of the entrepreneurial-values approach.[15]

Yet, if a value system is adaptive, the issue becomes why the behavioral traits acquired in one society are rewarded in another. To that question, Werner Cahnmann's comments on the historical experience of Jews offer an instructive response: "the era of liberalism . . . unleashed the energies of the Jews and gave them a free reign. The Jews had been conditioned to competitive risk taking for a long time. Now, the rules which had governed their conduct under specific circumstances, found wide application."[16] Thus, the entrepreneurial-values approach presupposes the existence of

opportunity structures congruent with acquired behavioral patterns. If opportunities are therefore a prerequisite of immigrant business growth, a good theory must explain the source of opportunities as well as their variation over time and space—neither of which requirement is met by the entrepreneurial-values approach.

The collective-resource perspective also elides the relationship between culture and the environment. Analysts such as Light and John Modell, whose book *The Economics and Politics of Racial Accommodation* is a study of Japanese immigrants in Los Angeles between 1900 and 1940,[17] base their case on Asian-American subeconomies of the pre World War II period, when nepotistic trade guilds and marketing organizations set prices, regulated output, and rationed entries to new firms. Undoubtedly, these economic activities sprang up out of preexisting cultural forms. But if culture is to serve as a predictor of ethnic business success, then the limiting case is the constraining power attributed to cultural norms: To what extent will cultural traditions influence economic behavior (as in the case of clan groupings that restrict competition) when nontraditional, individualistic actions elicit environmental rewards?

Reconsider, in this light, the evolution of those solidaristic organizations among Chinese- and Japanese-American business owners that served to set prices and regulate competition. These activities can be construed as rational responses to highly constricted market situations in which unimpeded business activity would have quickly exceeded the demand for ethnic products. Because these Asian immigrants were institutionally segregated, cultural consensus seems likely to have been less important in organizing the ethnic subeconomy than control mechanisms. In particular, confinement to the ethnic subeconomy made the threat of exclusion a potent weapon of associational control. Among the Chinese, collective economic organizations were instruments of elite organization whose efficacy derived from the autonomy that local authorities granted to Chinatown elites.[18]

If this reading is correct, then similar organizations are likely to diminish in importance if the environmental constraints lose force because more expansive market opportunities should diminish the need for associational controls while, at the same time, they stiffen the tension between guildlike regulation and economic growth. Indeed, ethnic economic associations occupy a greatly attenuated place in the Asian subeconomies that have arisen in the wake of the new immigration. In New York's Chinatown, for example, the proliferation of garment factories from 20 in 1965 to close to 480 in 1985

has helped fuel the growth of the entire Chinese subeconomy. Yet, in contrast to the prewar situation, when guilds and family groups controlled business transactions and guarded against saturating Chinatown's limited market, the Chinatown garment industry, as we shall see, is racked by the pains of overexpansion, with price wars forcing more than 30 percent of the businesses to change hands every year. Similarly, the ease with which Korean immigrants have been able to enter New York's fruit-and-grocery business has promoted intense intraethnic competition, completely overwhelming the ability of organizations like the Korean Produce Retailers Association to limit the entry of new Korean-owned stores.[19]

The point of this criticism is neither to dismiss the importance of culture nor to reduce it to an epiphenomenon. But one needs to remember that the bundle of traits, attitudes, and behavioral patterns that are "cultural" are themselves the product of previous interaction between a group and its original environment; consequently, if these cultural patterns can be successfully transferred from one society to another, then it is likely that the two societies resemble one another in some important respects. Just as culture is learned through childhood and adult socialization, so too are new cultural patterns learned and devised when the environment changes. Immigrants, after all, are unlikely to be the more traditional members of their original societies; rather, they are more likely to stem from those sections of the population already most inclined toward adaptation and change. Hence, culture will influence an immigrant group's economic life to the extent that it is congruent with the new environment of the host society; where the original culture does not apply, one can expect that, with some lag, its influence will gradually wane.

Middleman-Minority Theories. Another body of research identifies the business success of contemporary ethnic or immigrant groups as a "middleman-minority" phenomenon. Traditionally, middleman minorities have been associated with precapitalist societies where they have often dominated trading and commercial activities. For example, "Spanish Jews were indispensable for international commerce in the Middle Ages and Armenians controlled the overland trade between Europe and the Middle East as late as the nineteenth century"; in more recent times Lebanese Christians fanned out into middleman positions throughout the Near East and Africa, while in Lebanon itself, the small Armenian community remains disproportionately engaged in small and large industry. The importance of middleman minor-

ities can largely be ascribed to the characteristics of the minorities and their utility to then-dominant elites. The minorities possessed valued skills (a high level of literacy being perhaps the most important) and a network of family and personal relations that played an important role in facilitating long-distance communications and transactions. The elites, which were often drawn from a warrior class, lacked such skills and were constrained from engaging in commercial activities by virtue of the status considerations common to warrior groups.[20]

Though the precapitalist societies in which middleman minorities thrived have now largely disappeared, there is reason to argue that the middleman role persists. Edna Bonacich has contended that many of the historical middleman minorities (Jews, Lebanese, Armenians, Chinese, Indians) remain overrepresented in petty trade and commerce and that they appear to prefer business lines in which the firm can remain small. The form of their commercial activities, dependent as it is on personal ties and loyalties, still bears the hallmark of the traditional middleman-minority groups. Finally, the middleman minorities maintain a separate cultural identity and face "some hostility from the surrounding societies." These modern-day middleman minorities, Bonacich has argued, begin as sojourners, enduring short-term deprivations for the long-term goal of return and choosing portable and liquifiable livelihoods. This orientation elicits a hostile reaction from the host society; that antagonism, in turn, strengthens solidaristic behaviors and in-group economic ties. In a case study of Japanese immigrants in the United States in the first half of the twentieth century, coauthored with John Modell, Bonacich has argued that the Japanese' rapid penetration of small-scale, speculative lines in California agriculture-and-food retailing and wholesaling exemplifies the phenomenon of middleman-minority survival in advanced capitalist societies:[21]

[The Japanese] concentrated in a narrow range of lines, were overrepresented in commercial and service occupations, used the family firm as their main business form, depended on thrift and hard work, were able to utilize communal ties to generate multiple types of business aid, and were able to sell their goods and services inexpensively. . . . The nature of Japanese enterprise put [them] . . . in conflict with certain segments of the surrounding society.[22]

Exception to the middleman-minority approach can be taken on several grounds. First, it fails to specify the grounds for inclusion or exclusion with respect to both businesses and minorities. Any and all small business ac-

tivities undertaken by immigrants are classified as middleman-minority phenomena; similarly, the defining traits of the minorities are stated in such diluted form as to encompass almost any range of behavior. Second, the middleman-minority approach provides no account of the context in which middleman minority or, for that matter, any ethnic business develops. This neglect of contextual factors vitiates one crucial thrust of the argument, namely the assertion that "middleman minorities typically face considerable hostility from the surrounding society,"[23] which in turn promotes ethnic solidarity and small business activity in the middleman group. In fact, the historical record plainly shows that there was no "typical" host-society reaction to the classic middleman minorities: rather, host society responses ranged considerably, from recruitment of middleman minorities, to elite protection and mass antagonism, to discrimination, and possibly to extermination. What one needs, then, is a theory that will explain these variations, for which the middleman approach simply won't do.[24] A further consequence of downplaying contextual factors is that the middleman approach thereby ascribes the minorities' success to the cultural characteristics that the newcomers bring with them; for this reason it is liable to all the criticisms of the cultural approach advanced in the previous section. Finally, the interpretive and factual bases for the middleman-minority hypothesis are at variance with its fundamental claims, as shown by the following salient examples from the economic history of American Jews, a group cited by Bonacich as an exemplar of middleman-minority behavior:

• Modernization and the rise of capitalism transformed the economic activities of Jews. As is well known, Jews were heavily overrepresented in trade in preindustrial societies. With industrialization, the Jews shifted out of trade and rapidly altered their pursuits, perhaps more rapidly than other groups. One indicator of this change was the rise of a massive Jewish proletariat. Jews still engaged in the traditional trades, such as trading and dealing, were greatly underrepresented among those who left Russia for the United States, whereas there was a much higher proportion of newly proletarianized workers among the immigrants than among the Jewish population at large. The fact that the immigrants took up work in the needle trades and other similar industries upon arrival in the United States was one part of a large-scale abandonment by Jews of their traditional economic activities. Of course, the Jewish proletariat was short-lived, and American Jews moved into the middle class relatively soon after their immigration to the United States. In the process they moved further afield from traditional middleman pursuits, entering such new lines of business

as real estate, construction, movies, and high technology, while also developing a high level of professional self-employment. The Jews' continued concentration in business and self-employment is undoubtedly influenced by their past experience; however, their economic role in American society is in no way comparable to their place in the economic structure of preindustrial societies.[25]

• Although sojourning is purportedly a characteristic of small business minorities, Jews had the highest rates of self-employment among immigrants in the United States at the turn of the century, yet also had the lowest rates of return migration. In 1900, for example, when there were 124 Russian Jews employed as retail merchants for 1,000 employed Russian Jewish males, there were only 58 Italians so employed for every 1,000 gainfully at work. Yet return migration rates for the Jews was 7 percent as opposed to 75 percent for the Italians. As we shall see later on, similar differences in self-employment rates between permanent and temporary immigrant groups can be detected among the latest newcomers to the United States.[26]

• Another contention of the middleman-minority approach is that middleman minorities fail "to engage in the kind of activity that epitomizes modern industrial capitalism, namely, the hiring of contracted wage labor from which profits can be extracted." Yet the evidence on Jewish business activity provides no support for this assertion at all. In New York's garment industry, which grew up as an industry of immigrant Jews, Jewish factory owners rapidly began to recruit Italians, blacks, Hispanics, and others once the supply of Jewish labor began to diminish. Moreover, the growth of many Jewish businesses into quantitatively large concerns shows little foundation for the notion that middleman minorities are "pre-modern in their economic orientation" and hence limited to small firms. The same pattern held in Europe. In pre-Hitler Germany, 79 percent of all department store trade took place in Jewish-owned stores, and indeed anti-Semitic propaganda made much of the fact that non-Jewish women were employed in these Jewish-owned stores. In Poland, Jewish-owned textile mills employed an exclusively gentile work force.[27]

Rather than ignoring the context of minorities' business pursuits and baldly asserting that ethnic enterprise in modern societies is a carryover of earlier middleman minorities, it would be better to specify the relationship between the overall economic environment and the role and function of business minorities: on the one hand, traditional economies in which middleman minorities act as the engine of exchange relationships; on the other hand, market economies, with peripheral, if still dynamic ethnic enclaves.

But once we drop the assumption that immigrant business owners in capitalist societies are identical to the middleman minorities of the preindustrial past, then we can appreciate the importance of strictly market-based factors as preconditions of ethnic enterprise in the very case that Bonacich and Modell discuss. Land in Los Angeles was available to Japanese farmers because the city encroached on large holdings as it grew, and growth made extensive investments too costly and too uncertain for capital-intensive farming. As large-scale agriculture receded, land was bought by real estate investors who sought to rent out small parcels until higher-yielding uses could be realised—speculative practices that coincidentally lowered the costs of capitalization for would-be Japanese truck farmers. In contrast to precapitalist or developing societies, in which middleman minorities interject market relations into nonmonetized sectors, thereby undermining traditional producers, the role of Japanese farmers never altered the fundamental structure of truck farming. Nor did their basic orientation toward the market vary from that of their non-Japanese competitors, since both sought to maximize profits.[28] This interpretation suggests that the opportunities for immigrant enterprise stem from the social and economic structure of the host society in which the immigrants settle. That hypothesis is sketched out in the following section and is then systematically developed in Chapter 2.

Toward a Theory of Immigrant Enterprise. My argument thus far is that the prevailing theories of ethnic enterprise—most importantly, the cultural and middleman-minority approaches—are not so much wrong as incomplete. A penchant for risk taking, a preference for independence, the existence of ethnic economic organizations—all these culturally bound phenomena will facilitate the business of setting up a new firm and making it a success. But setting up a new firm is neither a trivial nor a random event. Industries vary considerably in the degree to which they breed new business births. For example, services made up the largest share (38 percent) of the 1,031,000 net new business formed in the United States between 1976 and 1982, followed by the financial-insurance-and-real estate sector and the construction sector (accounting for 14 percent and 13 percent, respectively, of all new firms); by contrast, manufacturing, transportation, communications, and utilities lagged behind, together producing only 9.3 percent of all net business births.[29] Business births and deaths cannot be tracked by the ethnicity of their owners, but minority self-employment rates (which include

black, Asian, and Hispanic immigrants) can be disaggregated by industry. What we find is that minority-business owners are overrepresented in trade and services, suggesting that these are the sectors where the bulk of new minority and immigrant businesses are born.[30] The point is that structural barriers—technology, capital needs, the level of competition—define the contours for the emergence of new firms; hence a culturally induced propensity for business may be a necessary, but is not a sufficient condition of entrepreneurial success.

Rather, there are two conditions that are logically prior to the creation of immigrant businesses: (1) access to ownership positions and (2) a niche in which the small firm can viably function. The first point is a reminder that immigrants usually have fewer resources than do natives; if ownership positions are equally coveted by immigrants and nationals, the former are not likely to win out. But recruitment to ownership may function similarly to those processes by which immigrant workers are recruited into the labor market.[31] That is, natives opt out of the supply of potential owners in a particular industry, perhaps because ownership in the industry generates too little status, perhaps because its economic rewards are insufficient to retain them compared with the alternatives available. If the supply of native owners runs short, there may be a replacement demand, and immigrants could then enter the industry to fill the ownership positions vacated by the natives.

But for immigrants to succeed natives in any small business sector presupposes that the small firm is a viable entity and the existing small business industries can be penetrated with the immigrants' limited resources. The literature on industrial organization identifies several barriers to the creation of new firms. Of these impediments, the most important are economy-of-scale barriers, absolute-cost barriers, and product-differentiation barriers;[32] as I shall argue in the following chapter, immigrant businesses proliferate where product-market characteristics tend to keep such barriers low.

It is in assessing what will happen in the existence of small business niches and vacancies for small business owners that the cultural and middleman approaches are helpful. Immigrants will be more likely to succeed should they possess a predisposition toward business. But, as I have argued, the immigrants most disposed toward business are likely to be those newcomers whose original environment bears a significant resemblance to their adopted society. The circumstances of migration—that is, whether immigrants move as settlers or as temporary migrants—will also influence their success in business.

Ethnic resources are another necessary condition of business success, and middleman and cultural approaches are correct in underlining the importance of ethnic solidarity. However, their assessment of these resources is incomplete. First, their mode of approach is the ethnic case study. This procedure tells us much about how ethnic businesses operate but provides little information on how ethnic firms are distinguished from native competitors, making it difficult to understand whence the advantages of the ethnic businesses stem. Second, neglect of the economic context leads cultural and middleman approaches to overlook the issue of environmental fit and the relationship between immigrants' ethnic resources and the requirements of the industries in which their businesses grow. Even in low-barrier industries there are significant liabilities associated with newness—how to learn and master new roles, how to wean away customers from their old vendors, how to establish trust—and the weight of these liabilities is evidenced by the high death rate among new concerns.[33] Moreover, small businesses, whether new or established, confront an additional set of problems by virtue of their smaller size. One such difficulty is access to finance; how ethnic firms might resolve this problem is handled quite nicely by both cultural and middleman approaches. Not considered by these approaches, however, is the fact that small-firm industries tend to have an unstructured labor market in the sense that there are few established institutions by which jobs are matched with workers and skills are maintained and transmitted; hence, a critical problem of the small firm is securing a skilled and attached labor force. One possibility, which I shall pursue at some length, is that immigrant firms enjoy a competitive advantage in small business industries because the social structures of the ethnic community provide a mechanism of connecting organizations to individuals and stabilizing these relationships.

This, in brief, is the line of argument to be developed in the chapters that follow. The next chapter offers a theory of immigrant enterprise, building on the propositions adumbrated above. The garment industry itself is then analyzed. Chapter 3 examines the historical development of the New York garment industry and the changes that have transpired since World War II—the internationalization of production and the rise of the large apparel firm. Chapter 4 shows why New York's garment industry continues to be a staging ground for new immigrant firms, despite the changes in structure and location analyzed in Chapter 3. The next chapters trace out the growth of New York's immigrant garment firms. Chapter 5 examines processes of ethnic succession in recruitment to ownership; Chapter 6 analyzes the conditions under which new immigrant businesses have arisen; Chapter 7 focuses on

the question of ethnicity at work and whether immigrant firms enjoy competitive advantages over their native counterparts; Chapter 8 asks what
accounts for the disproportional business success of some immigrant groups
and not others by comparing entrepreneurial careers and business organization among Chinese and Dominicans. The argument is then summarized and
reviewed in Chapter 9.

Background of This Book. Before turning to the heart of the book, a
summary is needed of the ways in which the material for this study was
collected and the analysis was developed. This book combines a variety of
research methods: nonparticipant observation; in-depth interviewing of key
informants; analysis of primary and secondary printed sources; and a series
of different surveys. My acquaintance with the industry began in 1975, when
I started to work for the International Ladies' Garment Workers' Union, first
in labor education and then in organizing. After two years with the ILGWU,
I began graduate studies; two years into graduate school I commenced the
series of research projects that culminated in this book. In the course of
these activities, I maintained and strengthened my contacts with the IL-
GWU; I began to work for the union as a consultant; and, without rupturing
ties to the ILGWU, later worked for the employers' association and for the
city of New York as a consultant on a number of projects related to the
garment industry. These various activities led to extended interaction with
key actors in the union and, to a lesser extent, in management. The sponsorship of union, management, and government also resolved some problems
of access, especially among owners of garment "manufacturing" firms, who,
despite extreme time pressures and a general reluctance to talk with outsiders, spent considerable time with me discussing the organization and
operation of their businesses. While the lessons learned from observation
and in-depth interviewing inform much of the analysis presented in this
book, I particularly drew on them in writing Chapters 3, 4, and 6. Information from these sources was supplemented by extensive reading of the industry's trade journals and by an exhaustive search through primary and
secondary studies and government reports related to the industry's structure, labor force, history, technology, and product markets. Much of the
relevant material gleaned through this research is cited in the notes to
Chapters 3 and 4.

In addition to these techniques, I also conducted a number of surveys.
The survey procedure was designed to take into account the particular

characteristics of the industry's structure and the ethnic composition of its entrepreneurial class. Garment firms, as I shall discuss in greater detail, can be distinguished between "manufacturers"—those firms that design clothing, purchase the textile out of which clothes are made, merchandise the clothes, but generally do not engage in the actual production of clothing—and "contractors"—those specialized firms that generally sew and finish garments to the specifications set by the manufacturers. The contractors include the ethnic groups that have traditionally furnished the bulk of garment capitalists—Jews and Italians—as well as the new immigrant owners, who are mainly Chinese and Hispanics, with Dominicans being the most numerous among the latter. While Jews and Italians are also the principal groups among the manufacturers, the new immigrants are still entirely confined to contracting. My main interests were in how and why immigrants became garment-factory owners; how immigrants were distinguished, if at all, from the older ethnic groups that had been active in the industry; and how one group of immigrant owners (the Chinese) differed from the other (the Dominicans). Thus, the bulk of the surveying work involved interviewing of contractors, both immigrant and nonimmigrant. A total of 136 contractors were interviewed during 1984 and 1985. Of these, 63 were Chinese, 41 were white ethnic (Jewish or Italian), and 32 were Dominican. The interviews with contractors followed a structured format, though most questions were open-ended. Details of the survey procedures are discussed in appendix B, and examples of the questionnaires used are presented in Appendixes C and D.

Two other surveys were drawn on to a very limited extent. The first was a survey of 35 New York-headquartered manufacturers; these interviews, which were conducted in 1984, focused on locational patterns and linkages between manufacturers and related suppliers and buyers. While this survey was concerned with a variety of questions, not all of which were immediately pertinent to the subject at hand, the relevant results are reported in Chapter 4. The second survey was part of a study of the migration patterns and strategies of Hispanic garment workers; this survey, which was conducted in 1979 and 1980, involved interviews with 100 Hispanic garment workers, selected on a random basis from the membership rolls of a large garment workers' union local. Some of the results from this survey are reported in Chapter 4.

[2]

A Theory of Immigrant Enterprise

This chapter develops a single, sustained argument for immigrants' over-representation among the self-employed and then inquires into the sources of ethnic differences in business success rates.

The Opportunity Structure

We begin with demand. For a business to arise there must be some demand for the services it offers. The initial market for immigrant entrepreneurs arises within the immigrant community itself: The immigrant community has a special set of needs and preferences that are best served, and sometimes can only be served, by those who share those needs and know them intimately, namely, the members of the immigrant community itself. Generally, those businesses that first develop are purveyors of culinary products—tropical goods among Hispanics, for example, or Oriental specialties among Asians. Businesses that provide "cultural products"—newspapers, recordings, books, magazines—are also quick to find a niche in the immigrant community. The important point about both types of activity is that they involve a direct connection with the immigrants' homeland and knowledge of tastes and buying preferences—qualities unlikely to be shared by larger, native-owned competitors.[1]

Immigrants also have special problems that are caused by the strains of settlement and assimilation and are aggravated by their distance from the institutionalized mechanisms of service delivery. Consequently, the business of specializing in the problems of immigrant adjustment is another early avenue of economic activity, and immigrant-owned travel agencies, law firms, realtors, and accountancies are common in most immigrant communities. Such businesses frequently perform a myriad of functions far above the simple provision of legal aid or travel information and reservations. As Hendricks noted in his study of Dominicans in New York City:

the typical [Dominican] travel agency encompasses a host of activities which, superficially, at least, seem unrelated to the travel business. A typical travel agency has available translations, notary public, income tax preparation, driving instruction, real estate and rental information, foreign Spanish language periodicals, the sale of money orders, and importantly, help in the preparation of immigrant forms.[2]

To a large extent, these services are confidential, unfamiliar, and unintelligible to the newcomer unaccustomed to American bureaucratic procedures. In some cases, they may impinge on the often dubious legal status of the immigrant and his family. Whichever the case, trust is an important component of the service, and the need for trust pulls the newcomer toward a business owner of common ethnic background. To this tendency may be added a factor common to many of the societies from which the immigrants come, that is, a preference for personalistic relationships over reliance on impersonal, formal procedures; this further increases the clientele of those businesses that specialize in adjustment problems.[3]

If immigrant business stays limited to the ethnic market, its potential for growth is sharply circumscribed, as Howard Aldrich has shown in his studies of white, black, and Puerto Rican businesses in the United States and (in research conducted with Cater, Jones, and McEvoy) of Indian and white businesses in the United Kingdom. The obstacle to growth is the ethnic market itself, which can support only a restricted number of businesses, both because it is quantitatively small and because the ethnic population is too impoverished to provide sufficient buying power. Moreover, the environment confronting the ethnic entrepreneur is severe: because exclusion from job opportunities leads many immigrants to seek out business opportunities, business conditions in the ethnic market tend toward a proliferation of small units, overcompetition, and a high failure rate—with the surviving businesses generating scanty returns for their owners.[4]

These conclusions may be too pessimistic in at least two respects, however. First, not all immigrant communities have enjoyed so few economic resources as blacks and Puerto Ricans in the United States and East Indians in the United Kingdom. One case in point is that of New York's Jewish community in the 1920s. As Jews moved into the lower-middle and middle classes they also dispersed from the tenement districts of the Lower East Side; their search for better housing created a market for Jewish builders who evaded restrictive covenants by constructing new housing and then recruiting Jewish tenants. While the real estate and construction firms that grew up in the 1920s have since extended far beyond the confines of the

ethnic market, the initial demand for housing provided the platform from which later expansion could begin. Quite the same process is being played out in New York's Asian communities today, where the housing needs of the growing Asian middle class have attracted Asian capital and stimulated the emergence of an Asian real estate industry.[5]

The immigrant market may also serve as an export platform from which ethnic firms can expand. For example, Greeks started out in the restaurant trade serving co-ethnics looking for inexpensive meals in a familiar environment. This original clientele provided a base from which the first generation of immigrant restaurateurs could branch out. More importantly, the immigrant trade established a pool of skilled and managerial talent that eventually enabled Greek owners to penetrate beyond the narrow confines of the ethnic market and specialize in the provision of "American food."[6] In the 1980s Dominican and Colombian immigrants active in the construction-contracting business in New York City appear to be playing out a similar development. Most of these immigrant business owners are engaged in additions- and-alterations work for an immigrant clientele; what leads these immigrant customers to patronize co-ethnics is not so much a search for savings as a preference for reliability, vouchsafed for by the immigrant contractor's reputation in the community to which he is linked. These initial jobs are important in two respects: they are small and therefore allow immigrants to start out at a relatively low level; in addition, the ethnic demand has supported immigrant contractors in assembling a skilled labor force and gaining efficiency and expertise, qualities that are gradually allowing them to edge out into the broader market.[7]

These examples notwithstanding, Aldrich's strictures still hold: the growth potential of immigrant business hinges on its access to customers beyond the ethnic community. The crucial question, then, concerns the type of market processes that might support neophyte immigrant capitalists. It is to that issue to which we presently turn.

Immigrant Business in the Open Market. As I noted earlier, the structure of industry is a powerful constraint on the creation of new business organizations; in that part of the economic world dominated by the demand for standardized products, scale economies, high absolute costs, and product differentiation bar the paths of entry to new immigrant concerns. But there are certain products or services where the techniques of mass production and mass distribution do not pertain. It is in these markets—those that are

most often affected by uncertainty or differentiation or that are relatively small in size—where the immigrant firm is likely to emerge. Consider the cases that follow:

Low economies of scale. As an industry where the entrepreneur is likely to be his or her own boss and nothing but that, the taxi industry illustrates one path of immigrant entry into small business. The passenger alighting in Washington, D.C., is likely to step into a cab operated by an African or a West Indian; in Los Angeles, Jewish refugees from Russia are more likely to be sitting behind the wheel; in New York one finds both Africans and Russian Jews as well as Israelis and a host of other immigrants.[8]

Immigrant concentration in this field is a result of the cost structure of the taxi industry and the barriers it presents to the realization of economies of scale. Economies of scale arise when the fixed costs of any operation can be spread over larger units, as a consequence of which the average cost per unit declines. However, the importance of economies of scale depends, in part, on the ratio of fixed to variable costs.

What is distinctive about the taxi industry is that none of the most crucial cost components—wages, benefits, and gasoline—are fixed; rather, they vary directly with the number of vehicles. Consequently, the ability of the taxi operator to lower costs by building up a fleet of taxis is highly constrained. The owner of two or possibly three taxis achieves the greatest possible scale economies; by contrast, a fleet of, say, twenty to thirty cars operates at essentially the same costs as the owner-operator of a single cab. Though scale economies at the firm level are thus negligible, one can attain sizable reductions in fixed costs by keeping the vehicle under the wheel for a longer period of time. One possibility is to hire operators to keep the cab busy for two shifts and possibly more. But an alternative exists if there is a supply of owner-operators amenable to self-exploitation, in which case working long hours results in the same economies of scale. As I shall argue in a later section, immigrants' restricted opportunities will make them more likely to work long hours than natives; hence the taxi field is one in which immigrant business has grown because the characteristics of this industry are congruent with immigrants' economic orientations.[9]

Instability and uncertainty. The basic notion of economies of scale, as noted above, associates declining average unit costs with increases in the number of goods produced. However, the length of time over which the flow of output

will be maintained is an equally crucial factor. Where demand is unstable, investment in fixed capital and plant is likely to be endangered. And if product requirements change frequently, the learning curve is low, since there is little time for workers to build up specialized proficiencies. Hence, when demand is subject to flux, versatility is preferable to specialization, and smaller units gain advantages over large ones.[10]

As Michael Piore has argued in his studies of economic dualism, industrial segmentation arises when demand falls into stable and unstable portions, and the two components can be separated out from one another. Where these conditions hold, one can expect an industry to be segmented into two branches: one, dominated by larger firms, that handles staple products; and a second, composed of small-scale firms, that caters to the unpredictable and/or fluctuating portion of demand. The consequence of this type of segmentation is that the two branches tend to be noncompeting; hence, where segmentation arises, it offers a sheltered position to small firms of the type that immigrants might establish.[11]

Such is likely to be the case in the garment industry. Some clothing products fall into the staple category, in which case they can almost be worn year in, year out. At the other end of the spectrum there are products whose existence is virtually ephemeral—for example, a bridal gown, which even in today's world is unlikely to be worn more than once. To be sure, most items of clothing have greater longevity than a bridal gown, but the nature of fashion is such that a dress or blouse sooner rather than later becomes out of date. Clothing purchases are also prone to various forces whose effects are often difficult to project: seasonality is one such factor (if winter is delayed, one postpones buying a coat until next year), and the overall state of the economy is another source of uncertainty (spending on fashion goods rises when one's pocket is full and falls when there is barely enough for necessities). The point is that these product-market conditions are correlated with particular types of production technology and organization: staple products involve long production runs and can be handled and merchandised by large, bureaucratized firms; those same technological and organizational features are much less suited to product markets prone to instability and unpredictable changes; consequently, these markets offer a suitable environment for small immigrant firms.

The importance of segmentation processes and their implications for immigrant business are evidenced in another industry with characteristics similar to garments—construction. One case in point is Carmenza Gallo's

study of construction businesses in New York City, which shows that the building trades have provided the staging ground for new immigrant firms that specialize in residential-and-renovation work. The reason for this development is that competition with larger, native firms for the residential-and-renovation market is limited. Large construction firms dominate the market for commercial and institutional building, where the projects are large and the lead times long; by contrast, small firms predominate in the highly volatile residential and renovation sectors where the demand is highly fragmented and the dollar value of contracts is considerably smaller.[12]

Small or differentiated markets. Still another environment favorable to small immigrant firms is one in which the market is too small or too differentiated to support the large centralized structures needed for mass production or distribution. One such example is the retail grocery industry in New York City, where the structure of the market is unfavorable to the large supermarket chains that dominate the industry nationally. One crucial reason for the weakness of the chains is the complexity of the New York market, whose heterogeneous mix makes it a quagmire for national chains with cumbersome and rigid central administrations. While chains reduce distributing costs by carrying only a few basic product lines, servicing the tastes of New York's varied populace is more costly, since it requires a much more diversified line than is usually carried. Similarly, the chains attain economies of scale in overhead by centralizing administrative functions, but to ensure that ethnic tastes are efficiently serviced—for example, stocking Passover goods in stores located in Jewish neighborhoods but not in black neighborhoods or providing West Indian specialties in a Jamaican neighborhood but not in the nearby Dominican area—a shorter span of control is preferable.

Thus, not only are large-firm concentration shares lower in New York than elsewhere, but the national chains that dominate the industry in the rest of the country have ceded place instead to locally based chains whose territory is often limited to one or two of New York City's five boroughs. These local chains are sufficiently small to process information about New York's highly differentiated market segments and then service those needs appropriately. On the other hand, because they are relatively small, these local chains also lack the economies of scale needed to achieve significant market power, with the result that food retailing has been easily penetrated by smaller, ethnic concerns that compete with very considerable success against their larger counterparts.[13]

In conclusion, what distinguishes the variety of processes giving rise to

immigrant business is an environment supportive of neophyte capitalists and the small concerns that they establish. Ethnic consumer tastes provide a protected market position, in part because the members of the community may have a cultural preference for dealing with co-ethnics, and in part because the costs of learning the specific wants and tastes of the immigrant groups are such as to discourage native firms from doing so, especially at an early stage when the community is small and not readily visible to outsiders. If the ethnic market allows the immigrant to maintain a business at somewhat higher-than-average costs, the other processes outlined above reduce the cost difference between native and immigrant firms. Low capital-to-labor ratios keep entry barriers low, and consequently immigrant businesses should be most common in industries where this condition prevails. Where there are problems in substituting capital for labor because changes in demand might idle expensive machines, immigrant businesses with labor-intensive processes can operate close to the prevailing efficiencies. When small markets inhibit the realization of economies of scale, small firms can achieve efficiencies close to, or better than, their large competitors and without the heavy overhead and administrative costs that the latter must shoulder.

▽ A second characteristic of all those industries supportive of immigrant firms is that the technical barriers to entry are also low. The best example is taxis where the essential skill—driving—is one that almost everybody has. As one Russian taxi driver pointed out, entry into other fields is barred because "we have lack of communication, knowledge of law, and so on," whereas in the taxi business one can "make a living without a lot of knowledge of the industry."[14] But, in most industries, a more specific skill is required, and thus the crucial factor is whether the would-be entrepreneur can pick up the needed business know-how while still an employee. One case in point is the rehabilitation-and-renovations sector in construction: not only are jobs smaller in size, but fewer master construction skills are needed, making on-the-job training easier to obtain. A similar situation applies in another province of immigrant businesses—restaurants—where the hierarchy of skills ranges from dishwashers at the bottom to cooks at the top. Although one way of going to the top in this industry is going to a culinary school, a newcomer can also move up through observation and learning through doing: today a dishwasher, tomorrow a sandwich man; eventually, a cook.[15]

▽ All three product-market conditions that favor small-scale enterprise—low capital-to-labor ratios, unstable product demand, and small markets—characterize the garment industry. In contrast to the rest of manufacturing,

garments remains an industry where much of the labor force works in small firms; whereas only a quarter of all manufacturing workers are to be found in firms of 100 or less, clothing firms of this size contain almost half the industry's workers. Not only is average establishment size in this industry small (45 workers), but it is smaller still in the urban fashion-market centers where immigrant firms are concentrated: an average of 29 workers per establishment in New York, 26 in Los Angeles, and 21 in Miami. As an industry of small firms, apparel is also an industry where relatively little capital investment is required. Average assets per employee in the women's outerwear branch, for example, are one ninth of the level of capital investments per worker in all manufacturing industries. Because so little capital is used, the skill requirements demanded of a clothing worker are quite high; but in large measure these are also the skills required to run a garment business, and they are such that the immigrant worker can acquire them on the job.[16]

Another factor conducive to immigrant business is that the garment industry is really a conglomeration of a variety of small markets. Men's and women's clothing are distinctive industries unto themselves; within the women's branch, barriers separate the various industries—dresses and coats, blouses and sportswear, undergarments and children's wear. As evidence, specialization ratios, which measure the percent of a firm's products sold in its primary product area, tend to be very high: 94 percent in women's dresses, the high for all subindustries in the women's apparel sector; 75 percent for women's coats and suits, the lowest for all of the women's apparel subindustries. Even these ratios understate the level of specialization, since each broad product category is in turn stratified by price-line and styling characteristics. Thus, the garment industry remains the immigrant industry par excellence, and what we learn from the conditions under which immigrant garment firms have arisen should apply to the other economic fields in which immigrant capitalists have thrived.[17]

Access to Ownership

Given the existence of markets conducive to small business, the would-be immigrant capitalist still needs access to ownership opportunities. At the turn of the century, rapid economic growth created new industries, allowing immigrants to take up business activities without substantial competition from, or displacement of, natives. In fact, the garment industry offers the classic illustration of this process. As we shall see at greater length in

Chapter 3, the garment industry became immigrant-dominated because the massive tide of Italian and Jewish immigration to New York occurred just when the demand for factory-made clothing began to surge. But in the late-twentieth-century U.S. economy, growth proceeds more slowly; there are fewer opportunities for self-employment; and, until recently, the ranks of the self-employed have been diminishing. Thus, the conditions of immigrants' access to ownership positions largely depend on the extent to which natives are vying with immigrants for the available entrepreneurial slots. If these positions are coveted by natives and immigrants, then natives should capture a disproportionate share. But if the supply of native owners is leaking out of a small business industry, then immigrants may take up ownership activities in response to a replacement demand.[18]

Consider how such a replacement demand might arise for the new immigrants who have arrived in U.S. cities since the liberalization of immigration laws in 1965. In most large cities, the small business sector has been a concentration of European immigrants and their later-generation descendants. The year 1970 is the last date for which we have information for both the immigrant and the foreign-stock populations; at that time the proportion of all self-employed persons in the five largest SMSAs (Standard Metropolitan Statistical Areas) who were first- and second-generation European ethnics ranged from a high of 57 percent in New York to a low of 30 percent in Los Angeles. Both immigrants and the foreign stock were overrepresented among the self-employed in all five SMSAs; but in all five cases rates of self-employment were lower in the second than in the first generation. Thus, for European ethnic groups, their initial placement in small business was already giving way to a pattern more squarely based in salaried employment as of 1970. All the evidence suggests that this trend has since continued apace.[19]

This drift away from independent business activities is exemplified by the case of the Jews. Jews migrating from eastern Europe at the turn of the century moved heavily into small business for a variety of historical reasons: their arrival coincided with the massive expansion of small business industries; this expansion made it possible for them to utilize previously acquired entrepreneurial skills and habits and also to pursue a culturally and religiously induced preference for independence and separation; finally, the tendency to concentrate in business was reinforced by discrimination, which at the upper-white-collar level persisted well into the 1960s.[20] Assimilation, occupational advancement, and the dwindling of corporate discrimination, however, have now diluted the Jewish concentration in small business:

"Jewish immigrants arrived in the big cities and took jobs as skilled workers and very small entrepreneurs; their children began to professionalize and establish themselves as white-collar workers or in more lucrative and stable businesses than those of the prior generation; and the immigrants' grandchildren competed successfully for the most desirable educational and occupational positions."[21] A variety of sources documents this shift out of small businesses. Analysis of the 1965 and 1975 Boston Jewish Community Surveys found that "while almost a quarter (23 percent) of the 1965 heads of households were self-employed outside the professions, only one in seven (14 percent) were so employed in 1975"; moreover, the ratio of business owners was higher for almost all age cohorts in 1965 than was the case in 1975.[22] Similarly, the 1981 New York Area Jewish Population Survey found consistently declining rates of self-employment from first generation to third, with much higher levels of education in the latter generation suggesting that much of its self-employment was concentrated in the professions rather than in business.[23] Finally, results from a study that examined Jews as well as a variety of Catholic ethnic groups in Rhode Island in the late 1960s, (French-Canadians, Irish, Italians, and Portuguese) show that "without exception the level of self-employment of fathers was higher than the level of self-employment of sons and the proportion of fathers of the oldest cohort who are self-employed is higher than that of fathers of the youngest cohort."[24]

As the occupational assimilation of the European ethnic population proceeds, it alters patterns of recruitment into small business. Just how this process is being played out is illustrated by a 1983 study of over 1,000 New York-area small businesses whose annual sales ranged from $500,000 to $5 million. On the one hand, the owners interviewed for this study foresaw considerable growth prospects for their businesses and expressed satisfaction with the business careers they had pursued: 55 percent said that they were "very optimistic" about their business' ability to succeed in the 1980s; 36 percent expected to create new positions within the next 12 months; 91 percent said they would choose to go into their own business if they had to do it all over again. On the other hand, these expressions of optimism and commitment were offset by a note of ambivalence regarding the businesses' future as family concerns. Only a fifth of the owners wanted their children to go into their own businesses; still fewer wanted their children to start up another business; and in considering their children's employment possibilities, the owners preferred that their children work for large rather than small concerns.

How this ambivalence affects recruitment patterns cannot be directly determined from this survey, but the data collected do show that the pool of talent entering small business has diminished. One indicator is that few new business start-ups have taken place: of the 1,057 businesses surveyed, only 9 percent had been formed between 1974 and 1983, with an additional 10 percent dating from the previous decade. Not only were there few new businesses among this group, but the small business population had greatly aged: with 52 percent of the owners surveyed 51 or older, and only 16 percent younger than 35, it appeared that few heirs were taking over these family businesses.[25] Further evidence of small business' dwindling ability to secure new recruits through established channels is attested by another study conducted in the early 1980s, focusing on 450 New York City manufacturing firms. While the results of this study pointed to the "basic vitality of most of the city's small industrial enterprises," another finding was that many otherwise viable concerns were going out of business for a variety of reasons, including sale of a small business to a large corporation, which then no longer sought to maintain the facility. A more frequent cause of business death, however, was the problem of succession:

Most often . . . small, profitable family-owned firms were closing because the owners were retiring and there were no potential buyers or family members interested in taking over the reins. We identified about 50 firms in just such a situation (out of a total of 450).[26]

What happens when a group falters in its recruitment to small business?—as is the case in New York, where the process of occupational assimilation has reduced the supply of potential business owners from the European ethnic groups that historically spawned the bulk of small entrepreneurs. One consequence is that a group's share of the small business sector inevitably declines, if for no other reason than the appallingly high death rate to which all small businesses are prone. David Birch's studies, for example, have shown that 8 percent of all firms in U.S. metropolitan areas are lost each year, which means that half of all firms in any area must be replaced every five years for the area simply to break even. For small firms and for new businesses the failure rates are higher still; indeed, the majority of new businesses do not last longer than four years.[27] Thus, as European ethnics seek out salaried employment as part of their shift toward higher positions in the social structure they are also setting up a vacancy chain. As older ethnic firms either go out of business or fail to transfer ownership to the next

generation, replacement opportunities for immigrant entrepreneurs should naturally arise.

But whether immigrants are poised to take over these positions depends largely on the economic entry barriers, the nature of which I discussed in the previous section. Where those barriers are low—because capital requirements are few, optimal firm size is small, and most activities are labor-intensive—ethnic succession can be expected to take place. Just such a case is provided by the proliferation of Korean fruit-and-vegetable stores in New York City, starting in the early 1970s. As Illsoo Kim explains in his book, *The New Urban Immigrants*:

The majority of Korean retail shops . . . cater to blacks and other minorities by being located in "transitional areas" where old Jewish, Irish, and Italian shopkeepers are moving or dying out and being replaced by an increasing number of the new minorities. . . . Korean immigrants are able to buy shops from white minority shopkeepers, especially Jews, because the second- or third-generation children of these older immigrants have already entered the mainstream of the American occupational structure, and so they are reluctant to take over their parents' business. In fact, established Korean shopkeepers have advised less experienced Korean businessmen that "the prospect is very good if you buy a store in a good location from old Jewish people."[28]

One other important aspect of this retail case is that succession took place in a patterned way: while the most competitive, lower-status fields were abandoned, higher-profit, higher barrier-to-entry lines retained traditional ethnic entrepreneurs. Thus, while grocery-store ownership has passed from Jews and Italians to Koreans, the wholesalers and food processors that supply these new ethnic concerns remain almost wholly dominated by older entrepreneurial groups. This phenomenon is further indication of how economic opportunity structures condition the growth contours of an immigrant economy. But it also discloses that growth proceeds more rapidly if there is complementarity, rather than competition, between new and old small business groups. With competition, natives might seek to inhibit business growth among newcomers; and given natives' greater resources, the likelihood is good that they might achieve some measure of success. But if newcomers and old-timers are complementary, the thrust toward ethnic protectionism subsides; rather than attempting to quell business growth among the newcomers, the established groups, which benefit from their patronage, will be more likely to respond in an adaptive way.[29]

Predispositions Toward Entrepreneurship

Thus far, I have argued that there are two preconditions for the development of immigrant business: a niche in which the small business can viably function and access to ownership positions. But if there is a demand for small business activities, why do immigrants tend to emerge as the replacement group? My answer to this question is that immigrants are predisposed toward business and that they also can draw on informal ethnic resources that give them a competitive edge. In arguing this first point, I am drawing on the cultural approach; my contention about the importance of ethnic resources is distinctive in that I emphasize the fit between the immigrant firm and the environment in which it functions.

The reasons why immigrants emerge as a replacement group rest on a complex of interacting economic and psychological factors. Blocked mobility is a powerful spur to business activity. Immigrants suffer from a variety of impediments in the labor market: poor English-language facility, inadequate or inappropriate skills, age, and discrimination. Lacking the same opportunities for stable career employments as natives, immigrants are more likely to strike out on their own and to experience less aversion to the substantial risks that this course entails.[30] The limited range of job- and income-generating activities also spurs immigrants to acquire business skills. Native workers will tend not to acquire particular skills if the returns to the needed investment in education and training are lower than those for comparable jobs; by contrast, the same skills might offer the immigrants the best return, precisely because they lack access to better remunerated jobs. As Thomas Bailey has shown, this is one reason for the prevalence of immigrants in the restaurant industry, where managerial and skilled (cooking) jobs offer lower returns to investment in training than other comparable, skilled and mangerial jobs.[31] Immigrants' willingness to put in long hours—needed to capitalize a business or to maintain economies of scale—is similarly conditioned. For those without access to jobs with high rates of hourly return, such activities as driving a cab or running a store from early morning to late night offer the best available rewards for their work effort.

There are also psychological components to the entry of immigrants into small business. Much of the sociological literature has characterized the small business owner as an anachronistic type impelled by a need for autonomy and independence.[32] Auster and Aldrich note that this approach assumes that entrepreneurship reflects the decisions of isolated individuals and thus ignores the issue of why certain groups disproportionately channel

new recruits into small business. Moreover, the traditional perspective also fails to account for the social pressures that condition groups and individuals for small business activity, among which the immigration process itself should be counted.[33]

The principal conditioning factor is the immigration experience itself. The process of leaving one's home to take up life in a new society is self-selective: the workers who enter the immigration stream tend to be more able, better prepared and more inclined toward risk than those who stay home. These same characteristics also give immigrants an advantage in competition with native groups in the low-wage labor market, against whom they compare favorably in terms of motivation, risk propensity, and an ability to adjust to change.[34]

Of equal importance, the immigrants' social origins alter the way in which they size up the chances of getting ahead. Michael Piore has suggested that immigrants have a more favorable view of low-level work than do natives because the migrants perceive their job's status in terms of the much-different job hierarchy of their home society.[35] Quite the same disparity would give the immigrant a distinctive frame of reference from which to assess the attractiveness of small business opportunities that open up as previously incumbent groups move on to other pursuits. Thus a young black or Puerto Rican aspiring to work as a manager behind the desk in a clean, air-conditioned bank might well look askance at the idea of taking over the candy store or grimy factory that goes vacant when its Jewish or Italian owner finally retires. Not so the immigrant, moved less by concern with unpleasant working conditions and impelled by status considerations of a different sort. In the newcomer's eyes, rather, taking over a petty proprietorship is likely to be a positive alternative to working for someone else and what is more, the best chance of getting ahead.[36]

Ethnicity as Resource. There are various dimensions to ethnicity—a common set of values and beliefs; a sense of shared identity; an interest in, or concern for, an ancestral homeland. My concern here is more with what might be called the subcultural dimension of ethnicity; that is to say, the social structures that attach members of an ethnic group to one another and the ways in which those social structures are used. These social structures consist, broadly speaking, of two parts: (1) the networks of kinship and friendship around which ethnic communities are arranged; and (2) the interlacing of these networks with positions in the economy (jobs), in space

(housing), and in civil society (institutions). Migration itself takes place under the auspices of these social structures. Information about the host society (true or misleading) is transmitted through communication or personal interaction between the migrant and his or her home community, and the picture portrayed by the migrant prompts yet another native to take his chances abroad. A similar chain of events conditions the process of settlement: once arrived in the new society, who does one turn to but those friends or relatives already situated with a home and a job? To be sure, home and job are not quite as glittering as the newcomer had imagined or the settler had promised, but importantly, the settler's neighborhood is home to other compatriots, and his job is one of many similar positions where other immigrants work. Because of a preference for familiarity, the efficiency of personal contacts, and social distance from the host society's institutions of assistance, the immigrant relies on connections with settlers to find shelter and work and thus finds himself in the ethnic occupational-and-residential ghetto. Should this process repeat itself time and again, two consequences ensue. First, intense interaction within a common milieu intensifies the feeling of commonality and membership within the group. Second, there is the buildup of that critical mass needed for formal ethnic institutions—a church, a mutual aid society, perhaps a trade union, maybe a political club—which in turn serve to reinforce ethnic identity.[37]

Thus far, this is a familiar, though greatly simplified story; however, we will use it to extract several less familiar lessons. The first is that immigrants may be vulnerable and oppressed, but, because they can draw on connections of mutuality and support, they can also create resources that counteract the harshness of the environment they encounter. The second is that the social structures of the immigrant community breed organizations, both informal and formal, in a context that might otherwise tend toward anomie. The third lesson, of particular importance to the discussion that follows, is that such informal organizational resources might give immigrants an advantage against natives should the institutionalized arrangements that normally connect individuals with organizations be undeveloped and/or malfunctioning.

Now let us consider the ways in which workers are attached to jobs in small business industries and the mechanisms by which the rules of the small firm are established. The labor market in small business industries tends to be unstructured in that it contains "few, if any established institutions by means of which people obtain information, move into and out of

jobs, qualify for advances in rank or pay, or identify themselves with any type of organization . . . for purposes of security or support."[38] The reasons why stable labor-market arrangements are undeveloped are various. In some instances, these conditions hold because the job is inherently temporary, as in the case of longshoring where workers are shaped up and form a work gang to unload a ship, only to return to the external labor market. In other cases, it is because skills are sufficiently general that they can be carried from one firm to another—as is the case in construction—and therefore, firms are reluctant to make an investment in training that will redound to another firm's gain. In other instances, as in the shoe industry, the firm will have a bimodal rather than a continuous distribution of skills, and the gap between the skilled and the unskilled positions is too great for on-the-job training to take place. And in all these cases, a problem is that small business industries are intensely competitive and that competition places a limit on firm size and thereby on the articulation of structured job ladders.[39]

Since small firms therefore rely on the external labor market, a chief problem is how to secure and maintain a trained labor force. One option is to lower skill levels so that the costs of training can be drastically reduced; this is the path that many small, low-wage employers in the "secondary labor market" have apparently pursued. As Piore has argued, jobs in the secondary sector "are essentially unskilled, either requiring no skill at all, or utilizing basic human skills and capacities shared by virtually all adult workers."[40] One case in point is that of the fast-food restaurant where the worker has been converted into an assembler and packer whose skills can be learned in a matter of hours.[41]

What the fast-food case also shows is that de-skilling is an alternative only when demand is standardized and tasks can then be broken down into repetitive components. However, this is the definition of mass production, and many small businesses arise in niches where specialty, not mass production, is required. One such example is construction, where new buildings are often custom-made jobs; another is the fashion segment of the apparel industry, where only small batches of highly varying products are made. In industries like these, where specialty work prevails, jobs involve a variety of tasks; the ability to adjust to changing job requirements and perform them with proficiency is precisely what is meant by skill.

Thus, the central issue confronting small firms is how to increase the probability of hiring workers who are capable of learning required skills and will remain with the firm and apply their skills there. "Hiring," as Spence

has put it, "is investing under uncertainty." The problem is that the employer "is uncertain about the productive capabilities of the job applicant"
prior to hiring and even for some time after the hiring decision has been
made.[42] One recruitment practice widely favored in industry, precisely because it reduces this uncertainty, is to recruit through "word-of-mouth"
techniques. When employers recruit by "word-of-mouth" the workers they
hire tend to have the same characteristics as those friends or relatives who
recommend them; employees concerned about their future tenure in the
plant are unlikely to nominate "bad prospects"; and finally, new hires recruited through the recommendations of workers already employed are likely
to be subject to the informal control of their associates once they are placed
on the job.[43]

Consider now the possibilities in an industry like clothing or restaurants
or construction, where nonimmigrants and immigrants both own firms, but
the first group recruits a heterogeneous pool of workers, all of different
ethnicities, while the second recruits primarily through ethnic networks.
The logic of word-of-mouth recruitment is that applicants resemble the
existing labor force; but, in the first case, social distance between native
employer and immigrant employee makes it difficult to accurately discern
the characteristics of the incumbent workers. As an example, many native
employers have but the vaguest impressions of the national origins of their
workers; thus, if one asks a native factory owner whether his Hispanic
workers are Puerto Rican or Dominican, the answer is likely to be: "How do
I know? They all speak Spanish. They're from the islands, somewhere."
Furthermore, the presumption of trust inherent in the process of assembling
a skilled work force through word-of-mouth recruitment is frequently weak
or absent under the conditions that seem prevalent in industries that employ
large numbers of immigrants and minorities. For example, personnel managers of supermarkets and department stores whom I interviewed as part of a
study of youth employment complained most vehemently about the high
level of theft among the largely minority, inner-city youth hired to work
in their stores. "The behavior of youth is impossible," noted one personnel manager in a typical comment. "The kids steal, they eat food in the
store, and they give food to their friends and relatives."[44] This recalls Elliot
Liebow's finding that stealing from employers was a prevalent practice among
the black street-corner men that he studied, but so was the assumption
among employers that their workers would steal, resulting in a consequent
reduction in the level of pay.[45]

Trust is further weakened when ethnic differences separate workers from employers. In some cases, this is due to stereotyping on the part of immigrant labor and native management alike—a matter to which I shall return in greater detail below. But it may also be the case that the situational constraints provide little room for trust to develop. For instance, many immigrants in an industry like garments work under assumed names, thus making their very identity uncertain. Similarly, a work force may be prone to high levels of turnover—which may occur because of seasonality or because of frequent travel or return migration to the immigrants' home societies. Whatever the cause, high turnover will hinder the development of stable relationships on which trust might be based. A firm with high turnover is also apt to be caught in a vicious circle, since the costs of constantly hiring make it uneconomical to exercise much discretion over the recruitment process.

Now take by contrast the immigrant firm. Immigrant owners can mobilize direct connections to the ethnic community from which they come in order to recruit an attached labor force. One means of securing a labor force is to recruit family members; because the characteristics of kin, unlike those of strangers, are known and familiar their behavior is more likely to be predictable, if not reliable; furthermore, trust may already inhere in the family relationship. Thus, Korean greengrocers tend to employ family members or other close relatives in the hope of "eradicating 'inside enemies'—non-Korean employees who steal cash and goods or give away goods to their friends or relatives who visit the store as customers," probably a better solution to the problem of "inventory shrinkage" than any policy that nonimmigrant retailers have devised.[46]

Of course, while some ethnic businesses may pivot around nuclear or perhaps extended-family relationships, the average size of many businesses makes it necessary to recruit beyond the family orbit. Still, kin can be used to secure key positions. Moreover, immigrants can also hire through other closely knit networks that will bring them into contact with other ethnics to whom they are tied by preexisting social connections. For example, migration chains that often link communities in the Dominican Republic to Dominicans in New York can funnel new arrivals into ethnically dominated workplaces and immigrant-owned firms. Similarly, Chinese immigrants may gravitate toward immigrant owners who speak the same dialect as they—and thus a Toisanese-speaking newcomer may opt for a Toisanese-speaking owner as against one who only speaks Cantonese. Moreover, trust may be heightened if an immigrant culture contains mechanisms for transforming

friendship relations into fictive kinship relations. For example, *compradazgo* (godparenthood) relationships between a child and godparents and between the parents and godparents are common to many Latin American societies and are seen as functional equivalents to kinship relationships. Similar relationships of fictive kinship are constructed among the Chinese.[47]

Just as newcomers turn to settlers for help in job finding, new arrivals may first seek out work in an immigrant firm, which offers the attractions of a comfortable environment and more familiar customs. Thomas Bailey, for example, reports that many immigrant restaurants in New York act as way stations for newly landed immigrants. It is commonly noted that the advantage of hiring such newcomers is that their dependence makes them likely to accept conditions with docility; but it is also the case that owners will be more likely to place trust in someone who depends on them.[48]

Ethnicity might also serve as a mechanism for mediating the strains in the workplace and providing the normative basis on which the rules of the workplace might be established. In the literature there are two conflicting descriptions of the industrial relations environment of the small firm. On the one hand, researchers working in the dual labor-market framework have argued that the small firm is riven by antagonism: supervision is tyrannical and capricious; there are no formal grievance procedures through which workers can seek redress for their complaints; and management and workers are caught in a vicious circle in which workers respond to the harsh exercise of discipline with further insubordination.[49] On the other hand, research investigating the "size effect" indicates that small firms garner favorable ratings when checked against large concerns on turnover levels, propensity to strike, job satisfaction, and a variety of other indicators.[50]

If size per se is unlikely to yield a particular industrial relations environment, these contrasting findings suggest that industrial relations outcomes are the product of the interaction of size with other factors. Compare the small concern with the large business, which is governed not only by a web of formal rules (promulgated by management or negotiated through collective agreements with unions) but also by informal understandings about how tasks are to be performed and jobs are to be allocated. Such understandings originate on the plant floor because workers, if put into stable and constant contact with one another, tend to form communities with norms, expectations, and rules of their own. These rules are often contested by management, and in unionized settings, much of the bargaining appears to center on the scope and permanence of these rules. Yet, management tends to abide

by central rules and to seek change on the margins. The reasons are twofold: first, workers have the economic power to punish management for breach of the customary workplace rules; second, management, especially at the lower levels, is socialized into the rules of the workplace as well and, to some extent, belongs to the work group itself.[51]

This being said, we can now assess the possible effects of ethnicity on industrial relations patterns in small firms. As I argued above, small firms where management and labor are ethnically distinctive have difficulty stabilizing the employment relationship. One consequence of their failure to do so is that turnover tends to be too rapid to permit the formation of social groups in which customary work norms might be embedded. Moreover, even where such groups take cohesive form, social distance between management and immigrant labor tends to preclude managerial acceptance of work-group norms. In part, this lack of acceptance is a consequence of ethnic behavioral patterns that are often so divergent that simple stylistic differences are perceived in deeply threatening ways. The conditions of duress that so often confront small firms (bottlenecks, short delivery deadlines, understaffing, etc.) further contribute to antagonism. Repeated conflict over production quotas, behavioral rules, absenteeism, and instability tends to take on an explicitly racial character as management interprets workers' behavior in racially stereotyped ways. And when immigrant or minority workers are employed by members of the majority group, the economic disparities between the two groups fuel discontent with wages, personnel policies, and general working conditions, making work just another instance of inequitable treatment.[52]

By contrast, ethnicity provides a common ground on which the rules of the immigrant workplace are to be negotiated. Above I argued that the social structures around which the immigrant firm is organized serve to stabilize the employment relationship. These social structures, however, are also relationships of meaning suffused with the expectations that actors have of one another. One consequence is that authority can be secured on the basis of personal loyalties and ethnic allegiance rather than on the basis of harsh discipline, driving, and direct-control techniques. Furthermore, ethnic commonality provides a repertoire of symbols and customs that can be invoked to underline cultural interests and similarities in the face of a potentially conflictual situation. Thus, Bernard Wong describes how immigrant entrepreneurs in New York's Chinatown use ethnic symbols and customs to bind outsiders to the firm:

The [restaurant's] labor boss does a great deal to promote efficiency and esprit de corps among the staff. . . . The spirit of brotherhood is deliberately cultivated. Everyone is expected to be fair with one another. The *Yi Hei* [trusting righteousness] is welcomed. In the kitchens of many restaurants, the portrait of the God of Justice, Gwaan Gung, hangs in a visible place. Some restaurants even have an altar of Gwaan Gung to remind everyone that they should be just to each other so that the deity will not be offended.[53]

But if ethnic commonality is a device for securing the immigrant worker's loyalty, the expectations bound up in the ethnic employment exchange impinge on the owner's lattitude as well. Immigrant workers can anticipate that standards of conduct prevailing in the broader ethnic community will extend to the workplace as well. For example, Harry Herman showed in his study of Macedonians in Toronto's restaurant trade that the egalitarian traditions of Macedonia carried over into the immigrant restaurants where workers and owners regarded one another as equals. Similarly, the terms under which immigrant owners obtain kin or hometown friends as laborers may also include an understanding that the employment relationship is meant to be reciprocal. In return for the immigrant worker's effort and constancy, the immigrant owner may be expected to make a place for newly arrived relatives, to accommodate work rules to employees' personal needs, and to assist workers with problems that they encounter with the host society or else lose his labor to a competing employer.[54]

Differences among Immigrant Groups

Thus far, I have sought to explain why immigrants are overrepresented in self-employment, but one major question remains: why do some immigrants do better in business than others? The historical record shows considerable disparities in self-employment among the various European immigrant populations: Jews, for example, were far more successful in business than were the Irish, and Italians achieved higher rates of self-employment than did Poles. Similar differences hold for the newcomers who arrived in the United States between 1970 and 1980. According to the Census of Population, Koreans ranked first with 11.5 percent self-employed; lagging far behind were the Mexicans, among whom less than 2 percent worked for themselves.

Various explanations have been adduced for these differences. Let us briefly consider one widely accepted account. This hypothesis, a version of the cultural approaches surveyed in Chapter 1, suggests that high self-

employment rates are largely a function of the skills acquired prior to migration and of previous exposure to an advanced market economy. One virtue of
the skills hypothesis is that it seems to do a nice job of explaining the
preponderance of Koreans among today's self-employed immigrants: Koreans
come with high levels of education (in 1980, 33 percent of the 1970–1980
newcomers reported having received a bachelor's degree); Korea is a rapidly
developing society whose competitive social system is in many ways akin to
that of the United States; and while Koreans have difficulty using their
formal and informal skills to gain entry into salaried professional and managerial positions, these same skills prove very useful in the competition for
small business positions.

The problem is that the situation of other immigrant groups does not fit
quite so neatly into the skills hypothesis. Koreans, it is true, report high
levels of education. Educational levels were considerably higher still among
Indians who came to the United States during the 1970s (63 percent of whom
reported having achieved a B.A.), yet Indians had less than half (43 percent)
of the self-employment rate of the less educated Koreans. The difference,
one might say, is that the Indians had the advantage of English-language
facility and therefore had fewer difficulties in getting jobs for which their
training qualified them, which might well be the case. But notice how
another factor has suddenly crept into the explanation and that, on concep-
tual grounds, language is almost certainly a component of skill. The difficulties become more grievous when one asks which group ranked number 2
among the self-employed. The answer is the Greeks, with 10.5 percent
working for themselves in 1980; but among this number 2 group, just over a
tenth of the 1970–1980 arrivals reported having a college education. The
problems are further compounded when one looks at the Chinese, similar to
the Koreans in educational background, exposure to industrialism, and
culture, and yet number 3 in the proportion working for themselves, with a
self-employment rate one half of the Koreans'. Of course, one could offer
various reasons for Greeks doing well despite their lower levels of education
and Chinese not doing as well as one might expect. However, the point of
this exercise is not to account for differences among particular immigrant
groups; rather it is to develop a general analytic framework. From this
perspective, what is wrong about the skills hypothesis is simply that it
is a single-factor explanation. The comparison among Koreans, Greeks,
Indians, and Chinese shows that a variety of factors impinge on the self-
employment process. Consequently, the most useful approach is multi-

variate, which implies that the terms of the interaction among the various factors is indeterminate. What one can do at an analytic level is to specify the variables that affect self-employment outcomes; it remains for empirical work to determine their effects on a case-by-case basis.[55]

In the broadest sense, one can separate out the conditions that influence the self-employment process into three categories: premigration characteristics; the circumstances of migration and their evolution; and postmigration characteristics. Under the former fall such attributes as skill, language, business experience, kinship patterns, and exposure to conditions (such as a high level of urbanization and industrialization) that would foster entrepreneurial attitudes. The circumstances of migration refer to the conditions under which the immigrants move, whether as temporary workers or as permanent settlers, as well as to the factors influencing their settlement type. Characteristics such as economic and occupational position, and discrimination (or the lack thereof) would fall under the postmigration rubric. It follows from the discussion above that no single characteristic—whether premigration or postmigration experience or circumstance of migration—will in and of itself determine the level of self-employment; rather, the critical factor will be how these various characteristics interact with another.

Premigration characteristics. The likelihood of succeeding in business is enhanced if an immigrant comes with skills that are useful to business success in both a general and a specific way. A good historical illustration is the case of turn-of-the-century Russian Jews who, by virtue of prior experience in tailoring, a high level of literacy, and a historical orientation toward trading, moved rapidly into entrepreneurial positions in the garment industry.[56] Since the educational level of the new immigrants is much higher than was true for the earlier immigrant waves, a considerable proportion do arrive with general skills that would be relevant for business success. As the comparison between Indians and Koreans suggested, it is not so much those immigrants with the highest or most developed general skills that will flock into business; rather, it is those whose general skills are not quite appropriate to the new context.

Relatively fewer immigrants arrive with skills that are specific to the business fields they enter. For example, New York's fur industry contains a high proportion of Greeks, both as workers and as owners, almost all of whom have come from the province of Kastoria where they were apprenticed as furriers at a relatively young age.[57] Yet the bulk of Greeks in business are

active in the restaurant industry, and cooking is not a skill that most Greek males appear to have brought with them, especially when one considers that Greek restaurants mainly specialize in "American food"! Thus, the crucial issue is how skills are acquired upon arrival in the host society. One answer, which follows from our discussion of ethnicity as organizational resource, is that groups with strong informal networks will do better in transmitting skills to newcomers. However, it is also true that these informal networks are important because of the conditions in small business industries; hence, for all groups, positional factors will be an important influence on self-employment rates.

Circumstances of migration. Whether newcomers arrive as temporary migrants or as permanent settlers, migration scholars increasingly agree, is a crucial condition of mobility and integration into the host society. Michael Piore, in his aptly named book *Birds of Passage,* has argued that most labor migrations to industrial societies begin as movements of temporary workers. In Piore's view, the fact that workers see themselves as temporary migrants explains why they constitute a satisfactory work force for dead-end jobs that native workers reject: as long as the migrants maintain the expectation of return, their concern is with the accumulation of capital to be brought home and invested in a business or farm, not with the attainment of social mobility in the societies to which they have migrated. Piore's discussion of social mobility largely involves access to the structured job ladders of large organizations, rather than the attainment of business ownership. But his argument also suggests a framework for evaluating how the circumstances of migration will affect entrepreneurial success.[58]

Earlier I contended that immigrants' predisposition toward business arises out of a response to blocked mobility. A better formulation would take account of Piore's argument and note that the opportunities or obstacles to mobility are likely to lie in the eyes of the beholders. Hence, the same factors that condition temporary migrants for work in low-level, dead-end jobs will also dampen the frustration that spurs other immigrants to start up in business on their own. As long as migrants anticipate returning home, as long as their stint in the host society is punctuated by periodic trips home, as long as they evaluate success in terms of their original standard of living, they will continue to furnish a supply of low-level labor. But those same low-level jobs will be unacceptable to permanent settlers, whose ambitions extend to the positions occupied by natives as well as to the rewards gener-

ated by those positions. Consequently, blocked mobility will impinge more severely on settlers than on their counterparts among the birds of passage.

Permanence is also likely to add an edge to the settler's quest for opportunity: if one does not succeed, there is no going back. It is for these reasons that permanent immigrants, as Piore points out, have a "reputation for being more aggressive . . . than temporary migrant groups."[59] And thus the circumstances of migration breed an affinity with the requirements of entrepreneurial success: only the aggressive immigrant will be foolish or desperate enough to start up a business when anyone can observe how many new concerns fall victim to a quick but painful death.

In addition to influencing aspirations, the circumstances of migration are also likely to affect immigrants' behavior in a way that will condition the likelihood of setting up on their own. One characteristic of temporary migrants is that their settlement and work patterns are too haphazard and variable to promote the acquisition of needed business skills and are also disruptive of the informal networks that play such an important role in organizing the immigrant firm and its labor force. By contrast, we can expect permanent immigrants to be more deliberate in their quest for economic progress. One nice example of this is Philip Young's description of Korean greengrocers in New York and the foresight and planning with which they pursue their trade: they may spend months scouring the city for the best possible location, and often deliberately open stores next to supermarkets so as to capture part of the latter's walk-in trade.[60]

The alternative to this argument is the possibility proposed by Edna Bonacich—that immigrants who move as "sojourners" with a clear intention of returning home will opt for business over employment as the better way of rapidly accumulating a portable investment capital.[61] There are two major problems with this hypothesis. One is that setting up a business is a far riskier endeavor than working for someone else. If we assume that even the most entrepreneurial of sojourning immigrants begin as employees, it is likely that they will accumulate a nest egg that can either be safely banked for returning home, or it can be invested in a small business whose chance for success is always open to doubt. Faced with these options, the prudent sojourner is likely to keep on working for someone else, as Robin Ward has shown in a study of East Asian immigrants in Britain. Though Bonacich has argued that these East Asian immigrants illustrate the influence of sojourning on ethnic business activity, Ward's study shows that they are in fact more likely to prefer employment over business in areas where high wages are paid to those

prepared to undertake hard and unpleasant work, resorting to business only in those cities where the available jobs are relatively poorly paid.[62]

Another condition of immigrant business activity is settlement pattern. Permanent immigrants usually either come with family or import immediate relatives shortly after settling; temporary immigrants leave family members at home. The consequence for temporary immigrants is that they must continue to funnel remittances that are needed to support relatives still living in the home country rather than use those monies to start up a business. As Kessner pointed out in his comparison of Italian and Jewish immigrants at the turn of the century, "the large sums of money sent back over the ocean to Europe drained [the Italians of] risk capital [for] investment and enterprise."[63]

Postmigration characteristics. Another factor that will exercise a strong effect on self-employment outcomes is a group's position in the economy. This factor follows from the argument made about opportunity structures, namely that certain environments are more supportive of small businesses than others. But the likelihood that immigrants will take advantage of these supportive conditions is greatest if immigrants are already concentrated in those industries where small business is the prevailing form. First, the motivation to go into business presupposes other conditions; for example, having some information about business opportunities that in turn can be used to assess the likelihood that one's efforts will be rewarded. Second, the neophyte capitalist will do better if he or she has some knowledge of the activities that the new role of ownership will entail; such knowledge is usually better if obtained at first hand rather than through indirect methods; and, as I have argued, one characteristic of those environments supportive of small business is precisely that the knowhow needed to run a business can be acquired through on-the-job training. Thus, immigrant groups concentrated in small business industries will have access to more and better information about small business opportunities and will also have more opportunities to acquire the relevant skills than those groups concentrated in industries where small businesses are not prevalent.

But emphasizing position begs the question of why groups occupy one position and not another. To some extent, this is a matter of prior skill; to some extent, purely random factors come into play, such as arriving at a time or place where small business industries generate a demand for immigrant labor. One important influence is the degree of native-language facility,

and looking at the effects of language provides a good illustration of how pre- and postmigration experiences interact to affect self-employment outcomes. Immigrants who arrive in the United States with English-language facility have a broader range of employment opportunities than do those newcomers whose English is virtually nonexistent or barely serviceable; and, having a broader range of opportunities, such immigrants are more likely to find employment in industries where the organizational form tends to be large. One case in point is that of West Indians in New York, who are heavily concentrated in an industry dominated by large, bureaucratized organizations, namely, health care.[64] Once ensconsed in this environment, the next logical step is not to go out and set up one's own business. Rather, the mobility-minded immigrant might acquire course credits or a degree, enroll in the job-training program run jointly by union and management, or simply accumulate the seniority needed to move up the next rung in the job ladder. What is at work here is in part a simple reference-group phenomenon: people act on the basis of imitation and follow the norms set by their peers. But the decision to enroll in a job-training program rather than setting up one's own shop also appears as a rational decision: the hospital worker knows far more about how to move up in the hospital hierarchy than about how a business might be run. One further point is simply that positional advantages or disadvantages tend to cumulate. In the West Indian case, this means that new arrivals are more likely to seek out jobs in health care than in an industry where there are few West Indians—simply because the existing concentration of West Indians makes it much easier for newcomers to get a job. At the same time, continued concentration in hospitals means that few entrepreneurial role models are created; hence, the tendency to seek mobility through the structured career ladder of the health-care system is reinforced.

Even within a small business industry some occupations are more strategic than others in terms of providing an employee with exposure to the skills and contacts needed to start up a small business. In the garment industry, for example, the typical new manufacturing business is set up when a salesman and a textile cutter get together: the salesman has the necessary knowledge of the market, and the cutter knows the production side. In restaurants, as Thomas Bailey has pointed out, waiting is the logical occupational bridge to becoming a restaurateur: the waiter learns how to size up the customer, direct him or her to the appropriate choice, and then hustle the customer off when a new patron is ready to take the table.[65] In retailing,

selling is also the point of departure for many employees who decide to start up on their own. For prospective immigrant capitalists, the question is how to gain access to these strategic occupations. This problem is particularly serious because many of these occupations involve face-to-face interaction, in which case natives' desire to maximize social distance from immigrants will obstruct the latter's recruitment into these key positions. What is at work is an instance of the principle of cumulative social advantage: immigrants belonging to a group whose characteristics favor business success will also be more likely to be hired by co-ethnics and thereby gain access to needed business skills. By contrast, those immigrants whose characteristics are less conducive to entrepreneurship will be more likely to work for natives, which in turn will reduce the likelihood of their gaining access to strategic occupations.

Conclusion. This chapter developed an explanation for immigrant enterprise that emphasized the interaction between the opportunity structure of the host society and the social structure of the immigrant community. The demand for small business activities emanates from markets whose small size, heterogeneity, or susceptibility to flux and instability limit the potential for mass distribution and mass production. Since such conditions favor small-scale enterprise, they lower the barriers to immigrants with limited capital and technical resources. Opportunities for ownership result from the process of ethnic succession: vacancies for new business owners arise as the older groups that have previously dominated small business activities move into higher social positions. On the supply side, two factors promote recruitment into entrepreneurial positions. First, the situational constraints that immigrants confront breed a predisposition toward small business and further encourage immigrants to engage in activities—such as working long hours—that are needed to gain minimal efficiencies. Second, immigrant firms can draw on their connections with a supply of family and ethnic labor as well as a set of understandings about the appropriate behavior and expectations within the work setting to gain a competitive resolution to some of the organizational problems of the small firm. While these factors lift the self-employment rate of the overall immigrant population, levels of business activity vary among specific immigrant groups. A group's success in attaining business ownership is determined by three characteristics—its premigration experiences, the circumstances of its migration and settlement,

its postmigration experiences—and how these characteristics interact with one another.

The next two chapters focus on the garment industry itself, considering the broader economic processes operating within this industry that have created the opportunities for the new immigrant garment capitalists.

[3]

From Tenement Sweatshop to Global Trade: The Changing Anatomy of the Garment Industry

Postindustrial New York meets the New York of production at the corner of Broadway and Broome. At 8:00 A.M., just hours after the last of the nearby punk clubs have closed, thousands of Chinese and Hispanic workers begin to clamber out of the subways, headed for the aging factory buildings that line the Broadway corridor. The elevators, slow and wheezing, take them to lofts packed with cut-up textiles and newly finished dresses and skirts. In the rear, older women and teenaged girls stand over the finishing tables, cutting off dangling threads and making last-minute adjustments. Behind them, steam already envelops the pressers, who are now placing a skirt on the ironing board, then shutting the press, now reopening it, then beginning the process time and again. Above the din blares the racy beat of salsa or the high-pitched voices of Chinese rock and roll, the latter transmitted through a local closed-circuit channel. Somewhere amid the clutter is the boss, perhaps straining over a sewing machine, perhaps haggling over prices with the manufacturer for whom the clothes are being made up.

Before we look directly at the immigrant firm, we need to know why garments are still "made in New York." That answer begins with the history of how the garment industry grew up in New York and then of how the industry evolved under the twin pressures of locational competition (both regional and international in scope) and of the growing importance of large firms; these are the issues to which we turn in this chapter.

New York City is the nation's principal concentration of apparel manufacturing and wholesaling. With almost 120,000 people employed in apparel manufacturing and another 50,000 working in apparel wholesaling, no other area begins to approach the level of this kind of activity found in New York.

New York City is also unique in the diversity of apparel activities that it offers. Not only is it the center of fashion design and creativity; it also contains an unparalleled number of buying offices, textile suppliers, accessory manufacturers, and specialized contracting facilities.

Strictly speaking, this and the following chapter focus on only part of New York's apparel complex, albeit its largest and its most important component, that is, the women's and children's apparel industry. This industry is composed of three main divisions: women's outerwear, women's and children's undergarments, and children's outerwear. These three divisions can also be broken down into a total of nine specialized subindustries. (These subindustries are listed with the Standard Industrial Classification [SIC] numbers assigned to them by the census and described in Appendix A.) These industries, which account for 63 percent of New York City's total apparel employment, are the backbone of its apparel complex. Some of the other functions classified as separate apparel industries by the census—beltmaking, pleating and stitching, and apparel trimming, to name the most notable—exist to service the needs of women's and children's apparel firms; other ancillary industries are not strictly in the apparel business at all but are in those wholesale lines that furnish needed inputs: textiles, buttons, needles, and thread. Of the remaining apparel industries, some have characteristics similar to women's and children's apparel but are not discussed here because they are too small (e.g., robes and leather clothing); other industries, such as men's clothing, are related to women's apparel but have distinctive features and have experienced a different pattern of development; still others, such as curtains and canvas products, have relatively little to do with the business of making clothing.

New York's present-day preeminence is a by-product of much earlier developments that date back to the turn of the century. Industrialization came late to the making of women's clothing and up to the late nineteenth century the bulk of clothing was still sewn at home. Starting in 1880, urbanization, the development of a national market, and rapid population growth spawned a market for ready-made women's wear, which then quickly began to supplant homemade clothes. During the next thirty-five years, clothing production shifted steadily from home to factory. In 1889 there were still 49,000 workers making dresses at home, whereas only 39,000 were producing women's clothes in factories; ten years later the number of dressmakers diminished slightly, while the number of factory-employed workers more than doubled; by 1919 the women's garment industry comprised 165,649 workers, almost all of whom were employed as factory help.[1]

The new, factory-based clothing industry grew up in the nation's cities. Boston, Philadelphia, Chicago, and Baltimore all gained sizable concentrations of clothing manufacturers. But in no city did garment manufacturing grow as rapidly or as greatly as it did in New York. The catalyst to New York's growth was the massive tide of immigration that flowed into the city just at the time when the demand for ready-made wear began to surge. Russian Jews fleeing poverty and persecution began to pour into New York City in 1880; by 1920 New York gained an estimated 460,000 eastern European Jewish immigrants. Roughly 12,000 Italian natives were living in New York on the eve of the great migration that began in the 1880s; over the next forty years approximately 390,000 of their countrymen and women landed and settled in New York.[2]

From the immigrants the garment industry gained a labor force that was poor, industrious, and compelled by want of other skills to seek work in a clothing shop. Many of the Jews had been tailors in the old country, and though most had worked with needle and thread, they quickly adapted themselves to machine production. Garments thus became the Jewish trade, and it soon attracted countless "greenhorn tailors" who had previously made their livelihoods in different pursuits but now found it profitable to claim expertise in the needle trades. Among the Jews, the garment shop was an employer of both men and women. Men went into coats and suits, the staple items of the garment business up to 1910. Shirtwaists, undergarments, and children's clothes, the lighter trades that developed after 1900, became the province of Jewish immigrant women for whom work was usually a limited stint that spanned the years between adolescence and childbirth. After 1900 the garment industry gained large numbers of Italians. In contrast to the Jews, Italian males were mainly drawn into heavy laboring jobs; and because these jobs were so unstable and low-paying, a high percentage of Italian women were compelled to continue working past childbirth, either in garment factories or as homeworkers.[3]

The industry was equally prompt in adapting itself to the newcomers. On the eve of immigration, most production was done in larger workshops, and as of 1889 the average establishment employed 31 people. Most of the factories were owned by manufacturers who were also Jews but were from Germany and were immigrants of a slightly earlier vintage. A new production system emerged with the advent of the Russian Jews. Rather than entering the larger manufacturers' shops, the newcomers went to work for smaller contractors, who often housed their factories in the same tenements where the immigrants lived. The contractors formed a convenient intermedi-

ary between the newly arrived working class and the established manufacturers. Usually also a Russian-Jewish immigrant, the contractor was better than the manufacturer in recruiting laborers, who were usually members of his own *landsleit*, the Yiddish term for those immigrants who came to the United States from the same hometown. These same connections also made it easier for the contractor to hold on to his labor force during the industry's wild seasonal fluctuations. And as long as the labor force consisted of newly arrived immigrants too bewildered and dependent to look for work elsewhere, the contractor could drive his workers to peaks of productivity that the larger manufacturer could not hope to rival.[4]

Thus, a new division of labor emerged: rather than supplanting the manufacturer, the contractor worked to specifications set by the manufacturer, simply taking over the arduous functions of recruiting and mobilizing labor. The distinction between the manufacturer, who was responsible for designing and merchandising, and subordinate contractor, who was charged with production, proved to serve other functions as well. The contracting arrangement allowed the manufacturer to limit investment in fixed capital and thereby reduce risks—an important consideration in an industry so prone to instability. Moreover, contracting permitted both firms to become specialists—the manufacturers in designing and merchandising, the contractors in production—and this proved convenient, since the small size and limited staff of most garment firms made it difficult for them to perform all the different activities efficiently. Hence, the tendency to divide functions between manufacturing and contracting has remained a distinctive feature of the industry up to this day.

With a massive labor force in place, other factors served to make New York the nation's clothing-manufacturing capital. As the nation's leading port, New York was already the chief entrepôt for the sale and exchange of textiles, both foreign and domestic. The sources of textile production were also located nearby. As Rischin points out, "Up to the first decade of the twentieth century, nearly all domestic materials handled by the wholesale dry-goods houses were manufactured in the mills of New York State and New England; and a combination of circumstances made nearby Paterson the nation's leading converter of raw silk."[5] Consequently, textiles were available at better prices and in greater variety than anywhere else in the country. New York's dual role as cultural center and gateway for travel to and from Europe also made it particularly sensitive to fashion change. These characteristics in turn served as a further attraction to the retail buyers, who by 1910 were massively congregated in New York.[6]

In the 1920s New York's premier resource—labor—was suddenly shut off. Passage of the Immigration and Naturalization Act in 1924 ended the huge flow of immigration and established particularly high barriers to those Jewish and Italian newcomers who had previously streamed into the garment industry in such large numbers. However, the impact of the immigration halt was not immediately felt, largely for two reasons. First, there remained a huge immigrant population, too lacking in skills to move into other trades and still so impoverished that it furnished an ample source of labor. To be sure, the composition of the industry's work force changed. Jewish immigrants had begun a transition from proletariat to middle class prior to 1920, and among the children of foreign-born Jews the movement into the middle class was more rapid. In the 1920s, as Deborah Dash Moore's portrait of New York Jewry shows, the city's Jewish population became firmly ensconsed in middle-class occupations and diversified beyond the needle trades into a broad array of business lines. This upward shift was particularly rapid among the American-born: by 1925, 63 percent of employed second-generation Jews were working in white-collar jobs. Mobility came slower to the Italians, however, as Thomas Kessner's comparative study of Jewish and Italian patterns found: a large proportion of the Italian immigrant population never moved out of low-level blue-collar jobs, and the second generation remained wedded to manual labor. Moreover, through the 1920s Italian men continued to be plagued by low wages and unemployment; as a result, Italian women were propelled into the labor force, where they mainly worked in garments, and the second generation was frequently compelled to leave school early to work in factory jobs.[7]

The growing influence of fashion was a second important factor reinforcing the tie to New York. The 1920s was the era of Gatsby and the flapper, and the loosening of life-styles that they represented was fully reflected in the clothes that women wore. Out went the rigid corset and the long, confining blouses and skirts: in came the dress. Stylishness became more important just as this new style—the dress—became in vogue.[8] At the turn of the century, fashion consciousness was mainly limited to the urban middle class, since the critical influences on taste—the large department store and the newspapers—were preeminently institutions of the large city. In the 1920s changes in communication and transportation linked city and small town, broadly diffusing the influence of big-city-generated fashion. In Muncie, as the Lynds found, the result was a "spread of the habit of being 'dressed up all the time.'" Girls and women gave "greater attention to dress, with increasing brightness and variety of color and costume," and the gener-

ation that reached adolescence in the 1920s placed a "taboo" on "plain appearance." While the Muncie newspapers printed virtually no advertising for ready-made wear as late as 1910, by October 1920 the leading Muncie newspaper was carrying 55,277 lines of advertising for factory-made women's clothes.[9] The cultural revolution in the Muncie's of the country had a far-ranging impact on New York's garment industry. As *Fortune* magazine observed in 1930:

[Before World War I] whether or not a manufacturer's line was what is now known as a "wow" made little difference. Dead stock in New York, Pittsburgh, Cleveland, and Chicago sold out quickly in Poughkeepsie, Beaver, Youngstown, and Peoria. [But] the movies now show the housewife, debutante and parlor maid in Poughkeepsie, Beaver, Youngstown, and Peoria just what Milady is wearing in New York, Pittsburgh, Cleveland, and Chicago. Conde Nast's *Vogue* and many another fashion periodicals circulate in quantities never before heard of. The motor takes Milady everywhere. No longer is any line saleable anywhere unless it is a "wow."[10]

With fashion thus more important, and New York very much the center of fashion, the city's early agglomerations of textile houses, department store buyers, designers, and, not least important, workers continued to give it a competitive edge in the production of style-oriented women's wear.

New York's Decline as a Production Center

While New York's garment industry continued to grow in the 1920s, and even in the 1930s, New York began to lose market shares to other producing areas. In 1909 roughly 61 percent of all women's clothing workers were employed in New York; by 1919 the city had almost 58 percent of the industry's total employment; but by 1941 only 39 percent of all garment workers were still to be found in New York.[11] In terms of absolute numbers, New York City's garment industry actually grew during these years, but its share of the industry dropped because new job creation mainly took place in other areas.

What accounts for the change? And why did it start in the 1920s and 1930s? The answer is threefold: the importance of labor; a shift upward in its cost to New York producers; and technologies that allowed firms to aggressively seek out cheaper labor elsewhere. In the 1920s and 1930s garments was a labor-intensive industry, as indeed it remains today. Made of soft material, a garment cannot be mechanically fed into a machine: a

worker needs to hold a garment or garment part and guide it through the sewing machine. Material-handling problems are compounded by the effects of style. Fashions change regularly; and since these changes alter the tasks of workers who sew the new fashions, the tasks cannot be fully broken down and standardized. For these reasons, labor counts for a very high percentage of total costs; such was the case in the 1930s, and such remains the case today.[12]

In the 1930s the labor costs of New York producers rose sharply because the International Ladies' Garment Workers' Union successfully organized the industry, first tying down coats and suits, and dresses, the two main branches, in 1934, and then mopping up the other, smaller industries (blouses, skirts, undergarments, etc.) over the next few years. Unionization had several effects, only one of which involved increased wages. The ILGWU also imposed a system of regulation that stabilized manufacturers' ties to their contractors, making manufacturers responsible for a steady flow of production to their principal contractors and thereby limiting their ability to rapidly build up and then level out production.[13]

The final catalyst to the dispersion of the garment trades was an increase in the mobility of garment-industry capital, such as it is. Considered against the steel mill or the auto assembly plant, there is an ineffable quality to the garment shop. The plant is usually a rented loft or storefront, and the machines are small, lightweight, and eminently mobile. Hence, when the price of labor rises in one location, in New York, for example, there are few costs entailed in closing down the garment shop and moving it to another location where the price of labor is somewhat less. The preconditions of relocation are two: means of physical access and availability of an alternative labor supply. In the 1930s both preconditions were met. The simultaneous collapse of the cotton textile industry in southern Massachusetts and the anthracite-mining industry in northeastern Pennsylvania created labor-surplus areas in close proximity to New York. Once the prevailing mode of transportation shifted from rail to rubber, the garment industry became less dependent on central locations like New York. Thanks to the new highways laid down in the 1920s and 1930s a truck could take on a load of cut textiles in New York on a Monday afternoon and deliver the material to a contracting shop in New Bedford, Massachusetts, or Allentown, Pennsylvania, the first thing Tuesday morning. Similarly, the spread of car ownership meant that the garment industry no longer needed to locate close to the tenement-housing districts, from which its workers walked to work, but

could instead rely on a dispersed rural population who drove to work along scattered country roads.

Thus, the outward flow of garment jobs began. With the start of World War II, the centripetal pressure on jobs momentarily waned, since improved economic conditions sparked a huge burst of pent-up demand, and manufacturers produced wherever they could find facilities and labor.[14] After the war the erosion of garment industry jobs resumed. Time-series data are not available for all three components of New York's women's and children's apparel industry, but only for the apparel industry as a whole: still, these data show the unmistakably downward trend. Between 1947 and 1958 total apparel employment declined by 54,000 jobs; in the succeeding decade, yet another 72,000 jobs were lost. The pace of job slippage accelerated further in the late 1960s and early 1970s. The 1969 recession produced a loss of 20,000 jobs in one year alone. And, in contrast to previous swings of the business cycle, the entire New York region remained on the downslide long after the nation moved into a period of renewed business activity. Between 1969 and 1975, employment declined at an annual rate of 12,500—twice as fast as during the previous decades. By 1975, when the garment industry had dwindled to just under 150,000 workers, one third of its 1969 labor force had been shed.[15]

In a sense, the explanation for the decline of New York's garment industry in the 1960s and 1970s is the same as the story offered earlier: the pressure on wages and the incessant drive to seek out still lower labor-cost areas. Other influences have since come into play, however. Once exclusively an industry of small firms, the garment industry is increasingly dominated by large entities. This transformation has altered the cost structure of clothing manufacture—putting New York at a further disadvantage—and it has also added a new dynamic to the pressure toward relocation. Second, the transportation revolution begun by the highway and truck has accelerated, making industry more footloose than ever. As a result, there is a new spatial division of labor that reaches far beyond the once peripheral areas to which garment manufacturers initially dispersed. It is the joint transformations in the structure and location of the garment industry to which we shall now turn.

Big Business Comes to the Needle Trades

"Apparel is the only major manufacturing industry in the United States," wrote *Business Week* not so long ago, "that has somehow escaped the 20th

century forces that elsewhere have led to concentration, automation, non-entrepreneurial managements, and a strong marketing orientation." This picture of apparel as a backwater of cutthroat capitalism may well be the standard portrayal, but the image it conveys is baldly anachronistic. In apparel, as in other types of industry, the small, family-owned firm has steadily lost ground; let us review the key indicators to trace the small firm's decline.[16]

Although apparel is still made up of a myriad of firms, many firms have been shaken out in a familiar process of contraction and consolidation. Between 1958 and 1982, the number of separate companies dropped by 5 percent, even though real consumption of apparel increased through the period: predominant among the losers were the smaller, labor-intensive firms. One indicator of the industry's changing structure is the spread of multiplant economies of scale. Single-unit firms prevail where product variations from plant to plant make it uneconomical for a company to share overhead costs among a group of plants. Historically, garment firms could attain only limited economies beyond those associated with a single plant of the optimal size. In 1954, the first date for which such data are available, less than a fifth of all apparel employees worked in multiunit firms. The extent of multiunit production was lowest in those product categories most influenced by fashion change: multiunit firms contained just over an eighth of all workers in the style-sensitive women's outerwear industry. By 1982, fewer than 8 percent of all apparel firms maintained more than one plant, but, as Table 3.1 shows, these same firms employed over 40 percent of the work force, indicating that substantially greater economies were now to be found by operating more than one factory. While women's outerwear continued to lag behind the rest of the apparel sector in this respect, employment in multiunit firms had grown substantially. In fact, the most notable gains were registered in the sportswear industry (SIC 2339), the most dynamic of the outerwear subindustries; by 1982, almost half of all sportswear employees worked in multiunit firms.

While employment is disproportionately concentrated among these multiunit firms and increasingly so, other indicators underline the depth of this trend. Shipments by multiunit firms (shown in Table 3.1) have grown even faster than employment, providing evidence of the internal scale economies generated by spreading overhead costs over multiple plants. Similarly, multiunit firms account for considerably more than their share of all capital investment. As Table 3.2 shows, changes in organization type have been accompanied by a shift toward larger plants. Whereas only a third of the

Table 3.1 Changes in Organizational Type
Women's and Children's Apparel Industry, 1954–1977

	All Industries	Women's Outerwear* (SIC 233)	Under-garments (SIC 234)	Children's Outerwear (SIC 236)
Percent of Employment in Multiplant Firms:				
1954	19.0	13.1	38.2	18.8
1958	22.9	16.7	42.0	24.8
1963	27.8	20.8	51.5	29.4
1967	35.9	26.5	59.5	34.2
1972	38.9	31.9	64.1	44.8
1977	42.4	33.3	70.4	56.6
1982	41.7	33.5	68.6	59.4
Percent of Shipments by Multiplant Firms:				
1954	NA	NA	NA	NA
1958	24.8	18.3	45.8	25.6
1963	30.2	23.1	54.4	30.0
1967	34.9	30.6	60.1	35.5
1972	45.0	38.8	68.6	47.1
1977	48.4	43.6	72.8	60.9
1982	49.5	44.8	73.1	61.8

Source: U.S. Census of Manufactures, 1954, 1958, 1963, 1967, 1972, 1977, 1982.
NA = not available.
*For full titles of industries, see Appendix A.

industry's labor force worked in plants of more than 100 in 1947, more than a half did so in 1982. The greatest changes took place in the more standardized lines, with average establishment size doubling in undergarments and almost tripling in children's clothes. The women's outerwear industry has been least transformed by these changes, but it too has experienced a shift away from smaller units. Of its various components, only the dress industry still retains a significant share of the work force in plants of less than 50. Dresses, however, has long been declining, whereas sportswear, which has grown significantly over the postwar period, employs 64 percent of its labor force in units of 100 or more, with more than half of these workers in plants of over 250 employees. The most recent statistics on establishment size and organizational type, however, do indicate that the trend toward larger plants and multiunit firms has slowed, which is largely due to the adverse effects of

Table 3.2 Changes in Establishment Size
Women's and Children's Apparel Industry, 1947–1982

	Avg. Establishment Size	Percentage Distribution of Employees by Size of Establishment Employee-Size Classes				
		1–19	20–49	50–99	100–250	250+
All Industries						
1947	32.9	13.3	30.1	23.0	20.6	13.1
1958	41.2	9.1	26.1	24.8	21.7	16.5
1967	50.3	6.1	20.5	23.6	25.6	25.6
1977	44.5	7.2	18.3	20.7	28.9	24.7
1982	45.5	7.6	17.8	20.7	27.4	26.3
Women's Outer-wear (SIC 233)*						
1947	31.0	14.3	34.3	23.3	18.3	9.8
1958	36.9	10.5	30.9	26.9	17.3	11.6
1967	43.4	7.3	24.9	26.7	23.8	17.1
1977	39.3	8.8	21.5	23.1	28.5	17.8
1982	38.7	9.4	21.2	22.7	26.6	20.8
Undergarments (SIC 234)						
1947	46.1	8.5	16.3	20.8	26.3	28.0
1958	67.7	4.7	11.8	17.9	29.7	35.8
1967	93.5	2.6	7.3	14.5	28.7	46.9
1977	104.5	2.3	6.3	10.1	27.3	53.9
1982	108.0	2.3	5.9	11.1	30.2	50.4
Children's Outer-wear (SIC 236)						
1947	28.5	16.4	29.3	25.1	24.5	4.7
1958	40.1	9.0	24.8	25.1	29.7	11.5
1967	58.6	5.2	16.9	21.0	30.6	26.3
1977	71.5	3.5	13.6	18.7	33.0	31.2
1982	73.8	3.2	11.4	20.0	29.6	35.7

Source: U.S. Census of Manufactures, 1947, 1958, 1967, 1977, 1982.
*For full titles of industries, see Appendix A.

international competition, treated in greater detail in the next major section (pp. 71–79); suffice it to say that the rising tide of imported clothing has robbed domestic clothing firms of the economies of scale needed to support a larger number of big plants.

Despite the growing importance of large firms, industry structure remains vigorously competitive, as can be seen from the data presented in Table 3.3.

Table 3.3 Four- and Eight-Firm Concentration Ratios, Women's and Children's Apparel Industry, 1947, 1970, 1977 (share of value of shipments accounted for by the four largest firms in each apparel industry)

| | *Percent Accounted for By* | | | | | |
| | *4 Largest Companies* | | | *8 Largest Companies* | | |
	1947 (or earliest date)	1970	1977	1947 (or earliest date)	1970	1977
Women's Blouses (SIC 2331)	7	22	12	11	29	18
Women's Dresses (SIC 2335)	6[2]	10	8	9[2]	13	12
Women's Coats & Suits (SIC 2337)	3[1]	10	15	6[1]	14	20
Women's Outerwear (SIC 2339)	14[2]	22	14	22[2]	31	20
Women's & Children's Underwear (SIC 2341)	6	16	22	11	23	29
Brassieres & Allied Garments (SIC 2342)	16	30	36	30	44	52
Children's Dresses & Blouses (SIC 2361)*	12[2]	14	15	20[2]	21	23
Children's Coats & Suits (SIC 2363)*	14[1]	22[3]	32	22[1]	31[3]	47
Children's Outerwear (SIC 2369)*	16[2]	22[3]	24	23[2]	32[3]	36

Source: U.S. Census of Manufactures, Subject Series, Concentration Ratios in Manufacturing, 1977.
*For full titles of industries, see Appendix A.
[1]1954 data.
[2]1963 data.
[3]1972 data.

Only in two of the specific apparel industries, brassieres and children's coats and suits, is the largest four firms' share of sales big enough to suggest the presence of oligopoly: in none of the other industries do the leading firms control a large enough share of the market to dominate price-setting. The more important consideration, though, relates to overall trend lines. In terms of seller concentration, the various apparel industries are evolving in

different directions. The undergarment industry, which was more concentrated than were the other apparel industries thirty years ago, has seen its large firms take up still more of the market. Children's clothing, which was previously characterized by small establishments and single-unit firms but now consists mainly of large establishments and multiunit firms, has also seen an upward drift in concentration levels. By contrast, women's outerwear remains almost as competitive as it was thirty years ago. What appears to have happened is that imports, to anticipate our discussion in a later section, greatly increased the number of sellers and thereby nipped off the potential for concentration.

Thus, large firms are of growing importance, especially in undergarments and children's outerwear, where seller concentration is up, as it is in women's outerwear, despite the persistence of competitive industry structure. What accounts for this change? The answer has three parts, the first of which stresses the importance of fashion change. New York gained dominance in women's clothing during a period of formal wear, a time when women were expected to wear distinctively feminine clothes, and both men and women were expected to conform to explicit and high standards of appropriate dress. However, the life-style transformations of the past few decades— suburbanization, the trend toward greater leisure, rising labor-force participation among women—have transformed patterns of dress. Women's fashions have become more casual, less constricting, less distinctive from men's. The best example of such fashion change is the emergence of blue jeans as an item of mass consumption.

The "blue-jeans phenomenon" was one of the major events in the popular culture of the 1960s and 1970s. Initially a standard item of proletarian wear, among 1960s youth blue jeans became a symbol of their rejection of the conformity and materialism of their parents' lives: What was a 1960s rebel without a pair of faded blue jeans, frayed at the knees, wearing thin at the hip pockets? A second transformation came when jeans became, not a symbol of disdain for status, but the very object of conspicuous consumption itself. The 1970s were the era of the "designer jean," when the name Vanderbilt was joined to a piece of denim cloth to lend a special aura to the wearer—at, of course, a significantly higher price.

The rapid rise in jeans consumption and other standardized items has now leveled off, with implications and consequences to be explored in the next chapter. For now, the crucial point is to note how suddenly jeans gained popularity and how fast the market for jeans grew. No company benefited

more than Levi Strauss, currently the industry's giant. In 1983 Levi Strauss's sales were more than two and a half times greater than its nearest competitor's, and Levi Strauss accounted for roughly a third of all U.S. blue-jeans sales and a seventh of all world blue-jeans sales. In the 1930s, however, the company was strictly a regional producer and its best-selling brand—Levi's 501—was virtually unavailable outside the Far West. Even as late as the 1950s, Levi Strauss's sales were largely confined to the West, with the company informally ceding other regions to its two principal competitors—Blue Bell in the Southeast and Lee in the Middle West. In 1965 a national survey commissioned by Levi Strauss showed that most people still considered the 501 a farmer's garment. But tastes then rapidly changed. From 1957, when annual U.S. sales of jeans of all kinds by all makers stood at roughly 150 million pairs, consumption rose to just over 200 million in 1967 and then skyrocketed to over 500 million in 1977, or more than two pairs of jeans for every man, woman, and child in the country. Levi Strauss rode the crest of this wave to become the nation's leading apparel producer. "Between 1962 and 1970 sales and net profits more than quintupled; between 1970 and 1977, after passing the billion-dollar-mark in 1975, sales almost quintupled again and profits almost septupled." By 1983 the Levi Strauss empire included 94 U.S. plants as well as 63 establishments overseas, altogether providing work to a labor force of 44,000 employees.[17]

For our purposes, the jeans story is important because it illuminates the link between changes in product markets and the growth of large firms. The trend toward jeans and other, more casual clothes involves a shift from an unstandardized product to a highly standardized item. On the one hand, there is the dress, made in small quantities and subject, thanks to fashion, to built-in obsolescence. On the other hand, there are the blue jeans or the T-shirt, fabricated in huge quantities and barely susceptible to the whims of style. Indeed, so little perishable are the blue jeans that Levi Strauss's best-selling 501 brand has received only minor modifications since it was first made in the late 1870s.

Standardization has important implications for industrial organization. First, it makes significant economies of scale possible. Components can be purchased in mass, with accompanying reductions in unit costs. Production runs can be lengthened, leading to savings through greater division of labor, which in the garment industry has involved a shift from full-garment sewing to "section work," an assembly-line-type process in which each operator sews together a single part of the garment. Long production runs also justify

investment in specialized, single-purpose equipment that would not be appropriate in fashion lines that involve constant changes in job tasks. Second, standardization yields economies of scale to multiplant operations. Once management no longer needs to keep its hand on the pulse of the market, since demand is relatively invariant, it can delegate functions and separate responsibilities. Problems at the operating level are at once less likely to occur, since these operations are more routinized—and less immediately important—since speed of delivery is no longer critical.

That standardization is related to larger firm size in the garment industry can be discerned from the data presented in Tables 3.1–3.3. Multiplant operations and large firms are most prevalent in the more standardized lines and are much less common in those product areas that are subject to fashion. Similarly, the highest level of sales concentration is in the manufacture of brassieres, perhaps the most standardized clothing item of all. In women's outerwear the effects of standardization on the size of both firm type and plant size can be grasped by comparing the data for dresses and for "other outerwear," the residual category that includes jeans and other casual items, popularly known as sportswear. The large-plant (250 workers or more) share of the work force in sportswear is four times as large as in dresses, while multiunit sportswear firms have twice the share of employment that similarly organized concerns do in dresses.

The Advantages of Large Size. If standardization has thus been the initial catalyst to the growth of large firms, a second set of considerations involves the use of size to attain greater market power and the strategies by which this is done. A large apparel manufacturer can mobilize significantly greater resources in pursuit of the retail dollar than can its smaller competitor. Large firms can wield significant muscle in their dealings with retailers, circumventing individual retail buyers who have authority over a single line or department to effect an alliance with top store management that ensures distribution throughout a store or chain. For example, large apparel makers often demand a minimum purchase order, while their smaller competitors will accept orders of any size. One top executive of Leslie Fay, the largest nondiversified manufacturer of women's wear, pointed out that buyers must purchase "a minimum of 15 styles. And if they don't, we don't take the account. We are tough people."[18] This policy is common among the larger firms, as one buyer at a major New York department store noted: "If we don't want one of its lines, a large manufacturer can, and sometimes does, hold

back other lines that we need."[19] Since retailers are increasingly cutting back on their advance purchases, the large firms' ability to obtain a minimum purchase order freezes out smaller competitors and confines them to late-developing components of demand. In addition, the role that large firms play as suppliers to retailers is often so important that manufacturers gain influence over how their lines are promoted and displayed within the stores.

Thanks to their own large sales, the major apparel firms also succeed in obtaining more favorable treatment from their textile suppliers—another advantage of large size. To secure large-volume orders, the textile mills will offer special services unavailable to low-volume producers, such as joint efforts in product development. Large manufacturers whom I interviewed offered these examples as cases in point:

We buy fabrics from both mills and converters, but generally our orders are big enough to go directly to the source. The mills work closely with us. Our designer will decide what she wants, and the mills will often design fabrics exclusively for us. There's a lot of interaction with mills and converters.

We grew by being the first firm to successfully market polyester. We used a fabric developed by "X" Mills, and they worked very closely with us in developing this fabric. There were problems in handling this fabric which we were the first to overcome, with their help, and this gave us a foothold in the department stores.

Moreover, since large firms plan their purchases early in close cooperation with their textile suppliers, the major apparel firms are in a stronger position to corner the best-selling materials and thus squeeze out smaller makers. Large purchasers are further rewarded with advertising funds that can either be used for institutional promotion to the industry or be advanced to major retail customers in cooperative advertising bids.

Distributional patterns are an additional source of advantage. Small firms typically rent a single selling office in a major market center; the smaller, New York-based firms depend on the drawing power of the huge New York market to generate business. By contrast, large manufacturers maintain selling offices in all the major marketing centers and also employ traveling salesmen who service customers from smaller cities and towns. Sales by localized producers are typically influenced by seasonal patterns (a warm fall dampens the demand for coats; a cold March or April discourages consumers from buying spring clothes), but large firms that sell nationally can offset regional losses by increasing sales in other areas. Access to the

broader national market provides additional justification for institutional advertising through the industry press.

While size is thus a source of significant market power, the large apparel firms have also developed strategies that mitigate against the effect of changes in consumer taste. One such option is diversification. The small maker is highly specialized in terms of both product- and price-line—making only popular-priced sportswear or only high-priced coats, for example—and hence is susceptible to any shift that might alter the demand in those particular categories. The large firms, by contrast, tend to span a number of product categories: the very largest usually make women's and men's wear, whereas those in the next tier span the full range of either women's or men's clothes. The result is considerably reduced exposure to the risk that demand for any one product might flatten out. As an executive for Palm Beach, a large men's suit concern that has moved heavily into other men's lines as well as women's wear, put it:

Our acquisition program was undertaken with the idea of balancing our product mix. We started out with a single product—men's white summer suits—and a single selling season—spring. Now we feel that cyclical downturns in any one or two lines will be offset by continuing improvements in all of the others.[20]

Since the large firms are also more likely to do much or at least some of their production in directly owned facilities, diversification is also a way of running these plants at high efficiencies. For example, in 1973 Palm Beach purchased Evan-Picone, a manufacturer of women's coats and suits, and then converted two of its idle men's suit factories to making women's sportswear under the fast-selling Evan-Picone label. In 1978 Palm Beach purchased another women's coat company whose assets included a highly efficient factory that had been underutilized because of seasonal swings in demand and leveled out production by bringing in less seasonal items during normally slow periods.[21]

Diversification is a way of adapting to the vagaries of style; developing a brand-name marketing program is a strategy designed to directly influence taste and sustain consumer demand in the face of fashion change. To begin with, the large concerns are long established, which makes it more likely that their products will be firmly identified in the consumer mind, as opposed to their smaller competitors, among whom the rate of failure is very high. Thus, even a discontinued line, if previously popular, may enjoy a considerable half-life: Jonathan Logan, for example, closed down its

"Jonathan Logan" label but sold the once popular name to Kayser-Roth, which sought the license to attract those consumers still loyal to the Jonathan Logan name.[22]

The advent of branded women's apparel on a large scale, however, was mainly a product of the 1970s, when large firms began a concerted effort to market brand-name apparel and to push those items through heavy investments in advertising and promotion. The next logical step was to use the name of a well-known couturier or high-fashion designer, whose name lent the cachet of fashion to easily produced standardized garments or accessories. These products were then marketed at a fraction of the designer's "regular" line but at a price that considerably exceeded the level of standard branded wear. The final twist has been to put the designer's name on a complete ensemble of women's wear—from coats to belts to pocketbooks— and then lease space in a department store where all the goods can be marketed together.

Transactional Economies and Their Importance. Yet another catalyst to the growth of large apparel firms has been a change in the industries to which apparel is linked. Historically, there was a strong element of symmetry in the relationship between the apparel industry and its suppliers and customers. On the selling side, apparel firms dealt mainly with independent department stores, specialty stores, jobbers, and resident buying offices. With so many small units active at the wholesale level, purchases were diversified and limited to short-term needs. A more formidable array of large textile firms confronted apparel makers on the input side. Yet the influence that uncertainty exercised on apparel firms led them to act much like their customers, holding back on textile purchases and delaying commitments until orders flowed in from the stores. Since the high-volume, massproducing textile mills could not afford to provide rapid deliveries of small, unstandardized orders, textile needs were mainly handled by locally based "converters" that purchased unfinished cotton or woolen goods and then dyed these materials to manufacturers' specifications.[23]

But big business has now come to both the retail and the textile industries, with important implications for their relationship to apparel firms. Retailing has been swept by a "retail revolution," in which department store- and discount-chains have exploded, largely supplanting their smaller competitors—the independent department store and the specialty store. In 1977, for example, only 331,000 of the almost 2 million retail enterprises

had more than one outlet, but these same 331,000 stores accounted for almost half of all retail sales. Big business is still more characteristic of those retailers that specialize in marketing apparel. In 1977 over 90 percent of all apparel was sold in either department stores or specialized apparel-and-accessory stores. More than 60 percent of all department store sales were made by chains with over 100 units; even within the apparel-and-accessory-store sector, the largest firms accounted for a quarter of total sales. These large-firm shares represented very substantial growth: twice the 1958 level for department stores and three times the entire volume for the specialty-store sector. Moreover, within the department-store sector, the trend is for the very largest chains to grab up a still larger portion of retail sales.[24]

The apparel industry has felt the impact of the retail revolution in two quite distinctive ways. First, the expansion of the large retail chains has created growth potential for those manufacturers with considerable capacity: the ability to produce quantities that are sufficient to supply an entire chain of stores gives the large apparel firm an important step up over its smaller competitor. And as the leading retail chains have relentlessly pursued market saturation, so has the volume of purchases made from major apparel manufacturers increased. Working with the large apparel manufacturer gives the retailer the further advantage of one-stop shopping. Rather than scurrying from one small maker to another in order to assemble a line, a large retailer can gain considerable transaction economies if it can negotiate a single purchase from a large manufacturer and thus obtain items from a variety of product- and price-lines. The search for transactional economies will also lead the large retailer to develop a new line in tandem with one of its major apparel suppliers. Thus, as one Leslie Fay executive noted, "The major stores are interested in developing key vendor intensification programs. They want to avoid shopping the whole market to know where their basic business will come from every month."[25] Finally, the larger retailer is also interested in reducing uncertainty, and for this reason it is also likely to buy from the time-tested major manufacturer rather than from the small manufacturer whose line might be "hot" but whose ability to maintain quality and meet deadlines is as yet unproven.

The retail revolution has had a second impact on the apparel industry by further standardizing demand. In part, this has come about through the influence that large retailers exercise on consumers, who are still more firmly wedded to stores than to the manufacturers of apparel, whose prod-

ucts so often go in and out of fashion and are often too thinly distributed to establish a "name." Advertising, which has grown with the expansion of the chains, has been another way of reducing instability in consumer buying patterns, and it is increasingly used to encourage consumers to "preplan" their purchases.[26]

In a similar process, centralization and concentration of textile production has undercut the market position of the small apparel maker. Though its changes have not been as far-reaching as the retail revolution, the textile industry has also undergone a trend toward larger firms and larger units of production. In 1977, 13 percent of textile employment was concentrated in the top three firms; the top ten firms accounted for almost one quarter of total industry employment. Given heavy investments in plant and technology, the textile mills seek large units of sale in order to obtain needed economies of scale and to plan future production lines. Like the retail chains, the mills also obtain significant reductions in transaction costs by selling to the tier of large apparel firms.[27]

These twin changes in both input and output markets have reinforced the trend toward large size among apparel makers. As noted in a report prepared for the Commerce Department, the retail chains tend to limit the number of apparel suppliers for any one price or style category to those few that do the best job of satisfying retail needs.[28] To satisfy the retail chains, the apparel makers must be able to fill their orders and deliver products on time; this, in turn, means that the successful claimants for the chains' orders are those apparel firms that are large enough to buy directly from the high-volume textile mills. Thus, as the president of one of the largest manufacturers of women's sportswear pointed out in an interview:

The chains are very demanding. Their pattern is to buy in huge quantities. To work with them you have to be able to back up your merchandise, and that involves buying your goods from the mills way in advance.

Run, Run, Runaway Shop: The Garment Industry Relocates

New York City's decline as a production center began in the 1930s when manufacturers and contractors started abandoning it for lower-cost, labor-surplus areas in the Northeast. Since then, the frontiers of garment production have widened. Today there are virtually no barriers to where the proverbial runaway shop can flee. The industry's new spatial division of labor is global; its internationalization is the result of the changes in product-market

and industrial structure discussed previously, to which has been added a revolution in permissive technology speeding the flight of the industry from one new production source to another.

Changes in product markets tell part of this story. As we have seen, the post–World War II period has been marked by a steady shift toward more standardized clothing products; New York lost out in the trend toward casual wear for several reasons. First, these changes in taste meant that demand for New York's traditional, more formal products declined. Second, New York producers were unable to compete in making the newer, more standardized wear, owing to the economies of scale and the reductions in labor cost made possible by the shift to standardization. Third, standardization was accompanied by a constantly mounting pressure on wages, since the shift toward less skilled labor increased susceptibility to lower-labor-cost competitors.

Standardization also loosened the other ties that had bound firms to New York's broad apparel complex. As long as the bulk of garment makers specialized in fashion goods, clustering in New York had the advantage of quick and easy accessibility to the multitude of fabric sellers and apparel buyers that also congregated in New York. However, standardization alters the size and tempo of production, thus freeing firms from their spatial dependency on related purchasers and suppliers. Since standardized makers use large quantities of inputs and can plan their material needs long in advance of actual production, fabric supplies can be routinized and directed over long distances. And since output is planned according to previous sales, standardized makers no longer need to depend on proximity to competitors and buyers for information about quickly changing fashion trends. Finally, the trend toward larger firm size, the result of economies of scale made possible by standardization, means that more firms have the material and personnel overhead needed to manage activities dispersed over space, thereby gaining greater access to remote, low-labor-cost regions.[29]

Just how changes in product markets and firm size influenced locational outcomes can be seen by tracing out the historical pattern of industrial dispersion. Initially, the outflow of apparel from New York was limited to those lowest-price, labor-sensitive lines that were relatively immune to fashion change. However, this mainly involved sewing operations, which were spun off to lowest-cost, labor-surplus areas; meanwhile, those aspects of the business that were difficult to routinize and required face-to-face interactions and prompt decision making—designing, textile cutting, buying and selling—remained in New York. This unevenness at the early stage of re-

location kept decentralization within bounds: the importance of rapid communication as well as the need to coordinate shipments among the different production operations kept sewing facilities within a day's truck drive of New York City.[30]

As long as the outflow of jobs from New York tended toward nearby areas, the wage differential between New York and its regional competitors could be partially contained. The ILGWU was immensely successful in organizing garment workers in Pennsylvania and Massachussets, though raising wages to the New York level proved a much more difficult task. In the mid-1950s there was a 33 percent wage differential between the heavily unionized areas of northeastern Pennsylvania and New York City; as of 1982 apparel wages in Pennsylvania were still 16 percent lower than that in nearby New York City.[31]

Nonetheless, the union's success in the Northeast spurred apparel makers to seek out new, lower-labor-cost areas. The South beckoned, with its history of compliant labor relations, supply of surplus rural labor, and poor towns offering substantial inducements to new employers. But migration to the South was tempered by the pace of standardization. Up through the 1950s, the firms moving southward were mainly makers of standardized wear, since only these companies had the resources to decentralize and the products that could be made with little attention to the fashion trends evolving in New York and other design centers. Indeed, northeastern producers benefited from New York City's decline. As Table 3.4 shows, during the 1950s the Northeast's share of national employment barely slipped in any product category; because the domestic industry experienced considerable growth during this period, absolute employment levels in the Northeast actually climbed.

But thereafter the spatial reallocation of garment capital increased in both pace and scope, as can be seen from Table 3.4. By the 1960s intraregional competition spilled over onto the interregional level, as first the South and then the Far West became poles of industry growth. Makers of standardized items stepped up their migration southward, while firms specializing in less standardized, women's outerwear lines joined the bandwagon in increasing numbers. Once the growth of the economy stalled in the 1970s, the terms of competition shifted decisively against the Northeast. With pressure on labor costs mounting, and more of the industry organized in a multiunit form that made relocation feasible, the southern drift of employment accelerated. As a result, the job base in the older producing areas suffered massive declines. By 1982 the South had surpassed the Northeast in its share of employment in

Table 3.4 Changes in Locational Distribution of Employment
Women's and Children's Apparel Industry, 1947–1982

	Total Employment (U. S.)	Percentage Distribution of Employees by Location			
		N.Y.C.	Northeast	South	Pacific
All Industries					
1947	456,096	41.7	70.8	5.7	5.2
1958	552,109	31.8	69.5	17.5	6.3
1967	601,700	26.0	57.1	26.8	7.0
1977	610,700	18.3	44.8	31.4	11.1
1982	572,500	15.5	41.7	39.4	12.8
Women's Outer-wear (SIC 233)*					
1947	313,402	44.5	70.1	5.7	6.4
1958	360,000	34.4	68.7	14.3	8.2
1967	410,000	29.3	59.7	21.1	9.0
1977	447,700	21.3	49.0	28.7	13.8
1982	419,300	18.0	44.8	34.1	16.8
Undergarments (SIC 234)					
1947	94,558	33.3	68.5	8.5	3.2
1958	111,300	26.0	63.2	24.5	1.9
1967	113,500	18.5	48.1	41.4	3.8
1977	91,800	10.1	32.0	36.4	4.6
1982	81,600	9.2	31.7	52.4	6.1
Children's Outer-wear (SIC 236)					
1947	48,136	39.6	80.2	7.5	1.9
1958	80,809	28.5	81.8	21.8	3.6
1967	78,200	19.8	56.7	35.5	3.9
1977	71,200	10.0	38.3	44.3	3.9
1982	71,600	8.6	35.5	55.3	4.2

Source: U.S. Census of Manufactures, 1947, 1958, 1967, 1977, 1982.
* For full titles of industries, see Appendix A.

the more standardized undergarments and children's wear lines; only in the more fashion-influenced women's outerwear lines did the Northeast retain a slender lead.

International Competition. In garments, as in so many other American industries, the struggle for the consumer's dollar is no longer just a matter of

regional competition. America's clothing needs are increasingly met by foreign producers. In 1959 imports were 6.9 percent of domestic production of all women's and men's apparel (a figure that includes both woven and knitted clothing, the latter technically a branch of the textile industry); by 1980 the ratio of imports to domestic production had reached the 51 percent level. Thereafter, import levels climbed dramatically, up 8.7 percent in 1981, up another 7.9 percent in 1982, and then up by still greater jumps of 14.6 percent in 1983 and 21.3 percent in 1984. Because the domestic market grew at a much slower pace, imports grabbed a growing share of domestic clothing consumption: by 1984 half of all clothing sold in the United States was made abroad.[32]

Initially, imports were concentrated in highly standardized items like slacks and brassieres, but as exporters gained experience and distribution networks were developed, imports increasingly penetrated more fashion-sensitive lines. With the exception of dresses, suits, and skirts, imports had climbed above the 50 percent penetration level in most important women's apparel categories in 1983, as shown in Figure 3.1. Even in the least af-affected categories, such as dresses, where fashion reduces the lead time needed to import, or sweatshirts, where bulk increases import costs, the trend is unmistakably upward. As the market for imported clothing has grown, so too have the number of clothing-exporting countries. It is no longer just Japan or Hong Kong trying to woo U.S. consumers; today, virtually every country with a developed clothing industry is trying to gain a piece of the U.S. market as well. In 1984 the Department of Commerce's *Major Shippers* report listed more than 80 countries as major exporters of clothing to the United States.[33]

A crucial reason for the explosion of imports is that U.S. makers are unable to compete on labor costs. The technology of apparel production is sufficiently simple so that developing countries have been able to establish a toehold easily, especially in the more standardized product categories. Moreover, there has been rapid diffusion from developed to developing economies of those technologies in the few areas of apparel manufacturing in which significant technological advances have been made. Consequently, export-based producers in developing countries can usually match, if not exceed the levels of productivity attained by the most efficient domestic makers, and the more established exporters have been able to upgrade their products in quality and style and have succeeded in diversifying from low-end to middle-range goods.

Figure 3.1 Imports of Women's and Children's Apparel as a
Percentage of Domestic Production (in millions of units)

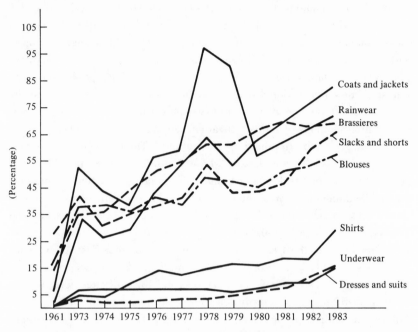

Source: International Ladies' Garment Workers' Union, Research Department.

While productivity is thus roughly comparable, U.S. wages in apparel are
almost five times the level of Hong Kong's, the single largest apparel exporter, and wages in Hong Kong are considerably higher than in the rest of
the "big four": South Korea, Taiwan, and the People's Republic of China.[34]
Moreover, since transfer costs are relatively low, garments being of high
value in relation to weight and bulk, the permeability to import penetration
is greater still. According to one British study, for example, transporting
individually boxed polyester/cotton shirts from Dublin to Liverpool amounts
to almost 0.5 percent of total production costs; the cost of shipping the same
type of shirt from Hong Kong to London adds only 14 percent to the total
Hong Kong production cost; substitute North Carolina for Dublin and New
York for London and the results are essentially the same.[35] Finally, what
Bluestone and Harrison have called a "revolution in permissive technology"
has shrunk international space. Owing to containerized shipping, the jumbo

jet and the wide-bodied cargo plane, the telex, and the worldwide computer network linked up through a satellite in space, the costs and time required for worldwide communication and transportation have been greatly reduced.[36]

Whereas the relocation of the domestic apparel industry took place as large, standardized producers succumbed to the lure of low wages, doing so with the aid of various decentralizing technologies, large domestics have played only a minor role in internationalizing clothing production. The industry's new international division of labor stems from two sources: the efforts of developing countries to follow export-oriented rather than import-substitution methods of industrialization; and domestic retailers' search to exploit the greater profits that importing affords. The first country to export clothing successfully was Japan, whose clothing industry proved highly competitive, thanks to low wages and substantial government export programs; the undervaluation of the yen; and a highly competitive textile industry, which kept fabric costs down. Exports from Japan began to permeate the U.S. market in the late 1950s, especially in certain standardized categories. Over the course of the 1960s, Japan lost its lead to other East Asian countries, most notably Hong Kong, Taiwan, and South Korea. One reason was that "voluntary restrictions" on trade with the United States agreed to by Japan in 1957 made it more difficult for Japan to maintain a high flow of exports. A more important influence was the effect of Japan's own rapid economic growth: labor grew short; the competition for labor yielded upward pressure on wages; and, since most producers were very small, they were unable to generate the gains in productivity needed to offset the increases in labor costs. Finally, the appreciation of the yen further added to the price of Japanese goods.[37] Hence, between 1960 and 1972 Japan sunk from first to eighth among the world's leading exporters, by which time Japan itself became a significant importer of clothing.[38] As of 1983, Japan was the world's seventh-largest importer of clothing and no longer ranked among the top fifteen exporting countries.[39]

Hong Kong's success was in part the by-product of Japan's growing difficulties: as Japanese production declined, Japanese trading companies contracted with Hong Kong factories to maintain their share of the market. However, the foundation of Hong Kong's clothing industry was laid just after the Chinese Revolution in 1949 when emigré businessmen from Shanghai brought both capital and expertise and founded the colony's fledgling textile/clothing complex. Initially, the orientation was toward the British market, with the connection established by Hong Kong's British-owned merchant

houses. Though successful in rapidly increasing exports, Hong Kong soon fell under pressure from affected British producers, which quickly limited the room for further growth. The colony's producers then looked for American trade, but in this endeavor they were handicapped by their previous experience in trade with the British, which had involved only the most standardized items. The crucial spur to Hong Kong's development came from the interest of large U.S. mail-order houses, chain stores, department stores, and wholesale distributors. The retailers were undergoing a significant increase in competition caused, in part, by the growth of low-cost discounters; consequently, the prospects of purchasing clothing in Hong Kong offered a welcome opportunity to cut costs and, to the dismay of domestic manufacturers, increase markups. U.S. retailers began making regular trips to Hong Kong, taking with them samples of goods to be made and negotiating contracts with Hong Kong producers.[40] As the Geigers write in their study of the economic development of Hong Kong:

On the one side, the Chinese manufacturers in Hong Kong were both eager and able to adapt their output to the style requirements and the stringent specifications of their U.S. customers, despite the many difficulties that had to be surmounted. On the other side, to inform and help their suppliers, American executives and buyers frequently visited Hong Kong to transmit samples and specifications of garments to be made and to negotiate the necessary contracts. Soon the largest U.S. importers opened Hong Kong offices so that they could continuously monitor the production runs, sample test the finished garments, and expedite shipments to the United States.[41]

What has evolved is a pattern known as "specification buying" in which retailers usurp the functions performed by domestic clothing manufacturers, actually designing the garment and making such decisions as which fiber to use, from whom the fiber will be obtained, who will make the fabric, and so on down the line. In their involvement with contractors, retailers furnish exact specifications, production schedules, and shipping instructions, while also providing technical and managerial assistance in production and quality control.[42]

In Korea and Taiwan, foreign buyers played a similar role in spurring the development of the clothing trade. Consequently, there are now tens of foreign buying offices and thousands of national and foreign trading companies maintaining full-time purchasing offices in Seoul, Taipei, as well as in Hong Kong; among the firms with such permanent installations are Macy's, Penney's, and other giants of American retail trade. The retailers have thus

provided the skill-intensive knowhow in marketing needed to complement the area's advantage in labor costs—the provision of outlets and the use of brand names, publicity, design, market research, and so on. Moreover, in their arrangements with East Asian subcontractors, the retailers absorb a substantial portion of risk, especially since the lead time involved in producing for export may range from six to twelve months.

With the buildup of East Asia's apparel complex, the cost of arranging for exports has fallen further. Though travel is still not cheap, there are ample connections between the United States and the East Asian exporting countries: Hong Kong alone houses the offices of thirty five international airlines. Moreover, communications links are well developed, an important consideration in an industry where buyer and clothing maker are in frequent contact. Finally, the spread of the industry through East Asia offers a further inducement to U.S. buyers. As a World Bank study notes, "A businessman who intends to travel to Hong Kong to place some orders can stop off in Japan to select fabrics and in Korea and Taiwan to look for potential new suppliers," and thanks to a special bargain fare, he can do so for the same price as for a regular round-trip visit to Hong Kong alone.[43]

Offshore Production. Most imported clothes enter the United States along the lines sketched above: a retailer or an importer travels to the Orient; arranges with a subcontractor to make clothes according to specification; and six to twelve months later, the clothes arrive in the retailer's warehouse. However, a substantial portion of clothing is imported under the direct aegis of a domestic manufacturer: this is known as offshore production, which falls into one of two categories. The first is when a domestic maker goes multinational, by investing in a directly owned facility for the purpose of manufacturing for the U.S. market. Often internationalization is a second-step event: many of the clothing multinationals first went to Puerto Rico, a source of cheap labor in the heyday of Operation Bootstrap; only later, when Puerto Rican wages began to rise, did they establish a foreign facility. Though a common breed for U.S. manufacturing at large, the multinational is a rare bird among clothing concerns, mainly found among firms specialized in highly standardized lines, such as bras and girdles. Thus, "related-party" data from the U.S. Bureau of the Census, which cover trade between parties in which an ownership relation of 5 percent or more exists between importer and exporter, show that in 1978 only 8.8 percent of all apparel imports were between related parties, as opposed to 91 percent for

semiconductor parts, 41 percent for television receivers, and 33 percent for motor vehicles. Moreover, related-party trade accounted for only a negligible portion of the apparel exports sent by the leading East Asian producers—Hong Kong, South Korea, and Taiwan.[44]

The second, more common arrangement is to supply a foreign contractor with textile parts cut in a United States-based plant. This procedure has two virtues. First, it offers a way of minimizing investment and maximizing flexibility, which are not so important when making bras and girdles but are crucial in any fashion-oriented line. Second, it allows a firm to take advantage of a special loophole in the U.S. tariff code, known as Item 807.

The importance of Item 807 is that it permits American-made articles assembled abroad in whole or in part to be returned to the United States duty-free. Moreover, what constitutes "an American-made article" and what is involved in "assembly" have been given broad and gradually expanded interpretation by both courts and the Customs Bureau: goods qualifying for Item 807 are not limited to products made of completely fabricated and finished U.S. components but may include products whose United States-made components undergo substantial change in shape, form, and even addition in the process of manufacturing. Under this definition, clothing eminently qualifies for Item 807 treatment.[45] Consequently, clothing imports under Item 807 have boomed. In the 18-year period from 1965 to 1983, the dollar volume of Item 807 imports advanced from $578 million to $9,226 million, a 1600 percent increase. As a result of this explosion, the percentage of all apparel imports coming in under Item 807 has also increased, moving from 0.3 percent in 1965 to 6.7 percent in 1983. For developing countries seeking export-oriented multinational investment, Item 807 has been a boon. The number of countries exporting more than $1 million worth of Item 807 production has risen from 1 to 21 since 1965. In 1983 Mexico topped the list, sending over $156 million worth of apparel into the United States under 807, closely followed by the Dominican Republic, with almost $130 million worth of Item 807 clothing exports.[46]

One important consequence of Item 807 is to change the geography of foreign clothing production aimed at the U.S. market. Whereas the bulk of clothing imports come from the Far East, most apparel brought in under Item 807 is made in and around the Caribbean Basin. Locating in the circum-Caribbean area has the obvious advantage of proximity to U.S. markets and hence drastically reduced transport costs, which in the case of goods made in northern Mexico are virtually nil. Under normal conditions, these advan-

tages are outweighed by other costs associated with Latin American and Caribbean Basin apparel manufacturing. The principal problem in these areas is that their domestic makers of fabric are expensive suppliers because they produce for relatively small markets and are protected by trade policies aimed at promoting import substitution. By contrast, East Asian apparel makers have access to the highest-quality fabrics at internationally competitive prices. Item 807 removes this cost differential from the equation by allowing fabric to be furnished by those U.S. firms that arrange for subcontracting.[47]

Consequently, many of the developing countries in close proximity to the United States have set up "free zones," designed especially to attract 807 production. The best case in point is the Border Industrialization Program (BIP) in northern Mexico. Established in 1965, the BIP provides inducements to foreign-owned companies, otherwise restricted in their investments in Mexico. Under this program, foreign companies operating within a band of territory running twenty kilometers wide at the U.S.-Mexican border are allowed to establish fully owned subsidiaries; staff these companies with U.S. managers; and import materials, supplies, and machinery duty-free as long as all the production is exported. Although there is considerable debate about the social and economic benefits that the program has generated for Mexico, with much of the opinion running on the negative side, there is little question that the BIP has stimulated considerable growth. In 1965 the BIP zone contained 12 offshore plants with 3,087 workers; by 1983 the zone contained over 600 assembly plants, called *maquiladoras*, which provided employment to more than 150,000 workers.[48]

The BIP has been a haven for labor-intensive industries. Most important in employment terms is electrical/electronics work, and as of 1980, 51 percent of the *maquiladora* labor force was employed in this industry. Running second is clothing and textiles, which in 1980 employed 14 percent of the border zone's labor force.[49] One important difference between these two industries has been the connection between U.S. manufacturers and the border plants that they utilize. The majority of the electrical/electronics plants operate as direct subsidiaries of the largest and most important U.S. manufacturers. In clothing and textiles, by contrast, only a few large U.S. companies—most notably, Levi Strauss, Warnaco, Puritan, and Kayser-Roth—have set up directly owned facilities. Instead, most production is done by small, locally owned contractors, among whom longevity is relatively uncommon.[50]

But if Mexico leads the list of Item 807 producers, the race is on among other nearby countries to capture their fair share of 807 activity. What the BIP pioneered is now standard fare on the menu of incentives drawn up to attract assembly operations, to which is added the allure of wages still below the Mexican level. Thus, Haiti, the country with the lowest per capita income in the Western Hemisphere, now has a thriving foreign assembly industry made up of 200 plants, employing over 60,000 persons. Other Caribbean Basin countries are similarly stepping up their efforts to garner 807 work.[51]

But whether 807 production will burgeon further is difficult to say. Several factors are to be found on the positive side of the balance sheet. First, the uncertainties involved in offshore processing have gradually diminished. Those companies yet to make an offshore venture need only consult the classified pages of any industry publication to find specialized U.S. contractors that will that act as brokers—finding a facility, coordinating production, and handling the paperwork.[52] Second, East Asia has lost some of its advantages, with a scarcity of quotas and lack of available capacity driving importers to find new sources of production. Third, some of the major U.S. textile companies are venturing into apparel production themselves, setting up offshore processing plants to be fed fabric made in U.S. mills. On the minus side are the operating problems associated with 807 production. Productivity in many of the 807 producing countries is low, and the industry press is replete with complaints about processing delays and bottlenecks that reduce the advantages of a nearby facility. Moreover, the small size of many of the circum-Caribbean countries places a limit on the possibilities for growth: what Hong Kong, Korea, and China with their huge populations can do is unlikely to be duplicated by the mini-states of the Caribbean.[53]

Domestic Responses to International Competition

No sooner did imports enter the American market than an outcry for protection arose; as the flow of imported clothing has swollen from a trickle to a flood the clamor for protection has incessantly grown louder. The response to protectionist pressures has taken a variety of forms and has evolved considerably over the past thirty years; since the subject is extremely complex and is not central to the issue with which we are concerned in this book, only the briefest summary will be presented.

Protectionist demands arose in the mid-1950s when imports of cotton textiles shot up just as textile profits turned down sharply. The first to loudly champion restrictions were the cotton textile makers, but apparel interests quickly joined in as imports of scarves and cotton blouses mounted. The campaign for restriction produced a bilateral agreement between Japan and the United States in 1957 in which Japan consented to restrain sales for a five-year period. No sooner did this occur than imports from Hong Kong took up the slack. When Hong Kong was importuned to restrain exports, it insisted on growth rates unacceptable to U.S. textile/apparel interests; to quell further increases in trade, the United States convened a conference of the major trading countries in order to get international support for a new trade arrangement.

This effort culminated in a one-year "short-term" agreement regulating international trade in cotton textiles, signed in 1961, which was then followed by a multiyear "long-term arrangement regarding international trade in cotton textiles" (LTA) beginning in 1962 and renewed in 1967. Rather than providing tariff protection, the agreements strove to regulate the rate of import growth, stipulating that trade in cotton textiles and cotton textile products would increase in a "gradual" and "orderly" manner; bilateral agreements between importing and exporting countries were then negotiated within this framework. However, these long-term agreements covered trade in cotton textiles only. Most exporting countries had initially worked on these coarser materials, but over time they moved on to higher-quality, higher-priced man-made fabrics. These fabrics were uncontrolled by the LTA and could therefore be exported in unlimited quantities. In reaction, the importing countries sought agreements that would bring these man-made fabrics under control; in 1973 a Multi-Fiber Agreement (MFA), covering cottons and synthetic (man-made) textiles, was negotiated to replace the expiring LTA.

Annual growth in exports under the MFA was not to exceed 6 percent, though the agreement did include provisions for any one year's unused quotas to be carried over to the next and for future annual quotas to be "carried back." But, under the adverse economic conditions of the mid-1970s, the growth rates allowed by the MFA greatly strained the textile and apparel industries in the developed countries; consequently, MFA II, which was negotiated in 1978, contained provisions for stricter import controls. Most importantly, MFA II included a clause for "reasonable departures" from the MFA framework in particular cases, which many of the importing

countries invoked in bilateral agreements. The United States, in particular, made agreements with Hong Kong, Taiwan, and South Korea that allowed little initial quota growth in 1978 over the 1977 level and then set subsequent growth contours at rates well below the 6 percent level with many more products covered than previously. The third Multi-Fiber Agreement, negotiated in December 1981 for a term of four years and seven months, contained new protecting clauses against sharp and substantial increases in imports of the most sensitive products, whose quotas had not been used previously.[54] These clauses have since been used often by the United States, which has had frequent recourse to "calls" for consultation with countries whose products show sharp increases in imports. The United States has also imposed monthly limits on imports in an attempt to limit sudden surges that occur when an entire year's quota is brought over in a single month and thereby swamps the market and depresses prices. Other measures have also been taken, including a curb on transshipments of partially finished garments from one importing country to another.[55]

As of this writing, the struggle over the course of apparel trade policy after the expiration of MFA III is intense. Industry interests have sought new legislation that would impose global quotas and push imports from major exporting countries back to 101 percent of their 1984 levels, with future growth to proceed at a 1 percent per annum basis. Because the nation's yawning trade deficit, now extending from apparel to video recorders and semiconductors, has stirred public opinion, legislators are anxious to do something to curb imports; hence, this latest attempt to push back imports has gained unprecedented congressional support. The Reagan administration is strenuously opposed to the measure, putting its future in doubt. But the repercussions of this battle have already been heard in Geneva, where the trade agreements are renegotiated. At the very least, the strength of Congress' desire to curb clothing imports will toughen the U.S. position in the bargaining over the successor to MFA III and induce the importing countries to compromise within the MFA framework, lest more stringent measures be unilaterally adopted.[56]

Compared with the advanced economies of the countries of western Europe, the United States has drawn a considerably tighter web over its textile/clothing complex; and yet imports have continued to grow, as we have seen. The reasons are at once complex and straightforward: the cost advantages of importing are great; the number of low-wage countries is virtually indefinite; and the protective structure is simply too weak to militate against

these incentives. While ineffective in halting the growth of import penetration, the attempts at protection have altered the structure of international trade in clothing, in terms of both the geography of apparel manufacture and the quality of export production. Once the exporting countries were slapped with restrictions on cotton textiles, they sought to stimulate output by moving into man-mades. The MFA regulated trade in man-mades, but it did so on a country-by-country, category-by-category basis. Given the huge cost advantage in favor of the exporters, an exporter that had reached its category limit could maintain output in the same category simply by switching to a higher-priced and probably higher-profit line. A second option was to enter another category; and since the bilateral agreements cover only those categories in which there has been a previous record of significant trade, this offers a short-term opportunity to export on an unrestricted basis. Within time a quota gets slapped down on the new category as well, but if by this point significant levels of importing have been reached, the quota begins from a very high floor. Individual country quotas have also led to a pattern of shifting trade as retailers and importers have developed new source areas to supplement the output of established exporting countries that have reached the ceilings imposed by their quotas.[57] As the *Wall Street Journal* noted:

Hunting for loopholes in import regulations has been an industry pastime. Retailers have become, as one puts it, "creative Marco Polos," roving the world for suppliers in countries like Sri Lanka and Bangladesh where apparel exports are in their infancy and haven't been hit with many quotas.[58]

Evidence of the retail Marco Polos at work can be seen from import data for the first four months of 1985. While shipments from Taiwan, Hong Kong, Korea, and China were down, smaller exporters achieved huge gains: Turkey up 339 percent, Portugal up 214 percent, Bangladesh up 402 percent, Mauritius up 175 percent, Jamaica up 84 percent, and so on.[59] In their "game of circumvention," retailers and importers have shown no lack of ingenuity. Transshipments are one widely practiced technique: partly finished garments are sent from a country whose clothing industry's capacity exceeds its quotas, to be finished and shipped from another country, whose quotas are unfilled. Another dodge is to import by sections: send sportjacket sleeves into Los Angeles, ship the body of the jacket into New York, and hope that the coat is put into a "basket category" for miscellaneous items that can be brought in without a quota.

Thus, the import trend has continued unabated; consequently, even the largest American producers have found themselves under severe competitive pressure. One option has been to offset the industry's disadvantage in wages relative to its overseas competitors by making labor more productive and efficient. Toward that end, numerous firms have sought to invest heavily in technology, an effort that has yielded some limited productivity gains. Value added per employee, a standard measure of productivity, increased 134 percent between 1963 and 1977. Yet these gains lagged behind the 164 percent increase registered by all U.S. manufacturing industries during the same period, a time when overall U.S. manufacturing productivity slipped relative to its international competitors. Consequently, apparel remains a highly labor-intensive industry. According to the 1982 Census of Manufactures, 84.9 percent of all apparel employees were production workers, a negligible change from 87.9 percent in 1963. By contrast, all manufacturing industries were lower in labor intensity and had shed a larger proportion of their blue-collar labor force during the same period: production workers constituted 72 percent of total manufacturing employment in 1963 but only 64.8 percent in 1982.[60]

The reasons for apparel's continuing productivity lag are twofold. One is that many domestic manufacturers have been so severely battered by imports that they lack the capital needed for investment in laborsaving equipment. Annual levels of capital spending, adjusted for inflation, showed virtually no increase between 1973 and 1982. Not surprisingly, then, a 1980 survey by the American Apparel Manufacturers Association disclosed that 68 percent of the firms queried reported no plans for computerizing sewing, seaming, and materials-handling operations.[61]

The larger firms, of course, are better endowed in capital; the 1970s and early 1980s saw a concerted effort among these large apparel makers to step up capital investment and increase productivity. But even these efforts have yielded a modest payback: the problem is that the potential for reducing labor content through technology is limited. Automation has found its broadest application in the grading and marking stages, where there have been continual gains since the 1960s. Historically, the industry has relied on handcut cardboard patterns of each distinctive apparel component, which would be graded to size and then traced on a fifty-foot-long sheet of paper used later in the actual cutting of the fabric. With computer-aided design (CAD), the operator simply traces the pattern with an electronic instrument called a digitizer. This converts the pattern's specifications into digital data

that are then fed into a computer, which generates the needed size grada-
tions for each part. Next, the pattern is transferred to paper by the unit's
automatic platter, creating a master stencil that serves as the pattern for
cutting cloth. Automating marker making significantly reduces fabric
wastage—a major cost consideration for the larger firms. It also reduces
labor costs, allowing firms to replace skilled manual workers with a smaller
number of easily trained "technicians" who can be assigned to staff termi-
nals around the clock, thus building up a stock of patterns to feed into
subsequent production flows. More recently, numerically controlled fabric-
cutting machines have been marketed, but these involve very high capital
costs, making them affordable to only the very largest firms, and they lack
the flexibility needed by fashion-oriented firms that change fabrics and
styles frequently.[62]

However, in the most basic operations, such as sewing and stitching,
there is no technological rescue in sight. The problem lies not in the sewing
machine—whose speed has been upgraded from an average of 4,500 stitches
per minute in 1950 to 10,000 stitches per minute as of 1985. Rather, the
constraining factor is that relatively little—only 20 percent—of the operator's time is actually spent using the sewing machine. The bulk of the time
involves handling and repositioning the various pieces of cloth that are to be
sewn together. And as long as most handling and repositioning is done
manually, further increases in sewing-machine velocity simply produce coordination problems for the sewing-machine operator.[63]

Thus far there has been limited progress in simplifying or automating
these functions. The most common line of innovation has been the introduction of special-purpose machines for high-volume, repetitive operations.
These machines have gone through two generations, one mechanical, in
which a template guided the path of the needle and, more recently, electronic, with microprocessors and numerical control units. In both cases
automated machinery has generated substantial increases in productivity at
the cost of limited flexibility; hence their use is widest among plants where
staple products allow for long production runs. The most recent technological advance has involved the introduction of operator-programmable
sewing machines that rely on a "record/playback" mechanism whereby the
operator teaches the machine a sequence of operations that it can then
repeat. Handling and repositioning must still be done manually, however,
and cost factors, both for equipment and software, have kept their use
down.[64]

Consequently, while the large firms have gone ahead with capital-deepening, they have also sought to expand operations abroad. The Kellwood Corporation, for example, a major supplier of standardized clothing to Sears, increased its imports from virtually nothing to 8 percent of sales after having built plants in Mexico and Central America in the mid-1970s and having set up a subsidiary to import shirts directly from Hong Kong. Warnaco, a diversified corporation with divisions making men's and women's clothing, is so heavily involved in foreign manufacturing that it maintains offices in Hong Kong, Taiwan, and Tokyo, in addition to the fourteen plants that it operates abroad. Jonathan Logan's Misty Harbor Division and Interco's London Fog subsidiary, branded lines that have long enjoyed strong consumer identification, have reduced their domestic operations and have shifted much production abroad.[65]

If many of the large firms have now joined the import game, they are still maintaining a domestic base as well; doing so means paring domestic labor costs as sharply as possible. One route to keeping U.S. operations competitive has been to step up the search for the lowest-labor-cost facilities in the United States. As Roger Schmenner found in his study of the locational decisions of major manufacturing firms, competitive pressures in the apparel sector are so intense that labor-cost considerations override all other locational criteria:

The predominant concern for labor costs, by both union and non-union companies, drives the location search of apparel companies and greatly simplifies that search effort. Typically, both the region/area choice and the choice of community within a region/area are driven by the need to uncover low wage locations.[66]

This search has taken the large apparel makers to isolated rural areas and to such mountainous regions as the Appalachians or the Ozarks, where the supply of female labor is still abundant. According to Schmenner, the types of community toward which the large apparel makers gravitate tend to be small and sparsely industrialized, with no other employer, especially one paying high wages or organized by a union, likely to be within a thirty- to forty-mile radius.

Only because the large apparel firms' drive to cut labor costs is so overriding can their desire to evade unionization be considered a secondary influence on their locational decisions. Historically, the appeal of southern locations to runaway employers in the apparel industry has rested on the

promise of more favorable—that is, docile—labor attitudes. A 1947 study, *Why Industry Moves South*, found that:

The question of unions presents the greatest contrast between the labor oriented plants and the non-labor (or market and material) oriented plants. Without exception, there was little concern about avoiding unions in locating the nonlabor oriented plants. [By contrast,] the companies locating new apparel, shoe, and textile plants were interested, on the whole, in staying away from labor unions.[67]

In the antilabor climate of the 1970s and 1980s, however, the desire to evade unionization has spread beyond the labor-oriented industries like apparel or textiles to the rest of American manufacturing. Schmenner notes that "there is scarcely a manufacturer in any industry which would not choose to remain nonunion," and his survey of Fortune 500 firms found that labor climate, along with proximity to markets, were the two most important "musts" influencing the site-selection plans of large manufacturing corporations. In the vast majority (80 percent), the new plants established by the nation's largest companies are opened up nonunion; this preference for nonunion plants leads the Fortune 500 to set up new operations in states with "right-to-work" laws that prohibit union shops.[68] As Schmenner notes:

There is no question, however, that the right-to-work states are booming: one half of all the new plants were sited in them as opposed to only 34 percent of the stay-put plants. Of the 76 percent of plant openings where non-unionism was a "must" factor, 58 percent were sited in right-to-work states. The data suggest that the edge for non-unionism in right-to-work states has triggered a more than proportional degree of plant openings there. The data also suggest that companies are well aware of the advantages of right-to-work states: 88 percent of the managers of new plants so sited indicate that remaining non-union is a "must" for them.[69]

For apparel firms, the staunchly "right-to-work" southern states remain a nonunion haven of undiminished attraction. North Carolina, for example— the most industrialized state in the South and the region's largest and the nation's fourth-largest apparel producer—also ranks number 50 among the states in percentage of the nonagricultural work force unionized; New York and Pennsylvania, numbers 1 and 2, respectively, in terms of apparel employment nationwide, rank numbers 1 and 3 with respect to levels of unionization. The other laggards in union membership are South Carolina, Texas, Florida, and Virginia, ranking 49 through 45, respectively, in share of the labor force unionized; each state is also a major apparel producer.[70] Indeed,

both apparel unions, the ILGWU and the Amalgamated Textile and Clothing Workers, have registered little progress in organizing workers on their southern front. Not only has southern membership in the ILGWU failed to grow; it has actually slipped, largely because the wave of plant closings that swept through the Southeast in the late 1970s and early 1980s hit the unionized sector worse than it did nonunion firms. Membership in the southeastern region of the ILGWU plummeted from a peak of 22,850 in 1973 to 11,002 in 1982.[71]

Symbolic of the ILGWU's troubles in the region was the closure of the union's one toehold in the giant, fiercely nonunion Kellwood. Organizing at Kellwood's 1,300-person Little Rock, Arkansas, plant began in 1966; later that year the ILGWU won the election, held under National Labor Relations Board auspices, to represent the workers. Bargaining over the first contract then began, but after eight months of little progress the union called the workers out on a strike that was to last 392 days. Though the workers returned to the plant without an agreement, a contract was finally signed in 1971. In 1976 the National Labor Relations Board issued an order that forced Kellwood to provide $1.6 million in back pay to 784 former strikers. By 1978 Kellwood began to send production overseas. The company closed its shirt division in 1980 and terminated the dress division in 1982. Meanwhile, Kellwood stepped up its acquisition of foreign plants: by 1984 it had acquired three plants in Sri Lanka, which brought with them rights to quotas in the United States and the United Kingdom. Finally, in March 1984, the company called union headquarters to say that the Little Rock plant would be completely shut down.[72]

This resistance to unionization is historical, rooted in southern culture and the fierce opposition of employers to unions. It is also the case that the apparel unions did little until the mid-1970s to meet the growing nonunion threat. After 1974 the ILGWU's organizing efforts were greatly intensified, though the results have been meager, as noted above. This is mainly due to the intensity with which employers, like Kellwood and others, have resisted unionization. Increasingly, their opposition has crossed the bounds of legality, as is indeed the case in much of American industry. The union's failure is also linked to the changing structure of the industry: with so many of the large firms operating on a multiunit basis, the threat of shifting production from one facility to another should unionism occur is a sword of Damocles hanging above the workers' necks. And as critics both internal and external to the union have charged, the ILGWU has yet to discover the tactics or

strategies that would win over southern workers—though in this respect its failing is no greater than that of the rest of American labor. But, whatever the reasons for the ILGWU's inability to organize the South, the existence of nonunion southern pastures continues to lure other companies and also to increase the pressure on the market position of those unionized, higher-wage firms that remain in New York or elsewhere in the Northeast.[73]

[4]

Why Garments Are Still Made in New York

New York's decline as an apparel-producing center is thus over a half-century old; in light of the trends we have just reviewed—the growth of large apparel firms, the internationalization of production, the continued search for domestic low-labor-cost locations—the pressure on New York's remaining apparel firms remains strong and is mounting. Thus, it is no surprise that New York City's apparel industry plunged into decline with the city's economic crisis, starting in 1969.

After 1975 New York moved into a different relationship to the national industry. Like other domestic apparel-producing areas, New York was battered by the rising tide of imports. By the mid-1970s imports were no longer taking away potential growth from domestic apparel makers but were taking away their customers; the results were felt in steadily declining employment figures. As the nation's apparel industry shrunk, so too did New York's. But, in contrast to the earlier period, New York's apparel industry began to hold its own in competition with the rest of the nation, reversing a thirty-year trend. As the data on Figure 4.1 show, New York held on to a virtually constant share of the national market from 1975 to 1985. New York firms in the fashion-influenced outerwear industry did notably better than those in standardized lines like undergarments, where the pressure to reduce labor costs was particularly intense. Moreover, the cyclical ups and downs in the national economy exercised less impact on New York's apparel industry than was previously the case: in contrast to the experience of 1969 and 1974, when national recessions sent New York's market share tumbling, New York retained its share of employment even after the nation's economy faltered in 1979 and again in 1981–1982.

The sources of the turnaround are to be found in a series of simultaneous shifts on both the demand and the supply sides. In part, what happened between 1969 and 1976 was that New York lost those low-priced stand-

Figure 4.1 New York City's Share of National Employment in Apparel Industries, 1969–1985

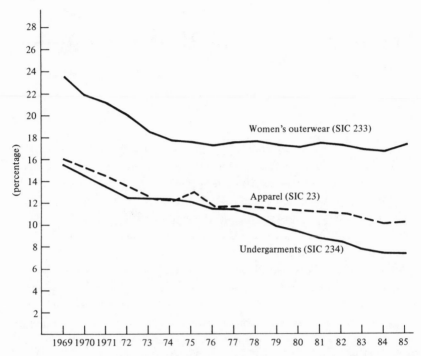

Source: National employment for 1969 to 1984 from U.S. Bureau of Labor Statistics, *Employment, Hours, and Earnings, U.S., 1909–84*, Bulletin 1312-12; employment levels for January through September 1985 from U.S. Bureau of Labor Statistics, *Employment and Earnings*, V. 32, 4-11 (1985); employment levels for October and November 1985 are from unpublished data, U.S. Bureau of Labor Statistics. New York City employment levels from 1969 to 1979 are from U.S. Bureau of Labor Statistics, *Employment and Earnings for States and Areas, 1939–1982*, Bulletin 1370-17; employment levels from 1980 to 1984 are from U.S. Bureau of Labor Statistics, *Supplement to Employment and Earnings for States and Areas, 1980–1984*, Bulletin 1370-19; employment levels for January through November 1985 are from unpublished data, U.S. Bureau of Labor Statistics.

ardized items that could be made just as well in Greensville, El Paso, or Hong Kong as in New York, but more importantly, could be produced at these other locations at a considerably lower cost. The remaining products were those style-sensitive goods susceptible to built-in fashion obsolescence or consumer uncertainty, as this comment from one local manufacturer suggests:

Ours is an item house. We don't have a planned production program. We're constantly making samples, and something new is always coming out of our design room and

going onto the racks in the showroom. I don't know what's going to happen two months from now. But what I do know is that the sportswear departments in the stores are more volatile than ever, and that requires turning around quickly.

While New York's firms are organized to respond to short-term market trends, the big apparel makers lack the flexibility to do so. Because planning is required to generate the economies that large size makes possible, "everything has to be projected in advance," as an official of one of the leading brand-name makers pointed out. By contrast, because New York's manufacturers are small and do their production in nearby facilities, they can extend a season's production run or suddenly introduce a new line in midseason—changes that would disrupt the large and decentralized operations that the big apparel makers maintain. As one New York manufacturer told me: "Our patternmakers can come out with twelve new numbers overnight if we learn that the market is turning in a new direction." Moreover, New York's firms can use their location in the center of fashion design and merchandising to deliberately accentuate fashion distinctiveness and create up-to-the-minute styles that set them apart from the products of their lower-cost, mass-production competitors. "There's very much fabric and color change," said one manufacturer. "The color on our items changes all the time."

The Liabilities of Size

However, New York's garment industry also owes its niche to the self-limiting nature of the locational and organizational processes examined in the previous chapter. In a market so prone to change as is apparel's, large firm size is often more of a liability than an advantage. Outside investment analysts have applauded the trend toward consolidation; Standard and Poor's, for example, considers that the decline in the number of apparel firms and the growth of large makers should "prove beneficial for the industry as a whole over the long run, since large firms tend to be stronger financially and relatively well managed."[1] The track record of large firms is not quite so convincing. First, merging one apparel firm with another has rarely produced meaningful economies of scale. Rather, larger firms have often found that swallowing up smaller concerns produces disastrous results. Takeovers by large concerns outside the apparel field have frequently yielded unwieldy structures. Revlon purchased Evan-Picone in the early 1960s and then burdened it "with the overhead of a vast warehouse, a batallion of traveling

salesmen, and computers so complicated that the subsidiary's employees never learned to use them."[2] Even General Mills, considered particularly adept at maintaining entrepreneurial management in subsidiaries removed from its main cereals business, has been humbled by its inability to cope with the vagaries of style. The company's Izod Division became a raging success in the late 1970s and early 1980s when the "preppy look" emerged as a major fashion craze. Profits first zoomed, but the division later faltered: Izod first proved unable to produce in sufficient quantities and then failed to realize that making a fashion item required constant change and updating. The consequence? Competitors grabbed large chunks of the retail business, and despite Izod management's attempts to update and diversify, General Mills gave up the effort, putting Izod on the auction block.[3]

Large apparel firms have not been particularly successful in digesting their smaller apparel acquisitions either. When Warnaco expanded from a small brassiere-and-girdle company into a full-line apparel conglomerate by making a string of acquisitions in the 1960s and the 1970s, the new divisions were put under centralized corporate control. But the corporate staff proved so distant from its sixteen different, principal markets that style changes caught the firm unaware, producing severe deterioration in performance during the mid-1970s. Warnaco has since recovered, but it has done so by sharply pruning its earlier acquisitions—eliminating several product lines and selling off subsidiaries—while also cutting down corporate staff and shifting operating responsibility to divisional managers.[4] This is typical of mergers in the apparel field, which have less frequently led to horizontally integrated giants than to holding companies that acquire new divisions principally to reduce risks through diversification.

Second, the effects of style pervade almost all apparel categories; hence, even the largest firms can find themselves imperiled if fashion changes make product lines obsolete and plant and equipment are too narrowly specialized to be converted to other uses. During the late 1960s, several major apparel firms integrated backward to obtain control over their supplies of knitted fabrics, which were in such strong demand that supply on the open market typically ran short. Having their own knitting plants gave these big apparel makers complete product control from the fiber to the finished item, and in the early 1970s the president of Jonathan Logan could still brag that:

Verticality—owning our own textile plants—has provided great strength for a number of our divisions. Verticality makes us much less vulnerable than companies that depend completely on outsiders.[5]

Then, when knits suddenly fell out of favor in the mid-1970s, these same firms had to retreat by divesting themselves of their textile acquisitions. Some apparel firms moved quicker than others: Logan waited until 1981 to shut down its textile mill—a $17 million loss—and until then its apparel divisions had been forced to churn out poorly selling knitted garments, simply to use up the mill's huge production.[6]

A third factor is that the administrative apparatus of the large firm, while a precise and well-ordered mechanism for making standardized goods at the lowest possible cost, can also shackle a company and keep it from adapting to the latest market shifts. In the early 1970s, Warnaco founded new divisions to keep abreast of fashion changes, but, unused to starting new products from scratch, the company discontinued these lines several years later after persistent problems with inventory buildups and delivery delays.[7] Many companies that grew fat during the 1960s and 1970s by catering to the large "baby-boom" generation were too cumbersome to switch product markets in the 1980s when that cohort aged and its tastes changed. Bobbie Brooks, one of the largest outerwear firms with $200 million in volume, landed in bankruptcy in mid-1982 because its merchandising division continued to promote clothes designed for a shrunken population of young adults and proved too unwieldy to adjust to more volatile, though thriving, markets.[8]

Compounding these disadvantages of large size is the fact that flexibility has become more important, for reasons relating to market structure, organizational capacity, and overall economic uncertainty. The market for mass-produced clothing has finally reached its limits: the aging of the baby-boom cohort and the proliferation of two-earner families has shifted clothing expenditures to higher-priced, more fashion-sensitive goods. The impact of this change is greatest on the large apparel makers that previously thrived on mass production, and the troubles that it has brought them tell volumes about the liabilities of size—as the case of Levi Strauss vividly suggests. Profiled by management consultants Thomas Peters and Robert Waterman in their best-selling book, *In Search of Excellence*, Levi's has done well in making standard goods.[9] Levi's problem is that 75 percent of its sales come from jeanswear, and demand for that product, as Levi's chairman has conceded, is "flat for the forseeable future."[10] To recapture its previous growth rates, Levi's needs to generate new, fashion-oriented lines; but despite repeated attempts to do so the company has yet to learn how to bring innovation to the large, multinational apparel firm. In the early 1970s Levi's created new operating divisions for sportswear and accessories and expanded its Levi's

for Gals marketing unit into a full-fledged women's wear division. The results were dismal, as *Fortune* magazine pointed out: "Levi was trying to penetrate unfamiliar, fragmented markets using a shotgun approach with a lot of unproven merchandise, and it did not work."[11] A similar disaster befell its European subsidiary in the mid-1970s, which tried to make too many fashion items cut from too many kinds of fabric and found that the multiplicity of lines caused production problems, built up heavy diversified inventories, and amassed excessive receivables. The end result was massive losses so large that the parent company—otherwise hugely successful in the 1970s—itself went profitless in 1973.[12] Having burned its hands twice, Levi's was slow to diversify as the once explosive jeans market faded in the late 1970s; while companies making "designer" jeans branched out into other lines, Levi's failed to anticipate the consumers' shift away from basic goods. By 1980 it was ready for a second try at diversification. The danger, as *Fortune* saw it, was that "the task of keeping track of all the ever-changing fashions and maintaining the huge assortments of sizes and styles could tax the company's managerial capabilities beyond their limits."[13] Indeed the results were two years of red ink. Once again, Levi's retreated and, looking for a large middle market for its standardized goods, aligned itself with Sears and Penney's as their basic supplier of jeans and other pants. In so doing, Levi's angered its smaller retail and department store customers, who had traditionally offered Levi's as a way of competing with the unbranded goods carried by the discount chains.[14] Thus, losses in trade ensued again: in 1984 profits were down 79 percent.[15] Of course, jeans represents a solid bedrock for Levi's and the company is unlikely to founder. But in a competitive industry like apparel, standing still means inexorable decline; for Levi Strauss to recapture its growth rates of the past two decades it must learn to operate more flexibly; as of this writing, the company is still tentatively searching its way.

In a sense, the solution to Levi's dilemma has already been discovered: to control style change by developing strong brand names in fashion lines with which the consumer will identify, though this strategy too has its drawbacks. But if brand-name identification can stem the threat to the large mass producer, the option is generally out of reach for the middle-sized apparel firm less endowed with the capital and resources needed for product development and consumer advertising. Thus, what is transpiring in the apparel industry is a tendency toward market segmentation. Staple goods are made under long-term contract and supplied either by domestic makers or brand-

name wear or, more frequently, by subcontractors that produce according to the specifications placed by the retailers' own buying offices in the Far East. Both options require a long lead time between design, production, and delivery to the store. Indeed, importing is a particular source of rigidity: in most of the key exporting countries, goods must be ordered a year in advance of expected sale to ensure that they will enter the United States before a country's quota is filled. Consequently, retailers and importers find themselves in the position of "playing craps," as the owner of one apparel buying business put it. "You have to tell what the economy's going to be like 12 months in advance."[16]

Faced with this situation, most retailers and buyers hedge somewhat; hence, there remains a need for suppliers that can fill in lines once fashion trends develop and the pattern of consumer spending can be discerned. The middle-sized firm can hope to supply these lines from stock—an increasingly risky option—or it can strive to offer a multiplicity of items and produce only as orders come in, which means forfeiting any remaining advantages of size. Thus, market segmentation is inexorably squeezing out the middle-sized producer, leaving smaller, flexibly organized firms to absorb the instability in the market.

Because the prolonged crisis of the American economy has upset the stability needed for mass production and mass distribution, the ability to repond flexibly to change has become of still greater importance. The uneven performance of the economy has steered consumer behavior on an erratic path, producing repeated and severe inventory-control problems among the retail chains. The 1974 and 1975 recessions forced them in to heavy write-offs; in 1976 the chains experienced costly markdowns in the face of consumer sluggishness; in 1978 inventories were once again advancing more rapidly than sales; and in 1982 the stores were able to avoid major inventory losses because the high rate of inflation had made the cost of inventorying stock prohibitive. To hedge aganst risk while still purchasing large quantities abroad, the current trend is to shift more and more business back to the vendor by buying close to the selling season, pressuring the apparel manufacturer to share the costs of markdowns, and taking back merchandise that does not move. Moreover, initial purchases are kept small, and reorders are closely calibrated to inventory flows, which can be carefully monitored thanks to the stores' heavy investments in electronic data-processing controls.[17]

The stores' attempt to reduce their risks means that the large domestic

manufacturer confronts the prospect of being caught with merchandise that nobody wants. The large domestics have responded to this dilemma in two ways. Some manufacturers have chosen to cut back on their more speculative production runs, limiting themselves to their most stable and predictable lines. Since the logistics of size and organization increase the costs of disrupting planned production operations to meet short-term shifts in demand, the result, as one big apparel maker noted in an interview, was that: "We take economic considerations into account by making less." Other manufacturers have been repeatedly compelled to dispose of promotional goods.

Consequently, the instability of demand—caused by both cylical ups and downs and changes in fashion—has upset one of the major means by which large makers have sought to increase their output of more standardized wear: aggressively marketing branded wear. This strategy took off in the mid-1970s but proved difficult to sustain, in part because of the recessions of 1980 and 1981–1982, and in part because manufacturers invariably produced more clothes than they could sell and therefore looked for an outlet where they could "dump" merchandise and unclog their inventories. As things developed, that outlet proved to be the "off-price" retailer. As *Fortune* put it:

His mission is to buy opportunistically, to take the cancelled order, the overruns, the irregulars, or the "end of seasons"—sometimes at a quarter to a fifth of their wholesale price.[18]

Thus, the same branded goods offered by a department store wend their way to a low-frills, high-volume "off-price" outlet, there to be found at a significantly lower price, which forces the department stores to compete with other nearby stores by drastically lowering prices. Unhappy with the lower profit margins that this has produced, the department stores have drastically pared back their purchases of branded apparel, seeking instead to contract directly for clothing to be merchandised under their own labels.

"The division of labor is limited by the size of the markets," argued Adam Smith in *Wealth of Nations* (1776), and in apparel the limits of the market for mass-produced goods have contained the growth of the very largest apparel firms. The market for style-oriented goods is quite large itself but since it is prone to instability and uncertainty, it offers a terrain at once too costly and too risky for the large apparel maker. Moreover, risk aversion has spread to mass producers and mass retailers, owing to a trend toward market segmen-

tation and to the very instability of the larger macroeconomy itself. Hence there is a space for a spot market in which small firms that specialize in both fashion items and overruns on standardized items can thrive.

Staying Together—The Persistence of Agglomeration

Why is the spot market preeminently located in New York? The answer is threefold. First is the magnetic pull of New York's unique concentration of designing, merchandising, supplying, and wholesaling activities on style-oriented production activities. Second is a lowering in the costs of New York's labor—thanks to a massive infusion of new immigrant blood. And third is the emergence of a group of immigrant business owners and the flexibility associated with their firms.

We will begin by considering the linkage of production to merchandising and design, relying heavily on in-depth interviews with selected manufacturers and on a second survey of 35 manufacturers designed specifically to examine locational interdependencies. What characterizes the locational arrangement of New York's garment industry is the tendency toward agglomeration. Designing, merchandising, and supplying activities are all clustered together in New York City's densely packed garment district—a 21-square-block area that in 1983 contained 51,000 jobs directly involved in, or related to, the garment industry. Production activities are either located in the garment center or are in close proximity to it.

This clustering generates significant external economies that are similar to those scale economies brought about by the growth of a large firm but instead are found outside the small firm where they are shared by the entire industry and hence are external. One type of external economy comes about through the massing of related and complementary firms: this practice allows firms to be highly specialized and yet highly efficient, because their specialized facilities are used by many customers. A second external economy comes about because so many firms are packed together in such a dense area, which reduces the costs of communicating information and of transporting goods from one specialized maker or supplier to the next. As we shall see in the discussion that follows, both types of external economy are crucial in the small apparel firm's ability to maintain a competitive position.[19]

Consider the impact of clustering on communication. As even the casual passer-by on Seventh Avenue might note, the garment center is filled with groups of men standing around and "schmoozing." Some of the "schmooze"

is incidental, but much of it is the stuff of which businesses are made. For small firms that may not have the money to stay abreast of fashion by sending designers to Milan, Paris, or Tokyo, yet need to be apprised of the very latest style trend, the physical market of New York's garment center is a place where market signals can be read through constant interchange with suppliers, buyers, as well as competitors. By being close to the source of style change and fashion information, a New York manufacturer can find out about the latest fad or novelty item, copy it, and "knock it off" cheaply, doing so before the item goes out of fashion. "We react fast to style," said one New York manufacturer in an interview. "We're not just copiers. We'll pick up a good idea and change the fabric or the style. We spot trends by talking to buyers. We've had some long-selling items, but they're not significant." Another manufacturer pointed out that, "We knock off what's hot, often at the suggestion of buyers. The fashion trends that we follow are the fashion trends that our customers in the stores set."

The concentration of firms in highly specialized selling buildings—one for better-priced dresses, a second for coats, a third for medium-priced sportswear, and so on through product- and price-line differences—points to another external economy. Few New York firms are important or well known enough to attract a busy out-of-town buyer who comes to New York on two or three buying trips a year. Moreover, most New York firms are too small to afford a heavy advertising campaign that might attract an out-of-town buyer. But combined together in the same building, a multitude of apparel firms provides the buyer with virtually all the types of styles and fashions available. Thus grouped together, they also make it efficient for the buyer, who usually also specializes in a particular price- and product-line, to visit New York and move speedily from showroom to showroom and from floor to floor. Indeed, of the firms queried in my survey, 86 percent maintained a showroom in a building specializing in their particular line. And, when asked how important a factor this was, 90 percent of the manufacturers located in specialized buildings answered "very important." To quote from some of the interviews:

It's crucial for me to be in 530 Seventh Avenue [a better dress building]. The buyers are constantly in the building: they pop in unexpectedly and pick up stock. When they're here, they can reach everybody in one fell swoop.

In the children's dress business every children's dress buyer comes into this building. These days, it's one-stop buying: the buyer spends three days in New York at most.

He's pressed for time; he makes fewer trips than ever; and it's easier for him to come into this building and stay here than to jump around the garment center.

A similar economy is provided by the concentration of suppliers of textiles and notions (the industry vernacular for buttons, zippers, and such goods) that is also found in the garment center. Take the case of the textile wholesalers: New York contains 45 percent of all textile wholesaling employment and 50 percent percent of all textile-wholesaling establishments. Most of the city's textile wholesalers work close to their principal customers in the apparel trades: of the nearly 18,000 people involved in textile wholesaling in 1982, 96 percent worked in Manhattan and 37 percent worked in the garment center.

What binds these two industries together? What gains accrue to the small apparel maker from proximity to suppliers? Part of the answer is rooted in the intangible qualities that lead a garment manufacturer to buy one type of fabric rather than the other and compel the manufacturer to look and examine the cloth in person. "You can't describe a color over the phone" was the way one manufacturer explained the importance of being close to suppliers. Also, New York's fashion-sensitive firms, which thrive by making constant changes in fabric, depend on the market to provide them with immediate access to a wide variety of textiles, as the following quotes from the interviews suggest:

We're a better dress house, and it's a necessity to have our suppliers close by. In our line, getting the right pattern is crucial. Every order must be eyeballed before we make a decision.

It's very important for us to be close to our suppliers. The fabric salesmen are in the place almost every day. You've got to have a constant flow of information about what's selling; you've got to see the fabrics; and you've got to feel them.

We buy goods hand to mouth. We only buy piece goods once orders have been received. Ours is not a planned operation; we work exclusively with piece goods jobbers.

A final consideration is the importance of speed. Since a style-oriented firm produces for orders, and hence keeps little stock, it depends on suppliers that can provide the needed material on short order, whether to make up a new sample or to start producing a new style. One source in the textile-wholesaling industry told me: "What happens is that a garment manufac-

turer suddenly gets a new order and yells to his supplier: get me those piece goods. I've got to get moving quick." Or, as one manufacturer put it, "When your suppliers are close by, you have the opportunity to get what you want when you need it."

As a result, New York's garment manufacturers purchase mainly from suppliers located right on their doorstep. Seventy-seven percent said that their suppliers are mainly located in the garment center itself. A slightly lower but still similar proportion (60 percent) said that having a supplier close-by was "very important"; only a minority (20 percent) said that it was not important at all. In communicating with their suppliers the manufacturers that I interviewed relied on a combination of person-to-person meetings and conversations over the phone: 51 percent said that they usually communicated with their suppliers face to face and by phone; 29 percent said that they usually communicated face to face; 11 percent said that they usually communicated by phone. Nonetheless, the manufacturers lent considerable weight to the ability to see suppliers face to face: when queried about the ability to communicate face to face on a regular basis, 66 percent responded "very important," and only 11 percent said "not important at all."

Agglomeration generates a further external economy through the presence of service businesses—pleaters, beltmakers, apparel trim manufacturers, and embroiderers. Relative to apparel as a whole, these industries are disproportionately concentrated in New York City, for two reasons. First, there is the linkage to the New York-based producers, which are more likely than others to use fashion-sensitive accessory items or applications, precisely in order to ensure their own style distinctiveness. Given this very strong local demand, service firms located in New York City are also best situated to handle those larger manufacturers that do their sewing in Pennsylvania or in North Carolina but want a belt to go with one line and a pleated bottom to go with another. Local and national demand interact to ensure a high level of activity: with strong local patronage, service businesses can specialize in a particular type of pleat or trim, and it is precisely this specialization that in turn attracts the national client.

For the New York-based manufacturer making a style-oriented line, proximity offers advantages because of the need for direct observation (does the belt really fit that dress right?) and because of the importance of speed. The skirt must be pleated quickly enough to be sent to the contractor's factory with time left for sewing and finishing and delivery to the store; the belt must be finished, sent down to the contractor, and attached to the dress

without running late and risking cancellation. A final factor is the problem of coordination: a single dress may have a pleated bottom, a belt, and a special collar made out of apparel trim. Each item in a line may take a slightly different pleat or belt. Often, a problem arises or an accessory is misrouted. By using close-by servicers, however, the time spent coordinating product flows from one independent business to the next can be kept to a minimum.

The importance of proximity to servicers is fully brought out by the manufacturers' responses to my survey. Of those manufacturers that use service businesses (and many but not all do), 93 percent depend on servicers located in the garment center; the rest use other Manhattan-based firms. Not surprisingly, 75 percent said that it was "very important" to have their service businesses located close by; only 7 percent said that it was "not important."

Similar, yet different from the service businesses, are those independent businesses—known as contractors—that specialize either in cutting up textiles into parts or in making them up into finished garments. Such contracting shops are in abundance in New York City; hence they provide still another source of external economies by reducing transportation and communication costs and by keeping lead times short. As with any other small-batch process, making small quantities of garments is really an experimental process, and consequently things often go wrong. Many of these problems—a collar that wrinkles when it is attached to the shoulder, a fabric that is cut against the grain—require personal interaction or oversight. Consequently, proximity is of particular importance for style-oriented producers:

Though we don't do all our work in New York, when we do ship from here we gain time, quality checks, and fewer problems. If we have a contracting shop in the garment center, we can send someone over there twelve times a day.

I'm always talking with the contractors: by phone, it's at least twice a day. My production man is in the shop at least twice a week. And whenever there are problems or special orders my partner or I go ourselves.

My production man is in the shop every day. The contractors come here at least once a week, and they also talk with me on the phone several times a day. And if there's a serious problem, my patternmaker jumps in a cab and is down in the shop in less than twenty minutes.

These external economies have become still more important as a result of the

trend toward market segmentation. With the long production runs made abroad or, if done domestically, sent to large, highly mechanized facilities, manufacturers in staple lines have little demand for the facilities of the medium-sized apparel factory of, say, 100 to 250 workers. Nor is the medium-sized factory appropriate for those manufacturers in fashion specialties. With each worker assigned the task of making a subdivided part of a garment, the medium-sized factory is ill-suited to making short runs of constantly varying styles; its size makes it difficult to coordinate several simultaneous production flows without running into bottlenecks. As one consultant wrote in one of the industry's major trade journals:

Many contractors are having trouble coping with the fact that traditional sources of work are no longer available. In the past, the contractor could rely on only one to three customers but that is no longer so. Styling and short runs stretch the organizational capabilities of most contractors. Turnaround times and delivery schedules no longer allow contractors the luxury of lengthy start-up times.[20]

By contrast, New York provides a huge concentration of small, highly flexible factories that are set up for small-batch production. As manufacturers have become more style-oriented in an attempt to escape import competition, a growing number appear to be pulling back from larger, regional factories in order to make use of these local facilities:

As late as 1975 we used to work with contractors all over, with at least 50 percent of the work done in New Jersey. Then the business got difficult. New Jersey contractors weren't willing to make smaller lots or, if so, would charge a premium. Instead, we've gone to Chinatown. The Chinatown contractors will accept every style in small lots. In their factories the work is done by two or three people, and as a result they can do smaller lots more efficiently.

About five years ago we had 80 percent of our production in Pennsylvania and New Jersey, with the remainder in New York. Now 60 percent is in Chinatown, and the rest is split between Jersey and Pennsylvania. The reason is that we went away from basic shirts-blouses which used to be made in Pennsylvania and moved into a styled blouse line. Our customers were importing their own shirts, but we find that we can turn over fancier goods faster.

A final advantage to producing in New York is that manufacturers need "captive" plants to ensure that their goods will be made on time, especially during peak periods of seasonal activity. New York's style-oriented manufacturers rarely do the volume needed to feed large plants and thus risk losing

priority to a larger user. Small plants, however, can more easily be controlled, and as one manufacturer said, "You can make sure that your work isn't being thrown under the cutting tables while someone else's goods are going through the machines."

Despite these various agglomeration economies, manufacturers are less dependent on local contracting facilities than on local suppliers or on local servicers. Fifty-six percent reported making significant, though not exclusive, use of New York City contractors, with 25 percent relying heavily on Manhattan. When queried about the importance of proximity, only 47 percent said that it was "very important" that contractors be close by; 34 percent said that it was "not important." But since almost all apparel lines are fashion-influenced and manufacturers usually send contractors several different lines at a time, communication between manufacturer and contractor is frequent. As one manufacturer noted: "A day doesn't go by when there aren't at least two calls from the contractor." Indeed, 63 percent of the manufacturers said that they communicated with contractors several times daily; 22 percent said once a day; and only 3 percent said once a week. However frequent the communication, the face to face dimension is of reduced importance: only 6 percent said that they communicated face to face exclusively. Though a larger proportion (47 percent) said that the ability to communicate face to face was "very important," this was less the case than with servicers or suppliers. Thus, the survey results show that ties to local suppliers and servicers remain strong, while linkages to local contractors are waning. Yet a substantial proportion of manufacturers—especially style-oriented firms—continue to use nearby production facilities. For this reason, as we shall see, the arrival of the new immigrants has been a crucial event.

Immigrant Labor—Cheaper Labor

Whatever advantages may be gained through agglomeration—and these external economies, as we have just seen, remain significant—New York still must compete on labor cost. Starting in the 1920s New York suffered from the liabilities of a high-priced labor market. Even in the late 1960s and early 1970s, when employment tumbled, the cost of labor continued to march up while the industry's effective labor supply turned down.

New York is still a high-priced labor town in garments, but it is competitive on labor in a way that wasn't the case a decade ago. The change

stems from the renewal of mass immigration to New York and its impact on
this quintessentially immigrant industry; taking an overview of immigration
trends will be helpful before we look at the specifics of the garment industry
case.

The new immigration started in 1965 with the liberalization of the nation's
immigration laws: as Table 4.1. shows, New York became a mecca for the
nation's newcomers once the doors were reopened, much as it had been
before. Between 1966 and 1979 New York absorbed over 1 million legal
immigrants. To the legal immigrants can be added an indeterminate, though
certainly sizable, number of illegal immigrants. Although for many, New
York is but a port of transit, large numbers arrive in Gotham and settle down
there. The 1980 census recorded 1,670,000 foreign-born New Yorkers, of
whom 928,000 had came to New York City after 1965.

In New York, as in the rest of the nation, the new immigration has brought
the Third World to the First World, as can be seen from the data presented in
Table 4.2. Although the older foreign-born population consists mainly of

Table 4.1 Immigration, United States and New York City, 1966–1979

(in thousands)

Years	United States	New York City	N.Y.C. as Percentage of U.S.
1966–1979	5,834.0	1,053.6	18.0
1966	323.0	61.2	18.9
1967	362.0	66.0	18.2
1968	454.4	75.4	16.6
1969	385.6	67.9	17.6
1970	373.3	74.6	20.0
1971	370.5	71.4	19.3
1972	384.7	76.0	19.8
1973	400.1	76.6	19.1
1974	394.9	73.2	18.5
1975	386.2	73.6	19.1
1976	500.5	90.7	18.1
1977	462.3	76.6	16.6
1978	601.4	88.0	14.6
1979	460.3	82.4	17.9

Source: U.S. Department of Justice, Immigration and Naturalization Service, *Statistical Yearbook of the Immigration and Naturalization Service*, annual editions.

Table 4.2 Immigrants Arrived in United States, 1965–1980, Living in New York City, 1980

Dominican Republic	98,420
Jamaica	76,280
China	62,420
Haiti	43,780
Italy	42,000
Trinidad/Tobago	34,300
Colombia	33,200
Ecuador	32,960
USSR	32,640
Guyana	29,420
Greece	26,000
Cuba	23,520
India	20,680
Philippines	18,920
Korea	17,620
Barbados	14,520
Yugoslavia	14,260
Panama	12,120
Poland	10,760
England	10,520
Israel	10,260

Source: Public Use Microdata Sample, 1980 Census of Population.

Europeans, relatively few of the newest arrivals have migrated from Europe; in fact, migration from Europe to New York has dropped more sharply than in the country at large. Rather, Latin Americans and Caribbeans account for the lion's share of the new immigrant population, with Asians furnishing another sizable component. Those Third World immigrants who settle in New York are distinctive from the overall group of newcomers moving to the United States. New York's Hispanic immigrants contain few Mexicans or Cubans, who are predominant nationwide; instead, the most important source countries have been the Dominican Republic, followed by Colombia and Ecuador, with substantial numbers from the rest of the Southern Hemisphere. Of the Asians, less than 2 percent have come from Vietnam; almost a third are from China; Indians, Koreans, and Filipinos account for 10 percent each.

Garments is New York's quintessential immigrant trade, and like few other industries it has been transformed by this latest influx of newcomers from

abroad. The needle trades' proletariat was already in flux by the late 1960s. Accounts by Gonzalez, Hendricks, and Chaney, based on ethnographic research among immigrants conducted in the late 1960s and early 1970s, all underlined the centrality of apparel for the employment situation of Hispanic immigrants at the time. Hendricks's study of immigrants from a small village in the Cibao region of the Dominican Republic, for example, found that almost a third of the villagers residing in New York were employed as garment cutters, pressers, or sewing-machine operators.[21]

Chinese immigrants also began to gravitate into the industry around the same time. In 1962 a study of Chinatown residents who had sought assistance from a social welfare organization found that the largest number were employed in the traditional trades of restaurants and laundries, with only 2.5 percent employed in garment factories. By 1969, according to a survey conducted by a group of Columbia University students, the garment industry had become an employer of prime importance for the Chinatown community, with 23 percent of the residents interviewed working in apparel.[22]

Tabulations from the 1 percent Public Use Sample of the 1970 Census of Population, displayed in Table 4.3, paint a portrait of an industry at the threshold of change. At that time native-born whites were the most numerous of all; white immigrants were not too far behind (though more numerous than the native-born among blue-collar jobs); and native-born Hispanics, who were mainly Puerto Ricans, were also a sizeable presence. Yet foreign Hispanics already constituted a significant contingent, especially at the blue-collar level, and Asians had established a foothold, probably for the first time.

By 1980 the transition to an industry dependent on new immigrants was in full swing, as shown by the tabulations from the 5 percent Public Use Microdata Sample of the 1980 Census of Population, which are displayed in Table 4.4. The white share of employment was down by one third from its 1970 level; and though native-born whites were still the most numerous group overall, immigrant Hispanics had become the number 2 contingent. Still more striking were the changes among the blue-collar cohort, which in ten years had changed from being mainly white to being mainly Hispanic, Asian, or black. Behind this shift was the upsurge in immigrant newcomers. In 1980 almost one fourth of all garment factory workers—more than any other group—were immigrants of Hispanic background. The Asian share of the garment industry proletariat—16 percent—represented a four fold in-

Table 4.3 Ethnic Composition of Resident Labor Force
New York City Garment Industry, 1970

| | Total | Percentage Distribution of Ethnic Groups | | | | | | | |
| | | Whites | | Blacks | | Asians | | Hispanics | |
		NB*	FB*	NB	FB	NB	FB	NB	FB
Total emp.	157,700	37.1	26.7	7.6	1.8	1.9	3.0	13.1	10.4
White col.	36,600	65.8	18.5	6.3	0.5	0.5	0.8	4.4	4.1
Mgrs. & admin.	9,300	65.6	29.0	2.2	0.0	0.0	0.0	1.1	2.2
PTK*	5,100	60.8	23.5	3.9	0.0	0.0	3.9	3.9	3.9
Sales	6,100	80.3	16.4	0.0	1.3	0.0	0.0	1.6	1.6
Clerical	16,100	61.9	10.6	1.2	1.1	1.3	0.6	7.5	6.3
Blue col.	120,200	28.5	29.5	7.9	2.1	2.2	3.8	15.6	12.2
Craft	12,800	45.8	28.1	6.3	1.6	1.6	0.8	12.5	7.8
Operatives	105,800	26.9	30.1	7.9	2.2	2.2	4.2	15.7	12.8
Trans. ops.	500	20.0	0.0	0.0	0.0	0.0	0.0	40.0	40.0
Laborers	1,100	18.1	9.1	7.6	0.0	0.0	9.1	36.4	16.2
Service wrs.	900	33.3	0.0	2.2	11.1	11.1	0.0	33.3	0.0

Source: 1 Percent Public Use Sample, 1970 Census of Population.
Note: Data are for New York City residents only; "garment industry" includes all apparel subindustries. Percentages add up horizontally.
*NB = native born; FB = foreign born; PTK = professional, technical, & kindred.

Table 4.4 Ethnic Composition of Resident Labor Force
New York City Garment Industry, 1980

| | Total | Percentage Distribution of Ethnic Groups | | | | | | | |
| | | White | | Black | | Asian | | Hispanic | |
		NB*	FB*	NB	FB	NB	FB	NB	FB
Total emp.	139,140	25.1	18.0	6.9	4.1	0.3	12.5	12.6	20.6
White col.	33,720	57.9	11.2	9.0	4.2	0.4	2.7	7.9	6.7
Mgrs. & admin.	7,960	65.8	17.6	2.3	0.5	1.0	4.8	4.5	3.5
PTK*	4,240	58.5	14.2	5.7	6.1	0.0	2.8	5.7	7.1
Sales	4,540	78.9	11.0	1.8	0.9	0.0	2.2	2.6	2.6
Clerical	16,980	48.4	7.5	15.0	6.2	0.4	1.8	11.5	9.2
Blue col.	104,140	14.5	20.2	6.3	4.1	0.3	15.5	14.0	24.9
Craft	14,620	24.9	25.2	8.2	3.8	0.1	5.6	13.1	19.0
Operatives	84,560	12.8	20.2	5.7	3.9	0.3	17.6	13.9	25.6
Trans. ops.	2,220	13.5	8.1	8.1	5.4	0.0	3.6	18.0	43.2
Laborers	2,740	11.7	6.6	12.4	8.8	0.7	19.7	19.9	21.2
Service wrs.	1,280	20.3	9.4	3.1	4.7	0.0	10.9	20.3	31.3

Source: 5 Percent Public Use Microdata Sample, 1980 Census of Population.
Note: Data are for New York City residents only; "garment industry" includes all apparel subindustries. Percentages add up horizontally.
*NB = native born; FB = foreign born; PTK = professional, technical, & kindred.

crease over the 1970 level. Meanwhile, the presence of native minorities—both blacks and the mainly Puerto Rican Hispanics—continued to decline.

In reviewing these numbers the question that arises is why the immigrants have come to New York and found a place in a declining industry like garments. The New York of the turn of the century may have been a golden door of opportunity and economic activity for immigrants lacking in skills but rich in willingness to work hard. But where are the sources of opportunity for equally unskilled immmigrants in a postindustrial city where the number of easy-entry jobs has been severely eroded? And why is it the needle trades that have again offered a welcome mat to New York's latest newcomers?

One answer to these questions is provided by Michael Piore in his book, *Birds of Passage*. Piore explains the migration of low-skilled workers to advanced postindustrial countries in terms of an argument about the requirements of employers and the orientations of immigrant workers. While the postindustrial economy has its concentrations of high-skilled jobs and well-paying firms, the labor market is split: alongside the primary sector of large firms with well-paying, stable jobs lies the secondary labor market—a substratum of low-paying, unpleasant, unstable, largely dead-end jobs. These jobs are to be found in the various industrial sectors of the economy, but regardless of specific location, secondary firms lose out in the competition for native labor; to the extent that native workers remain in the secondary labor force, both resentment over bad conditions and the absence of opportunities provoke militancy and strife.[23]

In response to this shortage of labor and the intractability of the native work force, employers turn to immigrant workers. Whereas natives shun secondary jobs whenever possible, the immigrants accept these same conditions. The explanation lies in the expectations and orientations of the immigrant workers. Most of the immigrants see themselves as temporary workers, hoping to accumulate funds to invest in some means of permanent livelihood in their home countries. Consequently, the immigrant workers are indifferent to the issue of upward mobility and are unconcerned with the instability in employment conditions that troubles native workers. And though the transient nature of their commitment leads to a high level of turnover, instability is compatible with the manning requirements of secondary jobs, since most of these positions are essentially unskilled.

Considerations of status also differ among native and immigrant workers. The accumulation of status is an equally potent motivation for work as is

money; hence, native workers find secondary jobs defective because they lie at the bottom of the job hierarchy—not simply because the pay is poor and the prospects for stability are uncertain. By contrast, the secondary jobs of the postindustrial society lie somewhere in the middle ranges of the job hierarchy of the immigrants' societies. Consequently, employment in secondary jobs confers higher status as well as a sense of upward mobility.

Ethnic Succession and Labor-Force Change. To the extent that we can reconstruct the conditions under which new immigrants entered New York's garment industry, the events seem to largely confirm Piore's argument. Indeed, a shortage of labor has been a recurring problem for the industry since World War II, and in its search for an appropriate labor supply the garment industry has cycled through a series of different migrant and immigrant groups.

As we have already seen, the garment industry grew up in New York because the city's huge pool of immigrants provided the ample and flexible supply of labor that the industry needed. While the first immigrant generation provided apparel with a full-time, permanent work force of both men and women, the second generation was often loath to work in a clothing factory. Incipient signs of a recruitment crisis were first noted in the 1920s, shortly after immigration restrictions went into effect. Benjamin Selekman, writing for the 1925 Regional Plan Association study of New York industries, found that employers were concerned about potential labor shortages and noted that the second generation seemed reluctant to enter the garment industry.[24] But the onset of the depression altered the labor situation. In his memoir, Irving Howe writes that both his parents became workers in the garment industry after his father's store was wiped out in 1930; for countless others who were also stepping into the lower rungs of the middle class during the 1920s, the garment industry provided the job of last resort once the depression dashed their chances for mobility out of the working class.[25]

Some of these new entrants to the clothing industry remained in a garment shop all their lives; but many left the industry as soon as wartime prosperity opened up other opportunities. By the early 1940s there was already a notable exodus of white ethnic workers; to replace them employers recruited black workers, who until then had virtually been excluded from the industry and were also arriving in New York in large numbers in their flight from poverty and oppression in the South. Herbert Northrup, who conducted field studies of New York industries during the 1940s, found that the number of

black garment workers increased by 60 percent between 1940 and 1943;[26] the number of black workers in one of the large ILGWU dressmakers' local doubled between 1940 and 1945.[27] After the war, when the outflow of white ethnic workers accelerated, employers became still more dependent on blacks. They also quickly added Puerto Ricans, who just then began their heavy migration to New York and often possessed some previous experience in making and repairing garments. The skirt industry, for example, which grew rapidly in the late 1940s and early 1950s, was almost exclusively dependent on newly arrived Puerto Ricans.[28]

In its search for new labor supplies, apparel was handicapped by a steadily sinking wage position and the need to compete with a growing range of alternative employment and income-generating opportunities. The earlier Jewish and Italian immigrants had been highly specialized in garments and a few related lines; consequently, apparel largely escaped those "orbits of coercive competition" by which industries adjust their wages and conditions to the prevailing wages in the area. Blacks and Puerto Ricans, however, entered a variety of service and manufacturing industries, dispersing further through the blue-collar sector over time. These other industries were better shielded from outside wage pressures and also promised higher wages than did apparel. And as competitive pressures from the outside mounted, apparel wages fell increasingly out of line with the rest of manufacturing.

The recruitment difficulties created by apparel's growing wage isolation were compounded by the importance of seasonality and apparel's low prestige. Those product lines that remained in New York were highly seasonal; hence, employment fluctuated considerably over the course of a year, and this added a large gap in full-time, full-year earning power to the differential in hourly wages. In addition, the long association of immigrants with apparel had created a distinct psychological deterrant: the descendants of Jewish and Italian garment workers were joined by northern-born blacks and New York-born Puerto Ricans in their reluctance to take up work in a garment shop.[29]

By the late 1960s the gap between supply and demand became increasingly severe because the boom years of the time gave a temporary reprieve to the industry's long decline. In this superheated economic environment, production facilities in garments, as in other industries, were being used at close to full capacity. Consequently, the quickest and cheapest way to secure additional output was to activate the underutilized capital and labor resources concentrated in an older center of production like New York.

As a result, New York's apparel industry entered a period of relative stability, in which firms that were located in the central business district and employed mainly minority workers quickly built up activity.[30]

But a chorus of complaints from employers indicated that recruitment difficulties had simply intensified in the process. In 1969 the local offices of the New York State employment service were able to fill only half as many requests for apparel operators as were needed.[31] Two surveys of New York City apparel firms, conducted in the late 1960s and early 1970s by the Wharton School's *Racial Practices in American Industry Project*, found that clothing firms were restricted by labor shortages that persisted through the period of relatively high unemployment in the early 1970s.[32]

The source of the recruitment difficulty lay in simultaneous changes in the supply of the traditional ethnic and the newer minority work force. Many of the remaining European immigrant workers were then nearing the end of their working lives. More importantly, minority workers began to leave the industry in larger numbers. In the 1960s growth shifted to the city's white-collar sector, and civil rights protests and equal opportunity legislation ensured that minority workers got a large share of the newly created jobs. But while the labor market situation improved for those workers able to move out of manufacturing, political developments greatly eased the economic pressures that had previously compelled minority workers to accept low-wage work. In the course of the welfare "explosion," allowances from public assistance began to approach, and in some cases to surpass, earnings from low-wage manufacturing jobs. Between 1960 and 1970, weekly earnings in apparel fell from 160 percent of welfare benefits to 130 percent; by 1970 the weekly welfare allowance in New York City exceeded the equivalent income from a minimum-wage job by 30 percent. Changes in administrative procedures that eased welfare eligibility rules coupled with welfare rights protest to further reduce the incentives to remain in low-wage manufacturing jobs.[33] These trends encouraged minority workers to leave the labor force in considerable numbers; the Wharton study reported that "field work conducted . . . in New York City . . . repeatedly elicited from employers the problem of scarcity of job applicants during periods when welfare rolls were climbing."[34] And those minority workers remaining in the industry were affected by the militancy and racial conflicts of the times, further reducing the quality and competitiveness of New York's labor force.

These changes thus aggravated New York's market position at a time of growing competition from outside. New York firms now found themselves

tied into an aging and increasingly uncommitted labor force. And just when market conditions were becoming increasingly unstable, the growing shortage of labor further reduced the ability of firms to respond rapidly and flexibly to sudden shifts in demand. More importantly, recruitment difficulties forced New York firms to overcome their wage isolation from the rest of local industry; as Figure 4.2 shows, wage increases in the apparel sector outpaced the rest of New York City manufacturing during the late 1960s. The competition for local labor also pushed wage levels for New York garment workers even further beyond the national average. As Figure 4.3 shows, despite the sharpening of competition from imports and southern producers, the differential in wages between New York and the rest of the nation actually increased in the early 1970s.

Enter the New Immigrants. Thus, the industry's chronic shortage of labor was exacerbated by the boom of the 1960s and the simultaneous exodus of its traditional labor supply. Under these conditions, employers sought out an alternative labor supply, as Piore's argument would suggest. Jewish and Italian employers whom I interviewed in the early 1980s reported that few blacks remained in the labor force. In their eyes, blacks had essentially dropped out of the industry's potential labor supply, and those few still seeking factory work were perceived as undesirable:

The blacks were never numerous, and now we don't have any at all. They seem to leave or disappear. The blacks are looking to better themselves, and I don't blame them. They go to the banks where it's a steadier job. Ours is a seasonal line, so even if you can't get a better job you get a steadier one.

I find that whereas there are fewer blacks in the factory, the office staff has become black and Puerto Rican. This has been the normal progression: the parents work in the factories, and the kids look for white-collar jobs. In the office we get young Hispanics and blacks who are second generation and have never set foot in a factory.

Black workers tend to stay away; they're not interested. I haven't had success when I've hired black workers; they think that it's below them. Those few whom I've hired have come from the unemployment office, and then they've walked off after a short time.

I used to employ a few American blacks, a few as pressers, a couple as operators. At the moment I have none. I've run ads in the *Amsterdam News* [New York's chief black weekly newspaper]. Usually I run ads in *El Diario* [the largest Hispanic paper]; they work better.

Figure 4.2 Earnings Differentials:The New York City Context, 1965–1985
*(New York City Apparel Earnings as a Percentage
of New York City Manufacturing Earnings)*

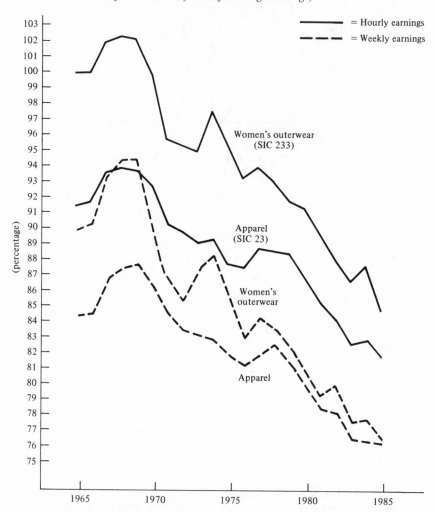

Source: Earnings for 1965 to 1979 from U.S. Bureau of Labor Statistics, *Employment and Earnings for States and Areas*, 1939–1982, Bulletin 1370-13; earnings for 1980 to 1984 from *Supplement to Employment and Earnings for States and Areas, 1980–1984*, Bulletin 1370-19; earnings for January through November 1985 are from unpublished data, U.S. Bureau of Labor Statistics.

Figure 4.3 Earnings Differentials: The National Context, 1965–1985
*(New York City Hourly Apparel Earnings as a Percentage
of Hourly Earnings of all U.S. Apparel Workers)*

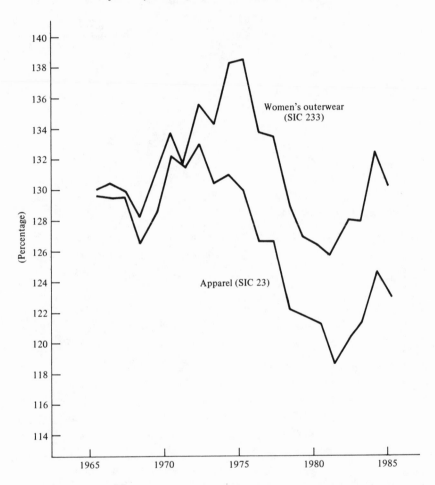

Source: National earnings from 1969 to 1984 from U.S. Bureau of Labor Statistics, *Employment, Hours, and Earnings, U.S., 1909–84,* Bulletin 1312-12; wage levels for January through September 1985 from U.S. Bureau of Labor Statistics, *Employment and Earnings,* V. 32, 4-11 (1985); wage levels for October and November 1985 from unpublished data, U.S. Bureau of Labor Statistics. New York City apparel earnings for 1965 to 1979 from U.S. Bureau of Labor Statistics, *Employment and Earnings for States and Areas, 1939–1982,* Bulletin 1370-13; wage levels for 1980 through 1984 from *Supplement to Employment and Earnings for States and Areas, 1980–1984,* Bulletin 1370-19; wage levels for January through November are from unpublished data, U.S. Bureau of Labor Statistics.

In place of blacks, and to a large extent Puerto Ricans, the employers in the lower-priced lines now reported recruiting immigrants: Dominicans, Colombians, Ecuadorians, and Haitians. As one large employer pointed out:

Most of my workers are immigrants; if native, they're minorities. The shop is predominately Haitian, then Jamaican, Spanish, some native black, with two Italian ladies and two Jews. If there were no immigrants, the needle trades would be out of New York.

By contrast, skill seemed to be an impediment to hiring new immigrants in the higher-price, higher-skilled lines in dresses and coats. These industries had never hired many blacks to begin with, and they still seemed to depend on an aging and rapidly declining corps of European-born immigrants, most of whom were Italians.

How the changeover to an immigrant labor force took place and how employers responded to the problem of labor scarcity is difficult to determine. Elaine Wrong's study of black workers in the garment industry, conducted in the late 1960s and early 1970s, suggests that one reaction to growing discontent and intractability among blacks was to recruit Hispanic workers.[35] However, none of the employers whom I interviewed appeared to have engaged in similar efforts to replace blacks. Some seemed to have been quite deliberate in their attempts to recruit a more pliable and highly motivated work force, as the following example suggests:

When I bought this shop the workers consisted of old Italian ladies. In that shop, if a worker took off three weeks I couldn't do anything about it. I changed over by getting rid of the older workers; now 80 percent of the workers are Spanish, and the labor situation is very good.

But for the most part the transition from older immigrants and native minorities to new immigrants appeared to happen in a more subtle way. Most firms experienced high levels of turnover and consequently absorbed immigrants as replacement labor for exiting workers. But, apart from the small number of cases similar to the instance cited above, few employers seemed to have replaced their departing workers with much selectivity. As Hendricks points out in his study of Dominican immigrants, the garment industry had previously "adapted itself to Puerto Rican workers and worked out organizational patterns, including bilingual supervisors or mediators between managers and employees"; hence, a changeover to a different set of His-

panic workers posed few adjustment difficulties.[36] Moreover, the instability of the labor force led most employers to simply rely on the casual flow of new recruits searching for work from door to door. Those employers who were more selective and discriminating, or who required higher-skilled help, encouraged workers to recruit friends and relatives, but the interviews produced little evidence that specific ethnic groups were targeted. Finally, given the competitive structure of the industry's labor market and the instability of employment in most garment shops, few employers had the economic power to directly influence recruitment patterns. It seems more likely that the typical garment employer was not so much an agent as the beneficiary of the replacement demand of the industry as a whole. Thus, when a neighborhood changed from Italian to Hispanic, the nearby employer found that the complexion of his work force evolved accordingly; and as more immigrants entered the industry, the shops located in the central business district gradually came to hire more immigrants. One employer offered the following story, and it seems to relate what happened in the rest of the industry as well:

In the 1960s my shop was mainly black and Puerto Rican, with a sprinkling of older Jews and Italians. Then one day I woke up and I found that I didn't have any more people from Puerto Rico. The only remaining black is my cutter. And the rest of my workers come from the Dominican Republic, with a bunch from Ecuador, El Salvador, and Chile.

While Piore's argument emphasizes the recruitment patterns of already existing employers, in the garment industry case another demand-side impetus to the new immigrant changeover came from the proliferation of immigrant-owned firms. From 1960 to 1970, the number of Chinese-owned garment firms in Chinatown grew from 16 to 102, and in the following decade the number climbed to 430 (see Table 4.5). The growth of the Chinatown garment industry spurred further Chinese immigration to New York: during the 1970s one fifth of all Chinese immigrants settled in New York City, and the city's share of arriving Chinese newcomers rose during the same period. For Hispanics, the relationship between business activity and immigration trends is more difficult to work out, in large measure because the trend data on Hispanic business ownership are not available. However, we do know that there was substantial business activity by the late 1970s, and the high levels of Hispanic immigration and the low occupational levels of the Hispanic population suggests that the Hispanic ethnic business sector helped fuel the demand for Hispanic immigrant labor.

Table 4.5 Number of Chinese Garment Firms, 1960–1985

1960	8
1961	16
1962	18
1963	15
1964	22
1965	34
1966	40
1967	49
1968	59
1969	73
1970	102
1971	118
1972	146
1973	185
1974	209
1975	247
1976	269
1977	316
1978	370
1979	388
1980	430
1981	429
1982	420
1983	429
1984	450
1985	480

Source: Administrative Records, Local 23–25, International Ladies' Garment Workers' Union.

Through the Factory's Revolving Door. The second component of Piore's argument involves a hypothesis about the congruence between immigrants' work orientations and the characteristics of secondary jobs; another set of interviews—these involving a random sample of 100 Hispanic immigrant ILGWU members whom I interviewed in 1979 and 1980—found that such a congruence was characteristic of immigrant garment workers. Virtually all the immigrants whom I interviewed moved to New York expecting to work. For the most part, they set their occupational sights low. "I thought that I would get a job," explained one Dominican immigrant, "not any office job because I didn't know how to take care of any responsibility in an office. I thought that I would get what I am doing . . . a factory [job] . . . manual labor . . . no? . . . what else can you do?" When asked what types of jobs

they expected to obtain, the immigrants invariably responded "whatever there was" or "anything that presented itself." Often, their statements underlined the instrumentality of their orientations, indicating that the meaning of a job derived essentially from its economic rewards:

I was told that here everyone who wanted to work worked. One could find work . . . of whatever type there was. But one could work.

I was hoping to find any job; it didn't matter to me as long as it was a job.

I was ready to do anything that presented itself because one doesn't arrive prepared to do office work or teach. English is very important for everything. I would take what came. I came ready to work in any place, whatever the job was.

Frequently, the immigrants' remarks suggested that the content of a job was immaterial, since work was evaluated in relation to a set of nonwork objectives: "I came to try hard," explained an undocumented Colombian when I asked about her job expectations, "to do something for my children." One immigrant, who had earlier spoken of sacrificing herself for her children, responded this way: "I came to plunge myself into whatever I could find. As I already told you, I am a poor person and I can accommodate myself with anything, no?"

Once on the labor market, low expectations translated into nonselectivity. Possessing few skills and knowing little if any English, the immigrants tended to accept the first job offered: "As I, as I did not know how to sew, as I did not know a trade, I had to go to work in the first job that I found." Their willingness to work and to do any job, the immigrants seemed to assume, would guarantee them employment. As one immigrant commented: "My sister-in-law said that I should come [to New York] and try. She said that I could find a job anywhere. Since I was a good worker, I would have no problem."

However, the majority of workers said that they had expected to work in the garment industry; those expectations also seemed to parallel the experience of the settlers to whom these immigrants were tied. The immigrants drew on the settlers for information about prospective job conditions. "My aunt talked to me about [working in] garments," commented one immigrant. "I didn't know what I was going to do," explained a recent Ecuadorian arrival, "but my uncle always told me that there was a lot of work in garments."

I expected to get the job that I have now. I knew that I would not be able to get a better one. I came prepared to do more or less what I am doing. My aunt told me that if I would come, she would talk with her shop, with her bosses.

Indeed, the most striking quality about the immigrants' expectations is that they seemed to have entertained few doubts about the likelihood of finding employment.

I always knew that here things would be secure, that as far as the economic situation was concerned, you always found work. I thought that I could find work without the necessity of having an advanced degree, as in my country. Here a worker can always maintain herself—with the necessities at least.

And despite the erosion of job opportunities, there was little in the immigrants' expectations that seemed to match the conventional picture of a depressed and declining industry:

I thought that I would work in garments. Everyone there knows that garments is what pays best in this country and where there is the most work.

They [my cousins] said that garments is what there is the most in this country . . . where you leave one factory and immediately enter into another where they take you.

In Santo Domingo they said that in garments there was a lot of work. And since I know how to sew I have never left the garment industry and I have never worked in anything that did not involve the sewing machine.

Thus, the initial demand for an alternative labor supply arose out of a shortage of native workers, and the changeover to immigrants took place because the newcomers were more accepting than were the natives of the industry's work- and wage-conditions. Once the immigrant population was in place, a somewhat different set of dynamics came into play. First, the presence of settlers, with their own information networks and established connections, encouraged additional immigrants to move. Glenn Hendricks, in his study *The Dominican Diaspora*, shows how villagers from a small town in the northern Dominican Republic moved and settled down under the auspices of migration chains that linked them to settlers: "Very often, the recruit arrives to find a position awaiting him, procured by his sponsor at his own place of work or scouted out for him among the sponsor's network of acquaintances."[37] Similarly, three quarters of the immigrants whom I interviewed reported that they had found their first job through connections with

relatives or friends. This happened in a variety of ways: in some cases, settlers acted as direct sponsors, bringing relatives and friends to factories where they themselves were employed:

I had a friend living in New York who wrote to me and said that when I wanted to come that she would receive me in her house. I wrote her, and she let me know that when I was ready she would receive me. And so it happened. I went to her house and she received me. I arrived at six o'clock in the morning. And at eight it was time to go to work. She said to me: "you stay or you go." And I said: "just as well." I opened my suitcase, took out a fresh dress, and took a bath. And on arrival at the factory, the other workers asked me: "Ai! And when did you arrive?" And I told them: "This morning."

On other occasions, the settlers served as a communication belt orienting the newcomers to the ways of the new environment and providing them with information about employment opportunities:

I had a good friend who was living here when I arrived. She received me very well, and she helped me look for work. She was a very good person with me. I lived in her house. Until I learned how to get around she took me out to look for work. For example, here [in the garment center]. She would say: "Here there are factories. Look for a job."

Thus, the net effect of settlement was to widen the garment industry's accessibility to the immigrant labor force; other characteristics associated with the immigrants further added to the supply of low-wage labor. For a variety of reasons, immigrants tend toward substantially higher levels of labor-force activity than natives. For permanent immigrants, as suggested in Chapter 2, the impetus comes from the drive to catch up to natives and to surmount the low-level, poorly rewarded jobs to which they are initially assigned. Temporary migrants are impelled by their desire to accumulate money that can be used for some investment back home; as one immigrant put it:

We strove very hard to put together a little money. My husband had two jobs, working at night and working during the day. I worked as well. We tried to form a savings so that we could get ahead. We made great efforts.

For temporary migrants the dream of return often fades—either because the immigrants cannot make as much money as they had anticipated or, as Piore emphasizes, they can no longer postpone consuming for pleasure. Whatever the cause, ties to relatives back home who are dependent on remittances

continue to fuel the demand for more and more income. Finally, those immigrants who are undocumented are ineligible for any form of income assistance, and hence the compulsion to work is particularly strong. Thus, when compared with blacks or Puerto Ricans, New York's immigrants have lower levels of unemployment, higher levels of labor-force participation, and less dependency on welfare.[38]

The transformation from native to immigrant labor has had still one further effect on the garment industry: it has stemmed the upward pressure on wages. As we have seen, wages for New York's garment workers grew increasingly out of line with the rest of the nation's in the early 1970s—despite the onset of massive job losses starting in 1969. After 1975 New York's lead over the rest of the nation began to decline, as Figure 4.3, which traces the differential in wages between New York and the nation, quite clearly shows. The presence of immigrants also buoyed apparel's position in the competition for labor with other local employers: as Figure 4.2 indicates, hourly wages and weekly earnings for New York's garment workers have steadily slipped below the average for New York's manufacturing sector—itself severely depressed.

While New York thus gained a highly motivated and lower-cost work force through this massive infusion of immigrant labor, its competitors elsewhere in the nation have been stymied by growing labor-supply problems. In the South, several decades of rapid industrial expansion have greatly reduced the region's once abundant store of surplus workers, and with the movement of higher-paying basic industries from the North to the South there are more attractive claimants for the southern labor force than apparel. The result is that southern garment manufacturers now also face a growing shortage of labor.[39] Not only are there fewer southern workers who wish to work in a garment factory, but those who do are of lower quality and lower morale. "Apparel's Next Problem: Poor Worker Attitudes," reads a headline in an industry publication, and indeed the trade journals are filled with articles ("The Bleeding Ulcer-Turnover"; "Hire Workers Who Won't Quit") that testify to the industry's recruitment difficulties. The manager of a Levi's plant in Tyler, Texas, reports having to hire one out of every two applicants. According to an industry trade journal, a well-run factory in a rural area with access to an ample supply of labor is still likely to have a turnover rate of 50 percent.[40] High turnover and tight labor markets mean that an appreciable percentage of the total labor cost goes to hiring and training. The American Apparel Manufacturers Association has estimated that the indus-

try wide average cost of training a sewing machine operator is $2,000 per worker. Thus, the recruitment problems in the once labor-surplus areas of the Sunbelt have further reduced the cost differential between New York producers and their southern competitors.[41]

Trying for the Main Chance. While immigration has lowered the costs of producing garments in New York, it has influenced the business of garment making in one other way. Mention of this leads us to the question of immigrant enterprise. As we saw earlier, New York's garment manufacturers still depend on the presence of contractors willing and able to run small plants in a cost-efficient way. In their absence, New York's manufacturers would be obliged to seek out larger facilities, whether fully compatible with their product lines or not. The crucial point is that the local New York City supply of contractors is great because immigrants have sought to move into the garment business in great numbers. Why and how they have done so will be explained in following chapters. But the fact is that the new immigration has boosted the supply of potential garment capitalists. Moreover, the characteristics of immigrant entrepreneurs are fateful for the survival of the New York garment trade. Because the immigrants are risk takers, as we shall see, they open factories to take advantage of fashion changes. Their search for opportunity through entrepreneurship also leads them to start up new firms at a high rate, which in turn provides New York manufacturers with the capacity needed to rapidly build up production in response to seasonal or style-driven changes. Thus, the availability of these small, immigrant-owned firms maintains the external economies associated with New York's production base. And without these immigrant entrepreneurs the spot market for styled items and late-developing clothing lines would be located somewhere else.

[5]

Exodus

For all the reasons discussed in the previous chapters, clothing remains a small business industry, and New York City is still the place where small clothing firms can best thrive. This provides part of the explanation for the burgeoning of immigrant firms in the garment industry, but there are other issues left unattended. As I argued in Chapter 2, the chances for immigrants depend largely on the extent of the competition. If petty proprietorship still attracts new native owners, then the outlook for immigrants will not be terribly promising. But for a variety of reasons—having to do with the status of a small business, the hours that it demands, and its rewards relative to other pursuits—natives may not be equally interested in certain small business lines as immigrants. Should the supply of potential native owners diminish, the door is opened to immigrants, who will be able to start up businesses in response to a replacement demand. This chapter attempts to show that the process of occupational assimilation has altered patterns of recruitment among the Jews and Italians that had traditionally furnished the bulk of garment factory owners—and has thus created vacancies into which new immigrant owners have moved.

Up from the Factory

The garment industry, as we saw in Chapter 3, has been a province of ethnic business owners since its growth took off in the late nineteenth century. Russian-Jewish immigrants entered the industry as workers at the onset of mass migration to the United States in the 1880s; shortly thereafter, the newcomers took over the bulk of petty ownership positions as contractors; by 1914, as Rischin recounts, the Russian Jews had become the dominant group among manufacturers as well:

[T]he industry's personnel had changed. . . . Employers were no longer of German Jewish stock, as they had been before the turn of the century. . . . Proprietors of the handful of leading German houses prudently abandoned the field and entered more advantageous fields of commerce. They became department store magnates, wholesale cloth and credit men, brokers, and bankers. By 1910, Alsatian-born Max Meyer was virtually the only one of the earlier generation who remained a big manufacturer. The thousands of women's garment manufacturers, led by Reuben Sadowsky's Sabbath-observing Broadway cloak factory, with thrice-daily prayer services for its 1500 employees, were almost all former East Side contractors.[1]

Italians experienced a similar trajectory, though their rise from workers to owners occurred at a somewhat slower pace, and the number who succeeded in moving further still from contractor to manufacturer appears to have been considerably smaller.

However permeable to these early immigrants, the garment industry has exercised a tenuous grip on the succeeding generations. As Glazer and Moynihan noted in *Beyond the Melting Pot,* the problem of succession proved particularly intense for those first-generation capitalists who had risen to success in immigrant trades like the garment industry:

When the father is an immigrant and not a college man, and not the sort of person one sees in the pages of *Fortune,* and the son has gotten a good education, there is great strain involved in his taking up the family business. Too, being a Jewish business it is likely to be of low status—a small clothing firm, an umbrella factory, a movie-house, a costume jewelry manufacturer serving Negro or Puerto Rican trade. Though such a business supplied enough to send the children to college and support the family, it might not seem quite the right thing to a son with an expensive education. Thus very often, the son of such a businessman goes into the professions, and the family business is regretfully sold or abandoned to partners.[2]

Chester Rapkin's 1962 study of an industrial area in lower Manhattan, which in a later incarnation emerged as the Soho of artists and art galleries, provided independent and contemporaneous evidence of this leakage of entrepreneurial talent. Even by this relatively late date, the South Houston industrial district still contained a concentration of thriving manufacturing firms in apparel and other related fields; indeed, Rapkin found that the apparel firms had enjoyed an average annual rate of growth of 10.7 percent during the 1950–1962 period. Yet, despite these favorable conditions, almost three quarters of the firms had been in existence for ten years or more, and only one tenth had been operating for four years or less—an indication that the garment industry was attracting few new entrants at a time, it should

be noted, when the competitive pressures were considerably less intense than they are today.[3]

What happened in the intervening years was that the older ethnic groups retreated from contracting to the higher-status, higher-profit activities involved in manufacturing. In the late 1970s Sharon Zukin restudied manufacturing firms in the same South Houston industrial district that Rapkin had examined almost twenty years before: though the area still contained over 7,000 apparel jobs, Zukin found that few new garment firms had emerged.[4] But the apparent stagnation obscures two diverging trends. Members of the older ethnic groups that historically dominated the industry are no longer setting up new firms of their own. Yet the garment industry is still experiencing a high rate of new-firm formation, thanks almost entirely to neophyte immigrant capitalists. For example, data furnished me by the largest garment workers' local in New York showed that in 1985, 57 percent of the 59 unionized firms owned by white ethnics had been in existence for at least 10 years, and only 12 percent had been established within the previous 2 years. By contrast, almost 66 percent of the 480 unionized Chinese firms had been in business for 2 years or less, and less than 5 percent consisted of long-established firms with 10 or more years of experience (see Table 5.1). Similarly, a comparison of all garment firms listed in the 1981 and the 1984 Yellow Pages for the outer boroughs of Queens, Brooklyn, and the Bronx (where a large portion of the contracting shops are to be found) yielded a total of 350 new listings. When the owners of these firms were surveyed on a one-in-five basis, only 25 percent proved to be United States-born. My survey of white ethnic and new immigrant firms confirmed this basic pattern. Longevity averaged 32.5 years among the 41 ethnic-owned firms sur-

Table 5.1 Longevity, Immigrant and Nonimmigrant Firms, 1985

Firm Type	No. of Firms	Year Firm Founded				
		1984	1983	1980–82	1975–79	1974 or older
Nonimmigrant	59	3 (5%)	4 (6.8%)	8 (13.6%)	10 (16.9%)	34 (57.6%)
Immigrant	412	137 (33.2%)	133 (32.3%)	80 (19.4%)	43 (10.4%)	19 (4.6%)

Source: Administrative Records, Local 23–25, International Ladies' Garment Workers' Union.
Note: Includes all firms under contract with Local 23–25, ILGWU, and in business as of February 1985.

veyed but only 5 years among the 95 immigrant firms. And whereas the vast majority of immigrant firms were new startups, only one of the ethnic-owned firms was established in the year prior to the interview, and only one other had been in existence for less than 10 years.

Thus, my survey found many Italians and Jews still active as garment contractors, but mostly they were aging, and few among them expected to pass on their business to a relative or a younger member of their own ethnic group. The average age of the Italian and Jewish contractors in my sample was 56, and many were near the end of their productive lives (the sample included 10 contractors aged 65 or older). Even the younger ethnic business owners were engaged in long-established firms. All those Jewish and Italian garment factory owners who were under 40 had succeeded their parents in business, and not one had established his own firm.

The career patterns of these ethnic contractors tell us a great deal about how ethnic specializations are born, maintained, and finally die out. Seventeen of the Italian and Jewish owners were foreign-born; for those who had come to New York as teenagers or adults, a combination of tailoring skills and high ambition had led them to careers in business:

[A Russian-born contractor, aged 78]: I went into business because I wanted to . . . you heard of Horatio . . . you know what I mean. I was willing to work hard, and I worked seven days a week. I still work hard at an age when most men quit.

Field notes: Interviewing an Italian-born woman who owns a garment shop; her sister, also Italian-born, who manages the shop, joins in. I ask the owner how much education she has and the question makes her embarrassed. She tells me [five years], but first says, "Please, don't ask. You don't really have to know that." Then her sister adds this comment: "You were asking why the children don't come in the business. Well, look at her. She grew up on the other side, she didn't have much education, but she was apprenticed at a young age, and so she learned how to sew. When she came here, this was her skill and was the only way to get ahead."

Similar motivations impelled a small number of native-born owners: lacking much schooling, they opted for ownership as an alternative to unemployment or as a way out of the low-level factory jobs in which they were trapped:

The last job I had was over thirty years ago, working in a shoe factory. I was making 90 cents an hour and getting kicked around, treated like dirt. The owners were always yelling and screaming and finally I decided to leave. My wife had been working in the industry as an operator, and we decided to make a go of it. We were overcharged for equipment, we made mistakes, but we learned from them. This is 1985, and we've been in business since 1948.

But for most native-born owners, the crucial factor was that "My family was always in this business. There was never a decision, never a question of not going in." Consider these cases:

[A sixty-year old Italian-American contractor]: During World War II, I worked on the planes, and when I came home I went to work for TWA at La Guardia. I was there for about a year when my dad told me that they needed me in the shop. So I came. [But did you want to go into the business?] In those days, I did anything my parents wanted. That's how we grew up. Most of the time they were right about what we should do. Of course, kids aren't like that today. [Is this your parents' original shop?] No, my parents' shop is upstairs. This shop used to belong to my father-in-law; when I got married—I met my wife at a dance of the contractors' association—I came here. My two sisters stayed with my parents upstairs; they're still there and so is my mother, who's now eighty-seven. This is all we ever did.

[A forty-two-year-old Jewish owner of a belt factory]: I've always been in this business. [You mean you never worked for someone else?] Well, the last paid job that I had was when I was a kid, running a knitting mill at night. After that, my brother and I went into our father's business. [Why did you want to go into business for yourself?] Money. My feeling was always that if you work for yourself you have opportunities that you can't get if you work for someone else. The true riches come from working for yourself. That's the attitude that we were both brought up with.

[A fifty-year-old Italian-American operating a garment shop with his wife and his mother in a heavily Italian section of the Bronx]: The last job that I had was working for All-American cable when I was sixteen. What happened then was that my brother went into the service; my father was sick; and my mother, who was running the shop, needed me to come into the shop and help her out. [But why did you decide to go into business for yourself? Is that what you wanted to do?] Look, I was brought up in the business. That was my way of life. My parents ran the shop ever since I was a little kid. I spent more time playing with cotton spools than with toys.

Thus, in the case of both immigrants and native-born, the conditions that led to careers as owners were mediated by their position in the social structure—their immediate ties to other owners and their acquisition of those skills needed in running a garment business. Moreover, many owners came from a milieu in which ownership was a common activity: 18 of the 41 owners had parents who were also active in the garment business, and another 11 owners reported that their parents had owned a business in some other field. What this setting seems to have furnished is not simply the information and connections needed to pursue a successful career in business but also a deeply ingrained preference for being on one's own. Thus, virtually all owners, whether Italian or Jewish, immigrant or foreign-born,

expressed a strong preference for ownership, in part because of the independence it promised, in part because it appeared to offer the most lucrative path to monetary gain. These two very representative quotations testify to this entrepreneurial bent:

It's been foreign to me to punch a card and to work for anyone else. I've always liked to make decisions and to do as I please. Working for myself has always had priority. There's the independence, freedom and pride that you take. I've found that running your own business is very satisfying. I've always looked forward to making a buck without taking orders.

In the long run, you're better off if you work for yourself. Eventually, you can improve your position in life. As a worker you work for the rest of your life and you don't get anywhere.

Further evidence of a propensity toward business emerged when I asked the owners whether they preferred the security of working for someone else and receiving a check every week as opposed to being one's own boss. The latter was chosen by virtually every owner, and their answers to this question underscore the appeals of a small business:

I could never work for someone else. I always wanted to be able to set my own time and pace. I don't mind the responsibility.

I would rather not work for someone else. You can go further working for yourself and you have more control.

Thus, the Italian and Jewish owners were embedded in a long-standing entrepreneurial milieu, and they had undergone an experience that apparently validated an entrepreneurial orientation. Hence, when asked about the best way of getting ahead in American society, it was not surprising that their answers embraced the values and attributes usually associated with small business. In fact, the question was meant to elicit the field or pursuit best suited for getting ahead. But the owners interpreted it as a question about attitudes, and their responses mainly took the form of answers such as these:

"ambition and hard work";
"intelligence and industry";
"do the best you can and that's all";
"work your tail off, there's no substitute for hard work";
"don't be afraid to get dirty working";
"common sense and hard work: book learning is nothing."

When the original question was followed up with a question about the field in which to apply these qualities, most owners suggested that business was to be preferred. As examples, take these somewhat hyperbolic yet true-to-form responses:

The best way of getting ahead is to go into your own business. But you have to have the type of mentality: you have to be willing to take chances, and you have to be logical enough to plan for success. Most people just want to put in their time and do the least amount of work and not have the headaches. Of course, going into business has a lot of headaches. [So what's the satisfaction?] The satisfaction is money. [Is there any particular business line that you would recommend?] I'd say any business in which you can be successful.

Don't punch a card! You know what I mean? As long as you're not afraid of hours money will come. What's the point of working for someone else? You put in the hours and you build up his business. If you're willing to work hard and you work for yourself, at the end you'll have a business. Look at me. I almost went under three times, and the only thing that saved me was the hours.

Yet, for all the congruence between world view and career, and despite the history of involvement in the garment trade and the satisfaction that it evidently generated, the possibility that the next generation should continue in the trade was an idea that the owners dismissed out of hand. "My kids going into this business?" asked one owner rhetorically. "As I told you, I told my daughter that if she ever went into this business, I'd break her leg." This generation of Jewish and Italian owners—so many of whom had taken over businesses from their parents—was uninterested in handing over the business to their own children because the garment industry was decidedly not the best way of getting ahead. Why this option should have lost appeal is rooted in several changes, but most important are the deteriorating competitive situation in the garment industry and an expanding opportunity structure of a type that the owners never enjoyed:

I'm a 100 percent believer in going for yourself. It's much better than working for someone else. But right now we're struggling in this business; each and every contractor is also struggling. If I were younger I would never be a contractor. You have to depend on the manufacturers. If they give me work I'm OK. If not, I sit around.

The garment industry in New York and in this country is on the way out. I would never advise anyone to go into the garment center. Not garment contracting . . .

Having a garment factory is definitely not the way to go in the eighties. Being a manufacturer or an importer may be better.

Why don't I think this is the best way to get ahead? The hours here don't compare with the money you get. Not here anymore, moneywise. Sure, I always made a living . . . but it's rough.

Going into the garment industry? I wouldn't wish this business on a dog. The imports are killing us. So far, we're hanging on pretty well, but I know that I'm eventually going to have to close the factory.

Thus, despite their strongly held entrepreneurial orientation, most owners were pleased that their children had chosen other pursuits. Several owners actually indicated that they had dissuaded their children from entering the business:

I would never let my kids into this business, and I never wanted them to go into the business. It's too taxing: you're fighting with the manufacturer, with the union, with the workers, and with yourself. It's not worth it. And anyway, they're doing something better outside the business. One of my kids expressed an interest, but I discouraged him: it's no way to spend a future.

Two of my kids are teaching, and the third is in computers. I never wanted them to go in. I thought that the kids could do better doing other things. My son even wanted to go into the business at one time, but I dissuaded him.

By contrast, two middle-aged brothers of Italian background had sought to convince one of their sons to enter the firm with the eventual aim of passing the business on to him; though they did so successfully, their experience testified to the recruitment problems of the older ethnic concerns:

The business is still very profitable, and we do a lot of volume. And in some ways things are even better than in the past, because so many of our older competitors have gone out of business, and there are relatively few people who can provide the type of quality service that we can. The problem, for most of the people in our age and in our situation, is that there's nobody to take over the business. In our case, there was somebody, although it took a hell of a lot of convincing. In the end, we made him an offer he couldn't refuse. Right now, he's learning the ropes and is working out well; hopefully, he'll stick it out.

And so, as the garment business has lost its appeal among even those Jews and Italians who remain active in this line, the pattern of succession that appeared to hold for an earlier generation at an earlier period has now worked itself out. Of the 18 businesses that had been handed down from parents to children, only one had attracted a third-generation heir. Only

three firms were run by owners under 40 who had succeeded their parents in business, and all these concerns were engaged in particular garment lines where contracting for manufacturers accounted for only a portion of the business. Indeed, those few younger Jews and Italians remaining in the contracting business were often aware of how exceptional they were. One Jewish owner in his mid-30s, for example, took the pains to point out:

I bet you're surprised to see me here. Most of the people who you'll find operating coat-contracting shops are old Italian men who think that it's still the 1930s and haven't changed their business since.

Moreover, in the present context succession represents not so much continuity but change. If for the earlier generations business was entrepreneurial in the Schumpeterian sense—that is, it involved a new way of doing things—for the current generation of successors it appears to be almost an atavistic habit to which business heirs resort for lack of alternatives. Thus, in contrast to the immigrant or older, second-generation owners, most of whom had not gone beyond high school and had often gone into the business immediately following service in the Armed Forces, all but one of the younger heirs had completed the B.A.—the exception having dropped out of college after three years. When asked why they had gone into business, the successors typically responded by saying that it was a business that they already knew. Yet, none thought that the garment business was the best way of getting ahead, nor did anyone think that the growth prospects for his own firm were bright. And when questioned about plans for the future, their answers gave no evidence of a strategy for building up the business.

Thus, ethnic succession has created a space for new immigrant garment capitalists whose investment calculus, as I shall show, is shaped by the lack of alternative opportunities for mobility. Patterns of succession are also influenced by the transformation of New York's garment industry from production center to spot market. As the level of uncertainty and instability has increased, the older ethnic firms have chosen to follow a risk-averse strategy. Consequently, immigrant firms have frequently been the first to benefit from short-term fashion trends.

For example, fashion changes have altered the nature of activity in New York in ways that have redounded to the benefit of new immigrant owners. Historically, as we have seen, New York firms specialized in the higher-fashion lines of dresses and coats. But demand for both items has long been

declining. Instead of dresses and coats, more sportswear is being produced; indeed, sportswear is the one subindustry that experienced growth in aggregate employment during the 1970s and early 1980s. As demand for dresses and coats declined, older Italian and Jewish contractors went out of business. Since few Italians or Jews were starting up new firms, the rise of sportswear meant that there was an entirely new field into which immigrants could enter with little competition from natives. Sportswear had the further advantage of requiring somewhat lower skills than dresses and a simpler division of labor than coats, which, as we shall see in the next chapter, further lowered entry barriers.

Another example is the case of the pleating industry, which shows how uncertainty affects the process of ethnic succession. Pleating and stitching, as pointed out in Chapter 4, is disproportionately concentrated in New York relative to the other industries that constitute the city's apparel complex. New York pleaters service both local and national manufacturers, and with such a large customer base, they are able to provide a wide range of specialized services. Although each customer accounts for only a small portion of business, the demand from many small customers justifies investment in specialized machines such as automatic pleating presses or those that make pleating forms. Similarly, the larger firms develop design capabilities and play an important role in the process of product development.

In the mid-1970s a shift in fashion expanded the demand for pleated dresses and skirts. One possibility was that the larger, ethnic firms would invest in new equipment, take on more space, and hire more help to meet this newly augmented demand. But precisely because pleating is so susceptible to fashion, and the ethnic firms tend to seek stability rather than expansion, a different reaction took place. One organizer for the pleaters' union offered this account, which was confirmed by interviews with owners of pleating firms:

When pleating took off, the larger shops had more business than they could handle. The owners preferred to concentrate on the fancy, specialized items—on which they could make higher profits. So what would happen is that the owner would go up to one of his workers and say, "Hey, Jose, you want to be a boss? You set up your own pleating shop, and I'll keep you supplied with enough work to keep you busy." Of course, Jose jumped at the chance and started out as subcontractor to his old boss. But before long Jose got to know his bosses' customers; and it wasn't much longer that Jose was out in the market getting business for himself.

Because Dominicans had previously become the most important work group in the pleating industry, they were the principal beneficiaries of this trend, and in the late 1970s scores of Dominicans set up small "renegade" pleating shops. In contrast to the larger firms, these "renegade" shops specialized in a few high-volume styles that allowed them to use simple, labor-intensive techniques: pleaters hand-folded a skirt into a cardboard form and passed it to a helper; the helper steamed the pleat and returned the skirt to the pleater; the pleater then unfolded the skirt and sent it back to a separate sewing facility.

However, the same market factors that facilitated immigrants' entry into pleating and stitching also left the immigrant firms highly vulnerable to changes in consumer demand. By the spring of 1982, pleated dresses and skirts, though fashionable, were no longer de rigueur; hence the market for the product that the immigrant firms produced collapsed. According to union officials, half of the firms owned by Dominicans in 1981 had gone out of business by the end of the second quarter of 1982.

There is, however, one alternative to the argument made in this chapter: that immigrant firms are growing, not because they are replacing older ethnic concerns, but because they can compete better and are driving the older companies out of business. Some of the evidence that we collected does point in this direction. Any small business rests on the strength and aggressiveness of its owner, and on average we can expect that younger owners will be more aggressive and harder-driving than their older counterparts; this will be all the more so in an industry as frenetic and competitive as garments. In this respect, the fact that those Italians and Jews still active in the contracting end of the garment industry were in late middle age (56 was the average age of the owners that we surveyed), while their new immigrant counterparts were a good deal younger (the average age of the new immigrant owners was 39) should work in the immigrant's favor. Moreover, the older ethnic owners do seem to be slowing down. Though they continue to work long hours and long weeks, the new immigrants work still harder: the old-timers averaged 47.3 hours and 5.4 days a week, whereas the new-comers reported working an average of 51.4 hours and 5.7 days a week. Still another factor is that the old-timers have a dimmer view of business prospects. Fifty-three percent of the Italians and Jews said that business was getting worse, whereas only 43 percent of the immigrants reported similarly deteriorating conditions. Furthermore, the latter figure is inflated by the

negative reports made by the Hispanic owners; when the Chinese are considered alone, those reporting that business was getting worse fell to 33 percent.

Despite these indicators, the available data indicate that immigrant firms fail at a higher rate than do their native competitors. Table 5.2 shows out-of-business rates for 1983 and 1984 for all immigrant and nonimmigrant firms under contract to the largest garment workers' union local in New York City. Though failure rates for both types of firm were high in both years, the immigrant firms went under at much higher rates.

But, given the differences between the two types of firm, this is what we could expect. The immigrant-owned firms are mainly new concerns, as shown in Table 5.1, and a very high failure rate is associated with new businesses of all types. Moreover, while the older entrepreneurs may be losing some of their competitive edge, their experience, knowledge of the market, and ties to customers and suppliers are assets that still work to their advantage. Nonetheless, the benefits that they derive from their experience provide only partial protection against the severe pressures of the industry; hence, many nonimmigrant firms are forced out of business each year. The crucial point, however, is that the old-timers are replaced by a negligible number of new Jewish and Italian business owners. By contrast, the immigrants are undeterred by the appallingly high rate at which garment firms are forced to the wall; hence, ethnic succession has created opportunities of which the newcomers have amply availed themselves.

Table 5.2 Failure Rate for Immigrant and Nonimmigrant Firms, 1983, 1984

	Immigrant Firms	Nonimmigrant Firms
Failure rate, 1983		
No. in business, $^{12}/_{82}$	420	88
No. out of business, 1983	213	18
Failure rate	50.7%	20.4%
Failure rate, 1984		
No. in business, $^{12}/_{83}$	429	74
No. out of business, 1984	156	15
Failure rate	36.3%	20.2%

Source: Administrative Records, Local 23–25, International Ladies' Garment Workers' Union.

[6]

Getting into Business

Ethnic succession, as the previous chapter has shown, has opened up vacancies for immigrants who are seeking out ownership opportunities in the garment industry. But we could imagine a situation in which businesses that arose under one environment no longer enjoyed the same competitive advantages and yet still remained viable for residual factors that are primarily a function of time and experience: long-standing ties to customers and suppliers, knowledge of the market, access to credit, and so on. If this were the case, old-time business owners would then depart from the scene without being replaced by newcomers.

In the garment industry, however, newcomers do replace old-timers; hence, our questions in this section concern those characteristics of the industry that make it supportive of new, immigrant-owned firms. Why can immigrant capitalists break the barriers to entry in this industry? And how important are ethnic group resources in the creation of these new immigrant concerns? In answering these questions, the framework will be both analytic and genetic. That is, I will attempt to examine the historical conditions under which an immigrant garment industry grew up in New York City between 1965 and 1985 and also to analyze those structural features of the industry that make it permeable to new firms.

Start-up Funds

The prospective entrepreneur's very first problem is how to obtain start-up funds. Most untested entities are too risky to merit a bank loan, and the very plebeian origins of the garment factory owner are unlikely to improve his or her credit rating. Thus, from where does the money come?

For immigrants the start-up problem may be somewhat reduced thanks to a habit of saving and frugality. The historical literature on immigrant groups

suggests that immigrants save at an unusually high rate, and saving seems to be a correlate both of temporary migration patterns and of familial chain migrations. There are also culturally sanctioned forms of saving that further expand the pool of financial resources beyond the ambit of the nuclear or even the extended family. Light and Lyman have shown how Chinese immigrants organized rotating credit associations (*hui*) that amassed funds for investment purposes by collecting small contributions from individual family members. Like other immigrant savings banks or mutual-aid associations, the *hui* then used these funds to give credit for small business ventures, but their unique organization minimized the risk of fraud or default. Small size limited participation to close friends and relatives, while the sponsorship of the family associations, which controlled all activities in Chinatown, ensured that additional sanctions could be levied against potential violators.[1]

Similar credit-raising mechanisms indigenous to the English-speaking Caribbean have been imported to the United States by West Indian immigrants, with quite positive effects on small business success. Small merchants in the Dominican Republic also accumulate capital through rotating credit associations referred to as *San*. Hendricks reports that *San* groups are maintained by Dominican immigrants in New York, usually organized within close friendship or extended-family groups and often with the capacity of raising quite significant sums.[2]

However, the emergence of immigrant-owned garment firms owes little to the role of ethnic credit-raising mechanisms. None of the Hispanic firms and only two of the Chinese firms attributed any assistance to family associations or rotating credit associations. The reason is that these social bases of collective economic organization have either been bypassed by market mechanisms or have been undermined by the attenuation of traditional social relationships, even among the Chinese, where the degree of institutionalization is strongest. In the first place, the post-1965 immigrants represent a wider cross section of Chinese society than the older immigrants. Only a minority comes from the six districts near Canton from which the old immigrants originated, with the result that few of the newcomers have gained access to association-sponsored forms of credit. Moreover, savings have not significantly spilled over from commercial banks or credit unions to immigrant-owned firms. While the family associations still maintain the traditional *hui*, savings mechanisms have been rationalized to attract funds from the newer immigrants: there are now six federally insured

credit unions operating under the umbrella of the local family associations. Furthermore, by rationalizing their savings institutions, the family associations have also limited the use to which their funds can be put: federal restrictions prohibit business loans and force credit officers to scrutinize personal loans more carefully. Savings are also put into more conventional institutions, and the large number of savings banks that line Chinatown's streets attest a high savings rate.[3] The banks serve little function as a source of start-up funds, however, since most are unwilling to lend money for capital investment to garment-factory owners, given the risk and uncertainty associated with the business. Still, some banks offer personal loans. Key informants, however, suggest that the practice is neither widespread nor of great consequence.

Rather, the critical factor is that the garment industry provides an environment that is at once permeable to small, new firms and that maximizes the importance of immigrants' informal resources. My survey showed that the immigrant owners' connections with the broader ethnic community played a critical role in capitalizing new firms: only 14 percent of the owners provided start-up funds from their own savings alone. In all remaining cases, start-up capital was pieced together from a variety of sources—some savings, some loans from relatives, some advances from friends.

But the more important condition of new immigrant business start-ups is that the prospective garment capitalist has access to external economies that offer an opportunity to go into business with a small investment and a short-term commitment. Perhaps the most crucial of these external economies are the market mechanisms within the garment industry itself that mediate the needs for credit and capital supplies. The crucial actors are those businesses that specialize in supplying the equipment and machinery that a garment factory needs. These equipment suppliers furnish machinery nationwide, but, like the purveyors of other needed supplies, they are concentrated in New York because New York is where they have greatest access to their customers. In selling nationwide, the equipment suppliers deal mainly in high-speed automated machines, and many provide special attachments or customized machines. The equipment suppliers also do a large trade in used machinery, much of which is too slow or inefficient for the modern producer of standardized goods, but can be recycled to the New York, immigrant-owned firm that specializes in styled items that cannot be worked on at high speeds. Thus, these equipment suppliers intervene in such a way as to lower the barriers to entry: for as little as $25,000 a neophyte garment

capitalist can purchase a 25- to 30-person factory, complete with a boiler needed to generate steam for pressing machines as well as the necessary electrical and gas hookups. Moreover, dealers provide generous financing terms: a down payment of $6,000 to $7,000 usually suffices, with the remainder to be amortized over an 18- to 24-month period at below-market interest rates.

Technology

Not only does the garment industry have built-in mechanisms that lower the barriers to entry, but its technology and organization keep down both capital and technical thresholds. The basic contours of immigrant enterprise are defined by the fundamental distinction between manufacturers and contractors. While low in comparison with the rest of American industry, the barriers to entry at the manufacturer level vastly exceed the resources that immigrants can amass. Minimum capital requirements for the new manufacturer run close to $500,000. One reason that so much capital is needed is that the cash-flow pattern makes the manufacturer highly dependent on credit: stores remit payments six to eight weeks *after* delivery, which means that the manufacturer must have access to considerable amounts of up-front money in order to purchase textiles, pay for contract labor, and maintain other overhead expenses. A second barrier to entry is the greater number and complexity of tasks involved in a manufacturing business. Whereas a contractor specializes in one function—production—the manufacturer must attend to merchandising, designing, and purchasing, as well as supervising, if not directing, the manufacturing work performed to his specifications. These functions are also difficult to routinize in the form of standardized rules or codes. Hence, learning takes place, not so much through formal instruction, but through a process of informal on-the-job socialization. Thus, a manufacturer may often have followed a career that involved positions in each significant component of the interrelated apparel complex: first, a stint as salesman for an apparel firm; then as buyer for a department store; next, possibly as a salesman of textile piece goods as well; and only then a manufacturer in his own right. What is acquired in such a career is not simply the mechanics of how things are done but also the codes for reading market signals through interpersonal communication as well as the networks through which information is generated and passed.

Consequently, the province of the immigrant garment entrepreneur is

contracting, a function whose essential component is purveying labor. As such, the manufacturing/contracting arrangement greatly lowers entry barriers because it spares the contractor the costs of purchasing raw materials as well as the risks of accumulating inventory. But even at this level patterns of ownership are circumscribed by constraints of capital, technology, and skill. For example, a contracting factory making high-priced dresses tends to be smaller than the average immigrant firm and requires even less investment in machinery and other equipment. Yet immigrant owners have only begun to branch out into this line, and they have done so in relatively limited numbers. The barriers to entry stem from several factors: the high-priced dress contractor uses difficult and costly textiles; the sewing must be done precisely; consequently the entire process must be very carefully managed; and finally, the contractor must be able to provide the manufacturer with advice on design and production problems. Similarly, immigrant firms have not successfully penetrated the mass-production lines—coats, men's clothing, and undergarments. In this case, capital requirements tend to be excessive, because these garments are made in assembly-line fashion; setting up this type of production line requires technical assistance, training, and costly, specialized machines—all of which have thus far deterred immigrant owners.

Rather, the starting point for immigrant garment firms are those low-priced, style-oriented product lines where volatility keeps barriers to entry low. In these lines, almost any existing factory space—lofts, storefronts, even apartments—will suffice. As we shall see, such low-cost space has been widely available—either in the vacant loft buildings of New York's manufacturing districts or in the empty storefronts that line the decaying commercial streets in the immigrant neighborhoods. Since the expensive, computerized machinery used to manufacture standardized goods is ill-suited to constant changes in style and fabric, the immigrant firms buy out-of-date, operator-guided machines, inadequate for mass-production operations but depreciated by previous use.

By specializing at the low end of the market, new immigrant firms can further reduce both their capital and their labor investments. As in high-priced lines, making variable products sharply limits capital outlays. However, the high-fashion firms substitute for capital with costly inputs of labor—using hand workers, for example, to sew on buttons and clasps. By contrast, the market position of the new immigrant firm virtually eliminates the need for skilled labor, thus generating savings on both the capital and

the labor sides. Since new immigrant firms use few of the time-consuming and costly finishing operations on which higher-priced firms depend, they can also utilize higher-speed sewing machines for which workers can be more easily trained. Similarly, many immigrant firms work on cheap, synthetic materials that enable them to use industrial hand irons in place of the heavier machine presses that are standard equipment among larger nonimmigrant firms; some immigrant concerns even ship garments unpressed. In this way the immigrant concerns cut down on capital costs for steam-driven machine presses and, more importantly, eliminate the skilled labor required in operating more complicated machinery.

One further consequence of these technological arrangements is that the traditional paths of movement from employee to owner remain permeable to the newest garment capitalists. Thus, the experience of the Jewish and Italian owners whom I interviewed, most of whom went into business in the late 1940s or early 1950s, has a striking parallel to the experience of the Dominican and Chinese neophytes. Thirty-four of the 41 Jewish and Italian owners had had some work experience prior to starting up on their own; of those 34, 14 had been garment workers, 7 had worked in other blue-collar jobs before going into business, and the remainder had previously been in a white-collar or some other self-employed position. Ninety-three of the new immigrant business owners had had some other job prior to setting up a factory: of those 93, 63 had been garment workers, 23 had been employed in other blue-collar jobs, and 7 had previously owned another business or had been salaried employees.

Obtaining Premises

Equipment is one of the key components of any business' fixed costs; the second is plant. New York City has long been distinguished by the largest supply of rental factory space in the nation. For new firms, this is an asset of considerable importance, since rental space makes it possible to go into business without further capital investments and limits the need for long-term commitments. It is precisely for this reason that New York City has historically served as an incubator of new firms.

How this supply of space came into being is worth noting. Virtually all the industrial loft buildings in Manhattan were built prior to 1935. A significant portion of the space was constructed for the small manufacturing firms that have historically been concentrated in New York. Although the longevity of

most such firms was short-lived, aggregate growth rates in the early twentieth century were high; individual occupants turned over, but the overall number of such firms increased, providing a strong market for the owners and developers of loft buildings. A second source of loft construction was manufacturing firms that were large enough to finance and require their own individual plants. These firms quit the city once their multistoried structures became inefficient and motorized transport made it possible to relocate to the suburbs. But as they did so, their vacant buildings were subdivided into smaller lofts, which added to the supply of space for small industrial users.

Thus, there has been a filtering-down process in which space is made obsolete for its original user and yet is wanted by a new claimant. The process has worked well for many small manufacturing firms, principally for two reasons. First, the original capital costs are mainly defrayed by the initial occupant; second, the newcomer can often obtain lower rents, since the value of the structure has been depreciated by extended use.[4]

In the 1970s the new immigrant garment capitalists—in particular, the Chinese—became the latest beneficiaries of this filtering-down process. Though New York's manufacturing sector began its decline after World War II, the supply and demand for industrial space remained pretty much in balance up to the 1960s, largely because urban renewal and stepped-up office and residential construction made large inroads into the existing supply of industrial buildings. Thus, in the early 1960s, vacancy levels for good industrial space in Manhattan were under 3 percent, and even in the older loft districts in lower Manhattan near Chinatown the vacancy rates barely exceeded 5 percent. Though many buildings had been vacated by large tenants seeking suburban replacement sites, the turnover demand was so great as to lead to a considerable rise in rents.[5]

However, with the precipitous downturn in New York's economy, starting in 1969, the market for industrial lofts was entirely transformed. As manufacturing employment in the Manhattan central business district plunged at a rate of 25,000 jobs a year, the vacancy rate in the industrial-loft sector soared to 30 to 35 percent. With demand so severely depressed, rents also fell, tumbling to levels that in dollar terms equaled the rates recorded in the 1930s. And because the commercial and residential sectors were greatly affected by the same adverse economic trends, there was little demand for this space by alternative users.

One area where space emptied out abruptly was the lower Manhattan

industrial district that bordered on New York's traditional Chinatown. Printing, machinery, and textile firms had long concentrated in this area, but the more competitive environment of the early 1970s knocked out many of these concerns, and the survivors invested in new technologies that required larger and better facilities. Thus, lofts went vacant; rents dropped severely; and Chinese garment factories became the inheritors. Throughout the 1970s, the filtering-down process continued apace, making available low-cost space at advantageous lease terms; as late as 1980, according to one major realtor, factory space in lower Manhattan went for $1.50 a square foot, with options for relatively long-term (5-year) leases widely available. (On average, a garment factory in Chinatown occupies 5,000 square feet of space.)

Customers

It is one thing to set up a spanking new shop but quite another to find customers to keep the shop busy. Among the liabilities of the new organization, as Stinchcombe has noted, is the problem of weaning away clients from older competitors:

One of the main resources of old organizations is a set of stable ties to those who use organizational services. Old customers know how to use the services of the organizations [and] are familiar with the channels of ordering, with performance qualities of the product, with how the price compares and know the people they have to deal with. . . . The stronger the ties between old organizations and the people they serve, or the larger the component of personal loyalty in the consumer-producer relation, the tougher the job of establishing a new organization.[6]

Yet, for the fledgling garment capitalist, the problem is not quite as severe as Stinchcombe suggests. Consider the importance of trust. In some industries, obtaining business depends heavily on one's standing in the community from which the firm's clientele is likely to be drawn. Such is the case in construction, as Gallo has argued:

Most contracts for construction depend on the knowledge of the firm's past performance or reputation. In turn, such a reputation depends more on factors associated with social acceptance like trust and reliability than on "objective" and easily established criteria like cost. The great heterogeneity of the product in construction makes cost criteria less significant because outcomes cannot be easily compared.[7]

Where important, as in construction, the need for trust may put immigrants

at a disadvantage when competing in the open market, but, conversely, it may benefit them in servicing the ethnic trade. Thus, as I noted in Chapter 2, a fruitful niche for Latin American construction contractors working in New York City is to do small-scale renovation and residential work for a Hispanic clientele. Similarly, immigrants successfully trade on their acceptance in the community to generate business, as revealed by the panoply of immigrant businesses located in ethnic communities where they specialize in services requiring confidentiality.

By contrast, the garment industry is a "low-trust" environment, whose intensely competitive nature leads most of its participants to look at the world through a Hobbesian lens. Why does a manufacturer cut his own textiles rather than have a contractor do it to his specifications? The answer is that the contractor will be tempted to steal a few inches of fabric for each part of the garment that he cuts and use the valuable remainder for goods that he makes up on his own. Thus, rather than let the contractor "butcher" the textiles, the manufacturer keeps a cutting room under his own roof. Or why does the manufacturer insist on having a production man regularly visit a contractor's factory lest the contractor "throw his work under the [cutting] tables" and give priority to some other customer? The reason is that "the typical contractor's eyes are bigger than his factory." The victim of seasonality, the contractor remembers famine even when times are good; acting on the assumption that a season, no matter how busy, will eventually turn slow, the contractor accepts more work than he can possibly handle.

Thus, the expectation of loyalty is low, and suspicion extends equally to newcomers and old-timers. That one will seek short-term, personal gain is an assumption made about Jews and Italians and Chinese and Hispanics alike. For these reasons, the normative tie between old organizations and their customers is not a meaningful constraint on change. To be sure, a record of reliability and performance binds a manufacturer to a time-tested contractor. In contrast to construction, however, it is neither difficult nor particularly risky to test a contractor's performance: the lead time needed to produce a lot of garments is short, as compared, let us say, with building a house; and within a given price-and-style category, the product is homogeneous (a dress is a dress is a dress). A further factor is that garments is a seasonal and cyclical industry in which the demand for contractors' services ebbs and flows sharply. For this reason, the typical manufacturer is regularly adding and subtracting contractors to produce seasonal orders; this further weakens the tie between servicer and customer and gives the new immigrant firm an opportunity to prove its ability.

Finally, the new owner's search for customers is lubricated by intermediaries. For some sewing-machine operators or waiters turned factory owners, the novelty of their new role is so great that they seek out a broker from among their co-ethnics to help them develop a customer base. Among the Chinese owners, such brokers appear to play an important role; one such individual is said to supply fifteen to twenty factories. However, opportunities for brokerage arise, not simply because the immigrant owners have difficulty developing a clientele, but because intermediation plays an important function for manufacturers as well. Consider this example, recounted to me by a large New York-based manufacturer with sales, as of 1981, of over $15 million:

When I started out with this man he had only one factory which he mainly staffed with family workers. Now he has eight factories, and in each one he has a separate partner. He comes up to the place [the manufacturer's office] every morning at 8:00 A.M., and I show him what has to be done and he decides to which factory the work goes. If I need more work, he gives me space in other factories. . . . The reason for this arrangement is that it's more efficient. You only have one person to deal with. And in any case, it is so difficult to control what goes on in the contractors' factories that it's not worth it. The owners don't respect the manufacturer's employees.

In addition to these ethnic brokers, there are also the trucking companies that haul cut textiles and finished products from manufacturer to contractor and back. The apparel industry has a division of the trucking industry all to its own. Among these apparel truckers there are further lines of specialization: some carry textile piece goods only; some ship to the stores; still others engage in so-called city work, and it is these that are the key. In addition to transportation, the truckers are purveyors of information: which contractors need work, which manufacturers need contractors, who is equipped for what type of work. Just as importantly, the trucking companies are interested in keeping their customers busy. Hence, when a contractor has excess capacity he is likely to turn to the trucking company; and since the latter has tentacles spread throughout the industry, it is well positioned to find new business.

Communication

An important and increasingly acknowledged component of any industry is the culture of doing business. Firms and industries tend to adopt a common way in which the self is to be presented and interaction is to take place;

these rules extend from matters of dress, to patterns of conversation, to accepted levels of emotionality or lack thereof. A business culture develops because it provides a set of shared understandings that makes for efficient communication. In the garment industry interaction is particularly important: information is gathered informally; much business is done face to face; and there is a myriad of relationships—to sellers, to buyers, to intermediaries, to creditors—all of which are maintained through personal contact.

But in most cases immigrants have yet to be fully socialized into the broader culture of American society, not to speak of the particular customs and ways of a specific business. And this is yet another reason that immigrant businessmen so often depend on the ethnic trade. As Werbner has noted:

Where immigrants feel lost and insecure at first, fearing they might stumble in a foreign culture, doing business with fellow migrants provides a sense of familiarity, an understanding, a sense of sharing a common "system of relevances." . . . Being able to speak a language fluently, to joke, to bargain, to act as though angry or sad, makes business relations easier to manage. This is particularly so for newcomers to the trade, and especially if they are non-professionals and first-generation immigrants.[8]

However, the division of labor between garment contractor and manufacturer is the one niche in the clothing industry where communication, especially in its more subtle and intangible aspects, is least important of all. Relative to the tasks of designing, selling, and purchasing textiles, the actual production of garments is a routinized job; it is precisely because the manufacturer cannot standardize these other functions that they continue to be done in house. (Consider, for example, a lot of 5,000 dresses; although of the same style, they may be made in 5 different colors, each one of which has to be dyed to specifications; fabricated out of different types of cloth; and then sold to a number of different customers in quantities ranging from 1,000 to 10.) And whereas communication between manufacturer and buyer or supplier has an etiquette and style of its own, interaction between manufacturer and contractor is stripped down to its essentials. As one highly successful Chinese contractor pointed out:

Handling uptown [the garment center] and downtown [Chinatown] are entirely two different things. Uptown people are quick and businesslike: we talk about what has to be done and that's it. Down here in the factory is where I have to do most of the talking.

Similarly, the manufacturers whom I interviewed reported that communication with immigrant contractors, though stilted and limited due to language differences, was not a problem. As one manufacturer said, "Language is not a major difficulty. If they don't understand, you simply sit down and show them."

Cash

Thus, the structure of the garment industry makes it relatively easy to enter, and its competitive, unstable nature levels out the advantages that older businesses enjoy over new concerns. Another problem of the new business is generating cash, and here again the garment industry offers favorable terrain. For the small store owner the critical problem is one of cash flow: groceries are obtained on credit from the vendor; in turn, customers want credit; and revenue must be constantly channeled back to the vendor to pay off his loan. By contrast, the garment contractor has only machines and virtually no stocks of materials in which to invest; hence, he has few creditors to whom loans must be paid back. What remains to be paid are salaries. Since the contractor is essentially a purveyor of labor, the manufacturer will pay the contractor on Monday for work delivered on Friday; the clever, if not so honest contractor, will wait till the second Friday to pay the workers for the labor they performed the previous week. Equally important is the fact that the typical immigrant garment shop does a very large volume of business. Thus, while profits per unit may be quite low (in a cheaper line, 25 cents per garment or less), high-volume operations, running from 3,000 garments a week among the Hispanic firms to 5,000–6,000 a week among the Chinese contractors, produce significant earnings in the aggregate. Recall again the very low investment requirements, and one can see how much money a garment business can turn over relative to the initial start-up costs and why there is a constant source of immigrant waiters and factory workers willing to try their hand at ownership.

Competition

The empirical material presented above and in the preceding chapter confirm part of the argument developed in Chapter 2: that immigrant businesses develop in environments supportive of small firms where vacant positions can be taken over by neophyte business owners. But there is an alternative

possibility raised by previous research on ethnic enterprise, discussed in Chapter 1. As Light and Bonacich and Modell show in their work on Chinese and Japanese businesses in the early twentieth century, clan- and kin-associations gave ethnic capitalists an advantage by regulating internal competition and by creating vertical organizations of producers, middlemen, and suppliers.[9]

I attempted to discover whether similar factors were at work in New York's garment trade: instead, I found that ethnic organizations played at best a marginal role in mediating economic activity among the immigrant firms. While Hispanic business associations existed in two of the neighborhoods where Dominican garment factories were surveyed, participation in the associations was limited to retail businesses with a direct stake in the continued viability of their business areas. Chief among the Dominican owners' complaints was the absence of any association that would tend to their interests. The problem, in part, was that the owners' extreme individualism precluded effective collective action. "Every Hispanic," said one factory owner, "wants to be the leader. That makes it impossible." Still a more important constraint was the industry's harshly competitive environment which undermined the trust needed to sustain an organization, as another owner pointed out:

What most prevents any union among the owners is the competition among the same Hispanic proprietors. The Hispanic business owners don't get together because they lack confidence in one another. People without a conscience will take the work that you get [from the manufacturers] and will make it at any price.

By contrast, there was a greater level of organizational mobilization among the Chinese owners. But the impetus to organization, as well as the collective resources, was greater in the Chinese case. Since the Chinese firms are all unionized, they are brought into a complex industrial relations system through a collective association that bargains directly with the union over wages and with the manufacturers' association over the prices set on contract sewing jobs. Because this contractors' association remains dominated by Jews and Italians, and is thus suspected of collusion with both the union and the manufacturers, the Chinese have formed associations of their own. But, as with other Chinatown groupings, political dissensus has undercut the basis for traditional ethnic solidarity: the Chinese employers are predictably riven into rival pro-Beijing (the Chinese Garment Makers Association) and pro-Taiwan (the Oriental Garment Makers Association) factions. Interests

are also fractured according to business size and stability as well as with respect to broader economic linkages. Leadership quality in either association is poor, since organizational politics must compete with the burdensome (and far more lucrative) obligations involved in running a small business. More importantly, neither association possesses sanctions that can be effectively deployed to maintain ethnic cohesiveness.

The ultimate source of associational weakness lies in the same market factors that have given rise to new immigrant garment businesses in the first place. Contracting is the path of entry for these new immigrants for reasons that have already been discussed. It also makes immigrant firms the reactive and subordinate partners to the manufacturers with whom they are engaged in a division of labor because manufacturer/contractor linkages are inherently unstable, reflecting New York's role as a spot market for late-developing demand. A small core of Chinatown's 480 garment factories works as satellites, receiving continuous runs from manufacturers for whom they churn out garments on a full-year basis. But seasonality creates tremendous swings in production. During slow seasons, the manufacturers cannot adequately supply their satellites; consequently, these contractors must search for other sources of work. When demand becomes more intense, the same satellites cannot produce in sufficient quantities, and then the manufacturers engage additional firms to produce their excess goods.

This shifting and uncertain pattern of demand structures the opportunities to which actual and potential garment-factory owners respond. Given the ease with which new firms can be founded, and, as I shall show, the paucity of alternative routes of social mobility, the garment contracting business attracts a flock of new entrants. Yet the violent oscillations to which the industry is subject quickly shake out the majority of these newcomers. Owners enticed by the shortage of production capacity during periods of seasonal activity find themselves without a reliable supplier once demand subsides. A bidding war ensues; most of the new, already undercapitalized contractors fall by the wayside; but when demand revives there is little to prevent a new cohort of immigrant capitalists to enter the game, and so they do.

[7]

Ethnicity at Work

Small business industries, as I argued in Chapter 2, are the places where immigrant firms are most likely to start up, providing, of course, that there are vacant positions for prospective immigrant entrepreneurs. These industries are the breeding ground of new immigrant firms because they demand little in capital investment and technical knowhow and thus provide a protective environment for the small concern. But there is another characteristic of small business industries conducive to neophyte immigrant capitalists—namely, that they lack institutionalized arrangements by which workers are attached to jobs and the rules of the firm established and accepted. Consequently, firms in small business industries are often prone to a high level of turnover and experience difficulties in securing and maintaining a skilled labor force. The competitive environment in which small firms function also exposes them to considerable duress, which often translates into antagonism on the shop floor.

These characteristics led me to argue, in Chapter 2, that immigrants' ties to the broader ethnic community might be a source of competitive advantage, especially when the competitors are native firms recruiting immigrant workers. I proposed two hypotheses. First, whereas native firms will recruit through the external market, immigrant firms will be likely to mobilize their ties to kin and ethnic workers, thereby increasing the probability of hiring labor capable of acquiring skills as well as the likelihood that these workers will remain with the firm and apply their skills there. Second, I argued that small firms where management and labor are ethnically distinctive will tend toward a highly conflictual industrial relations arrangement; by contrast, the understandings implicit in ethnic relationships that originate outside the workplace will reduce conflict within the immigrant concern. This chapter assesses these hypotheses by looking inside native-owned and immigrant garment firms. We begin by looking at the labor processes of native firms and then turn to their immigrant competitors.

The Nonimmigrant Firm

One way of understanding how workers are matched to jobs in the nonimmigrant sector is to simply walk down a street in the garment center. Workers looking for a job begin here because of the concentration of factories that are piled up one on top of the other in the area's many multistoried lofts. One sees them, often in pairs, walking patiently from building to building, making inquiries with a building superintendent or elevator man, traveling from one loft to another asking for work. Around them are help-wanted signs—taped up on the walls of the factory buildings or posted on lampposts or on subway entrances. Some are in English, some in Spanish. Some simply advertise for help in a general way ("se necesita operarias—piso 11"; operators are needed—11th floor); Others announce vacancies for workers with special skills ("se necesita operaria de merrow"; merrow machine operator—a worker who operates a high-speed double-needle machine—is wanted).

Though the passerby might think that there is an ample supply of labor, the interviews indicated that there is actually a mismatch between these casual job seekers and the job requirements of the typical garment shop. For those firms making more standardized products at the low end of the industry, the external labor market is the pool from which they directly hire. "I only hire walk-ins," commented one employer. "The reason is that it's easier. You put a sign downstairs and you get help right away. People are more aggressive and reliable than from unemployment. If you hire from unemployment, they're already collecting . . .and they're happy to keep on collecting." For reasons to be explained shortly, however, most of the nonimmigrant factory owners who were interviewed were looking for experienced help, and too many of those workers who flock to the factory districts in search of employment have no meaningful skills at all. As one employer put it: "What's the labor situation like in this area? For poor operators, it's very good. But to get good, skilled help it's very, very tough." Similarly, another noted:

These days you get lots of people who move around, knocking on doors, looking for a job. They don't know what they're doing. They don't have experience. They don't know how to finish a garment.

One alternative to the external market is to hire through word of mouth, asking workers to recruit friends and relatives, but this is an option that few owners pursued. Because the labor force on which the nonimmigrant owners

drew was heterogeneous—composed of Italians, Puerto Ricans, Dominicans, other Latin immigrants, some Portuguese, a few Jews—informal networks were highly fragmented. Consequently, the yield from word of mouth recruiting was often small and slow developing. As one owner said: "I don't recruit by word of mouth because it's not reliable and you can't get an immediate response." A second liability was that network recruitment was seen to alter the balance of power in the shop and consequently exacerbate, rather than relieve, the owners' difficulties in securing qualified labor. "Hiring friends and relatives always leads to problems," one owner put it. "If you have problems with one relative, you end up having problems with the others." In a similar vein, another owner commented, "If you hire relatives, what happens is that you yell at one worker, and then she, her sister, and her friends will all get up and walk out of the shop. A shop can empty out real quick." The consensus among the nonimmigrant owners was that "strangers are better," and consequently their hiring efforts mainly relied on formal labor-market institutions, such as the State employment service or the referral services operated by the various local unions. The advantage of these procedures was that they furnished a supply of experienced workers; the drawback was that they limited the employer's access to the existing sources of labor, the implications of which will be explored below.

Most of the nonimmigrant firms experienced a shortage of labor, despite the high level of unemployment in the industry and the loss of more than 34,000 garment industry jobs between 1976 and 1985. "It's hard to get skilled help," noted one longtime owner with a factory in the garment center, "and it's getting worse and worse. All the workers are getting out of the industry." One explanation for these recruitment difficulties involves a story about ethnic succession. As I noted in Chapter 4, the garment industry began to lose its hold on Italian and Jewish workers, starting in the 1940s. However, that process was still working itself out in the late 1970s and early 1980s. The higher-priced, higher-skilled lines that had long been dependent on a skilled Italian labor force were most affected by the withdrawal of experienced ethnic workers. As one employer commented, "The mothers of my workers had previously worked in the trade, but these workers refuse to bring their kids in." Similarly, another employer pointed out that "my people work to put their children through school so that their kids won't have to go back to the factory."

Another explanation, consistent with the one above, is that that the indus-

try can no longer compete for a high-quality labor force. The main problem is that wages and conditions have slipped so grievously that many workers "can get more money doing something else," and they have simply moved out of the industry's effective labor supply. The quotations below underline the squeeze on the industry's source of potential recruits:

There is a shortage and the reason is that the pay is too low. It's just a shame: they [the workers] have a profession, a skill, and they never get paid par to other industries.

Even though there are factories shutting down there is still a shortage of labor. What's happening is that when a place shuts down, people go to work in another industry. Over the past year and a half, many of our own people have gone to work in other industries. The reason is that people are looking for steady, weekly paychecks. But our business is seasonal, and we have to lay people off for four months every year.

I would say that our workers fall into two groups. The older workers are stable. The younger workers [who are they?]—I mean those workers in the forty to fifty age bracket—they want to get out of the line. For example, I've had workers who went to work in a hospital rather than stay here.

A further source of recruitment difficulties lay in the employers' need for a skilled labor force. Twenty-four of the 41 nonimmigrant firms required mainly skilled workers; in another 13 firms most of the workers were semi-skilled; only in 4 firms was the bulk of the labor force unskilled. The problem for those firms requiring significant amounts of skill was how to transmit needed skills to new workers. As the quotes below indicate, training was impeded by several factors: firms were too small to set aside a special area for training; the owners, who often doubled as supervisors, lacked the time, and often knowhow, to instruct workers in sewing skills; even if they knew how to train new hires, the risk calculus worked against training, since a newly trained worker could easily apply those skills in another factory; and finally, the skill levels were sufficiently high to make training a costly investment:

I don't train unskilled workers anymore. The thing is that salaries have reached such a plateau that you can't play with the unskilled. The minimum wage for an operator is $5.75. I have girls [sic] working here who are making over 7 bucks an hour. The average is about $6.50 an hour. I just can't afford to play around while someone learns how to make out.

In this shop the work is skilled and the garment has to be A-1 when it comes out. What's done here is not cheap stuff: you're talking about garments that go to the stores

and might sell for as much 1,500 bucks. On this type of work the operators have to know what they're doing. First of all, it just doesn't pay to train; secondly, when I'm busy, I don't have the time; and third, when the shop's busy, the people don't want to bother themselves.

There's too much quality work in this shop to train. It's too aggravating, and the work's not easy. Once a new operator ruins you a dress, it's ruined. Training is taking a chance.

I don't train because I don't have the patience and because they need a high level of skills. It takes too much time. And finally there's human nature: you train them, break them in, they learn how to do the work, and then they leave you.

Conflict and Its Sources Dual labor-market research, as I noted in Chapter 2, tells us that instability is the salient characteristic of small firms in competitive industries like clothing: the jobs are unstable, whether because of seasonality or cyclical sensitivity; and the workers also evince little attachment to any particular employer, because the jobs promise no chance of advancement or the pay is inadequate. This was the picture that I expected to find in interviewing the Jewish and Italian garment factory owners, but in fact, the pattern that emerged was distinctive and more complex. Only a small number of firms fit the anticipated model. Most of these firms were actually in the accessory trades of beltmaking or pleating and stitching, where seasonality is even more of a factor than it is in garment manufacturing, and skill levels are considerably reduced. For example, the owner quoted just below ran a large contracting firm that made the orders sent in by belt-manufacturing firms, which in turn produced to the specifications set by garment manufacturers. Thus, this contractor's role was to absorb the overflow in a highly style-sensitive item like belts, which resulted in tremendous volatility on the factory floor:

Our turnover is tremendous: last year we employed 105 people and we ended mailing out 700 W-2's [income tax forms]. The main reason for the turnover is seasonality. Only twenty-five to thirty of our people can expect to work steadily year round; the rest work forty weeks maximum, and that's usually interrupted by spells of inactivity. What happens is that we'll hire someone; that person will work three or four months; then we'll lay them off for a week or two; and when we call them back, they've already found another job.

Though instability often imposed additional administrative costs, those

firms with highly varying labor requirements relied mainly on unskilled workers who could easily be substituted for one another.

In most firms, however, turnover was limited to a smaller minority of employees. Often the least stable workers were newer hires, and in these cases turnover was mainly due to employers weeding out less productive workers on the ground that "the wage scale is such that new workers can't be kept on if they're unskilled and not easily adaptable." But, on balance, most employers reported that turnover was low and that key workers attained considerable levels of seniority. Employers tended to explain the attachment of their workers in terms of the soft labor-market conditions of the time, arguing that workers tended to remain on the job rather than risk what little stability they had by seeking or trying out other jobs. However, an equally important factor was the institutional arrangements that cushioned the impact of instability. Although most of the firms were subject to seasonality, the fluctuations came at regular and predictable intervals, making it possible to use the unemployment system to absorb the effects of instability. Thus, as one employer explained:

The workers stick with you because if you can give them forty, maybe forty-four weeks of work, then they can collect unemployment insurance when you lay them off. And if they went anywhere else, they wouldn't do much better than unemployment.

A second, less common approach to the problem of instability was adopted by those employers who appeared to offer workers an implicit promise of full-year employment in return for greatly increased levels of productivity during the busy seasons. "I require certain loyalties from our workers," noted one owner. "They break their tails during our busy seasons, and we'll tolerate a slowdown when there's not a lot of production,"

While the dwindling demand for manufacturing help bred somewhat higher levels of attachment than expected, the poor competitive position of most of the garment firms deprived them of the resources needed to motivate the labor force. The prevailing view was that "today people are not interested in working hard." Most owners thought that skill levels were inadequate. Another complaint, echoed throughout the interviews, was that "the workers don't care, they're not responsible." Workers' reluctance to work overtime—which made it difficult for firms to meet short-term delivery dates or get out rush orders—was a further source of repeated dissatisfaction. The owners' explanations for their difficulties with the work force, as in the quotation below, suggested that the root problem was the industry's low wages.

Today there's no commitment whatsoever. They don't care, they just have an "I-don't-give-a-damn attitude." You're dealing with a low-quality labor force. Lots [of workers] come in sporadically; some come in early, some late. The basic work pattern is to sit rather than work. And there's been considerable deterioration in work habits. But the truth is, I don't blame them in view of what they're making.

While the owners lacked positive incentives needed to induce work commitment, they were also too dependent on their skilled workers to exercise meaningful sanctions. "It used to be that people wanted more money so they worked harder," noted one dress factory owner. "But today workers know that they won't be fired because of the difficulty of finding workers." Competition with welfare was also seen as a source of bad work habits, especially among those owners whose firms were located in minority neighborhoods in the outer boroughs. "The problem is that our wages are very low," complained one Jewish owner with a shop in East New York, a poor, minority neighborhood in Brooklyn. "People can afford not to work and go on welfare." Similarly, the owner of a sportswear factory in the South Bronx contended that "We can't get good workers because of welfare—people can get a hundred dollars working or they can get it from welfare."

The owners' sense of dissatisfaction with their work force was exacerbated by two additional factors. One was simply the fact that most owners had themselves started out as workers. The phrase, "when I was a worker," was a common refrain in many of the interviews. While the owners seemed to view their own success as a reward for hard effort, their sense of self-worth also seemed to rest on a history of work and self-support. Consequently, the owners' own past, or at least their view of that past, served to distance them from those workers whom they perceived as being unwilling to work and support themselves. Yet one also had the sense, as suggested by the following quotations, that the owners were indignant at their workers' perceived ability to get by without working or doing a full day's work because it made a mockery of the owners' own past efforts:

The workers these days are not willing to work, they're not responsible. The attitude of workers is that if you have no work I'll go to unemployment. But during the many years that I was an operator, I only collected two weeks of unemployment.

Today, people don't want to work, they don't want to work overtime. Today, I have to worry about the worker, the schoolteacher, the child, the baby-sitter—I'm hoping that everything goes well so that the mother can come into work. And, in any case, there's not enough commitment—partly because of welfare. When I was a worker, I never thought about not working because I could collect welfare.

Today workers aren't willing to work overtime. But when I was working and the boss told me I was going to have to work overtime for the next two weeks—my reaction was always, "no problem with me."

A second factor contributing to distance and antagonism was ethnic difference. With the exception of those firms making low-end products, which were first to switch from white ethnic to black and Hispanic workers shortly after World War II, most of the shops surveyed had mainly employed Jewish and Italian workers until the late 1960s or early 1970s. But, as has been noted, most of these firms had gone from white ethnic to minority workers by the time of the interviews. Not surprisingly, some employers evinced severe dislike for their newer, minority workers. "PR's [Puerto Ricans], they piss on the walls," said one owner disdainfully. "And blacks, I don't like them, they're always expecting something." While relatively few employers showed such direct hostility toward minority workers, most offered an unfavorable evaluation of their characteristics and work habits. The general feeling among the Jewish and Italian garment-factory owners was that work habits and work quality had deteriorated and that this deterioration could be linked to the changeover in the industry's ethnic composition. The owners contended that skill levels had dropped; that the new workers lacked the same pride in work; that the older workers were more concerned than their successors with making money and getting ahead; and that the older European groups were more responsive to economic incentives. Ultimately, owners seemed to link the differences between older ethnics and new minorities to broader disparities in the two groups' value systems. On the one hand, the white ethnics were responsible; by contrast, the minorities were unwilling to take care of themselves. "The Hispanics are good workers," noted an Italian immigrant woman, who had started out as a seamstress, "but the Europeans have higher skill, more responsibility. The Europeans were independent and wanted to build themselves through work. Now, if you don't make it with working, the newcomers will try to make it without working." A European-born employer with years of experience commented similarly: "The Europeans were more committed to work: they'd do more work, especially overtime, because they wanted more money. The Latin American workers would rather not work than have to pay taxes on the overtime."

The Immigrant Firm

Whereas nonimmigrant firms tended to match workers to jobs through market mechanisms, the immigrant firms relied heavily on the mobilization of kinship and ethnic ties. Social and economic roles were interpenetrated at the ownership level: most firms were owned either by relatives or by partners of the same ethnic group. This pattern of recruitment was one way that immigrants could mobilize scarce resources. "Relatives are a must," noted one owner who had come over from Hong Kong in 1981. "You need people to take care of all of the departments, and when you start out you don't have enough money to hire as many people as you need." Similarly, another owner pointed out that she was able to start up in business because "the family was able to cover almost all the departments." Family members provided labor if the firm suffered a labor shortage, if it experienced production problems due to antiquated and poorly functioning equipment, or if additional work needed to be done in order to get a delivery out on time. "Whatever it is," noted a Dominican owner who had opened her shop six months before the interview, "relatives help more than others. The others, they finish their hours of work and they leave. Relatives stay with you until the work is done." More importantly, family ownerships and ethnic partnerships facilitated the allocation of managerial tasks. "Relatives aren't needed on the shop floor," said one Chinese owner, "but on the management level, people should be good and reliable, and therefore you are better off with relatives." Running a business with kin and co-ethnics also allowed many of the immigrant garment firms to resolve problems of trust and delegation. Commonly, one partner or relative would supervise internal operations while another managed relations with "outside" parties—the manufacturers that furnished work; the truckers that hauled goods back and forth to the manufacturers; and the suppliers that provided needle, thread, and other required items. Dividing managerial functions this way also saved on overhead costs because, as one Chinese owner said, "You don't have to pay relatives."

In all cases the size of the firm made it necessary to recruit beyond the orbit of the owner's kinship network; nonetheless, the employment relationship remained mediated by friendship and ethnic ties. Immigrant firms built on the social structures that connected immigrants with settlers and reproduced them in the workplace. Whereas Jewish and Italian owners tended to recruit minority workers of varying origins and ethnicities, the

immigrant firms were tightly encapsulated in their own communities. Dominican owners invariably recruited other Hispanics, with Dominicans furnishing the vast bulk of their labor force. With but one exception, the Chinese-owned firms were staffed by other Chinese workers. In the majority of cases, Chinese owners shared a common point of origin with their employees, with owners from Hong Kong recruiting other arrivals from Hong Kong, while those owners from the mainland tended to hire workers of mainland origin. Recruiting premigration friends and hometown acquaintances was also another means of obtaining labor, though it was more common among Dominican firms where migration chains would link much of the factory to a common hometown in the Dominican Republic. In general, recruiting through word of mouth, or through the recommendations of workers already employed, was a far more common technique among the immigrant firms than among their nonimmigrant counterparts. Whereas the latter contended that assembling a group of related workers created the potential for disruption, most immigrant owners thought that "if you recommend someone to me, then I assume that you know who that person is." The immigrant owners, as the quotations below suggest, saw network recruiting as a way of screening out unqualified or inappropriate recruits, of obtaining trust, and of reducing the likelihood that workers would leave:

I prefer to hire by word of mouth because if they are recommended by my own workers they will usually feel confident with my firm, and they will work for me for a longer period of time.

Recommendations are more secure. Usually, if you know that the source [of the recommendation] is a good person, then it works to your advantage. Usually they send you good people.

When workers are hired through recommendations, they know our requirements and what we want them to do. They also tend to stay longer than workers who don't know anybody else in the shop.

Immigrant firms also served as points of entry for the newly arrived relatives and friends of workers already employed in the plants, and most owners said that they hired new arrivals upon the request of their workers when conditions allowed:

When we do need someone, usually we get a new person from someone already working here; that's the way we operate when we have openings. If a worker knows that another employee is leaving, then that person tries to recommend a substitute.

One further consequence of network recruiting was that most firms would take on unskilled workers and provide some rudimentary training in sewing skills. In part, training unskilled workers was seen as a way of obtaining goodwill among newcomers and older employees alike. More importantly, however, training took place because it was managed through an implicit contract between owners and workers. Owners provided some instruction, material, and a place to work, and the new recruits started out as simple piece-rate workers, earning only as much as the price of the garments they produced. For example, the Dominican owner of one large factory explained that:

Usually when newcomers arrive looking for a job and we hire them, they usually ask for training. What this means is that they'll work for basically nothing; and once they learn how to make out, they'll stay.

Recruiting through kin and friendship networks promoted a paternalistic relationship between immigrant owners and their employees. Acting as intermediaries was one way by which employers could develop a "good relationship with our workers," "make workers happy," and thereby "increase the rate of production." "In order to get people to work for you," noted a large Chinese employer who had been in business for more than ten years, "you have to let them know that you'll help them." Though a minority of owners indicated that their involvement with their workers was strictly limited to matters of work—"I don't mind their business," was how one Chinese owner put it—most immigrant owners claimed that they helped their workers with problems of adjustment, assisted employees with social and legal problems, or provided short-term loans to cover rent or emergencies:

We have to help them; they're like part of the family. We depend on them, and they depend on us. We're the people they know and we should help. We all live on that.

You have to help them. When the worker has a problem, whether it's family or financial, you have to help them. If you help them, the worker ends up giving you more. If you don't help them, they don't forget it, and they'll let you down. In our factory it's like a family. When you help them, when you lend them a hand, they feel protected. When there's a sickness we make a collection; when they need money, we give them a loan; when there's an immigration problem, we write them a recommendation.

As noted in the above quotations, ownership was also a source of strategic influence in immigration matters. Employers assisted workers in bringing

relatives over from the home country or sponsored prospective immigrants who needed a guarantee of employment in order to obtain permanent residency.

Ethnic commonality also provided a repertoire of symbols and customs that owners invoked or manipulated to underline the cultural interests and similarities that they shared with the work force. Chinese employers, for example, celebrated holidays and shop anniversaries by holding banquets or luncheons to which workers were invited. On the Chinese New Year, they passed out gifts (the traditional "red envelope" stuffed with five dollars), and shops also held raffles whose proceeds go to the workers. Although my survey precluded extended observation of employer-worker interaction, Wong's ethnographic study of Chinese garment factories has shown how values and symbols can be cultivated on a more routine basis to broker patron-client relationships:

The owner . . . is aware that he is more than employer to [his workers] and that he is consciously cultivating *Gam Ching* [sentimental feeling] with the workers. [He] used all possible ways to instill loyalty among his workers. He has had most of them since 1969. Kinship terminology such as *Je, Mui, Gai, Dai, Sou, Suk,* and *Baah* are deliberately used. He often tells them, "You are one of the family. You can count on me."[1]

The Limits of Ethnic Solidarity. I expected that informal networks linking the immigrant firm to the broader ethnic community would play an important role in securing the labor force and establishing the terms of the relationships at work. However, the interviews also pointed to the limits of solidarity and underlined the tension between the instrumental nature of the employment exchange and the reciprocity implicit in noneconomic relationships. Though most owners actually recruited from among their co-ethnics, the vast majority of Dominicans claimed to hire without preference to nationality, and a similarly large majority of Chinese indicated that a worker's point of origin in China was a matter of little interest in the hiring decision. What emerged in response to our query about hiring preferences were the refrains that "people are people"; that "a worker has to work, whether he's a friend of the owner or not"; that "I believe in individuality, not in nationality—all of us are equal"; and that "business is business [straight business, no personal feelings]":

[A Dominican employer employing mainly Dominican workers]: It's not necessary that your workers come from your country. The owner requires that every worker produce, regardless of nationality [*raza*].

[A Dominican owner with a heterogeneous Hispanic work force]: I'm of the opinion that whoever does the work best, that's it. I don't have to see where he's from; rather that he does his work. If a compatriot doesn't do his work well and someone who isn't a compatriot doesn't do it badly, I'm going to have to go with the one who produces.

[A Chinese employer]: Hiring depends only on your working ability and whether you can produce. Working and personal relationships are two different things.

[A Dominican employer]: Everyone is equal. Once one wants to work, they're equal. Friendship is something different. The only thing I care about is production.

Similarly, only a minority of owners among both the Dominicans and the Chinese thought that relatives were needed for business success, with some exception taken for immediate family directly involved in running the business. "Other than your wife, it's a pain to have relatives in the factory," commented one Dominican owner. "My opinion is that it all depends on the owner how to run the business" was how one Chinese owner evaluated the importance of family involvement; that sentiment was echoed quite neatly by a Dominican who said that "Relatives aren't important; the only thing is to have people who have the desire of working."

One possible advantage of the immigrant firm is that it can hold on to its employees: this would be a source of added competitiveness in an industry like garments where seasonality makes it important to be able to build up production rapidly. In general, the owners attributed turnover to a variety of factors, but most explanations emphasized economic factors—insufficiency of work, low piece-rate earnings, better job opportunities—suggesting that workers' sense of personal loyalty to the owner was subordinated to their own material concerns. The comments of Chinese owners, in particular, underscored the individualism of the workers. "In Chinatown they just go around all the time" and "they all go from factory to factory" were two common refrains. One key to maintaining a stable work force, it appeared from many of the interviews, was the ability of the owner to secure runs of high-earning styles; as one owner commented, "Workers leave when they can't get used to the styles." Stability was also endangered by slowdowns in production. In these cases, most firms attempted to retain their workers by sharing the work rather than laying off employees. Yet slowdowns also prompted workers to seek out new jobs in one of the many neighboring factories:

There's no need to lay workers off. They go as soon as there's any sign of work getting slow.

[When work gets slow] they leave before I tell them to.

I don't layoff people; the workers lay me off.

Owners, both Chinese and Dominican, also lent little credence to the idea that loyalty to the firm would win out against the search for opportunity, even among those workers with whom they shared closer ties and common characteristics:

No matter who the workers are they will take the job with higher wages.

If they think that you don't treat them well or they're not satisfied with the job, they'll leave you no matter what.

They leave. They don't know anything about this relationship between worker and boss and friends and friends.

All of the Chinatown garment workers come and go very easily, no matter whether you're a hometown acquaintance or not.

A complex of factors account for the limits of ethnic solidarity in the immigrant workplace. While the employment relationship tends toward paternalism, the conditions of immigrant business in the garment industry make patron-client relationships inherently difficult to sustain. When authority is secured on the basis of paternalism, the hierarchical relationship of boss and employee is overlaid with the assertion of communal or familial identity. But this assertion tends to legitimate the primacy of personal considerations and claims over the demands of economic efficiency. Thus, as Newby points out, paternalism involves an "acceptance of liabilities which require expenditure upon literally unproductive obligations."[2] This conflict between efficiency and paternalistic obligations was precisely the point underscored in our interviews when the immigrant owners insisted that "these are relationships of work, not of friendship":

When you hire compatriots, they think that they can get away with more. If you hire strangers, then they give you more, knowing that you can hire people from your own country.

The people from my country, they don't produce. They say it's too much work. The first week is OK; by the second week, they leave.

Hiring relatives is not a good thing. They give you problems. They think that they can take it easy and that they have a safe job. They don't produce what they should.

Not only did recruiting relatives or friends impose obligations; it also constrained the exercise of authority. Thus, one common concern was that "relatives will only interfere with your decisions." Moreover, employing relatives tended to increase the costs of conflict. As one Chinese owner pointed out: "Hiring relatives is good because you can rely on them. But it's also bad because sometimes if they did something wrong it's very hard to tell them." "Sometimes it's hard to work with compatriots and hometown acquaintances," noted one of the largest Chinese garment capitalists. "Arguments are difficult, and it's hard to open your mouth when he or she is doing something wrong."

While paternalism imposed unwanted costs on immigrant employers, workers' experience tended to weaken their allegiance to paternalistic authority. Paternalistic firms are "greedy institutions," to use Lewis Coser's phrase, and greedy institutions make total claims on their members, seeking exclusive and undivided loyalty.[3] The more complete the institution, the more likely it will succeed in defining its members' role; not surprisingly, the more successful greedy institutions are those with the resources needed to build a distinctive social world or those that are isolated by physical boundaries. The immigrant garment factory possesses neither of these characteristics. The prestations made by the garment factory owner are designed to increase loyalty. But the greedy institution secures allegiance by inducing dependency, whereas the resources available to the immigrant owner—advancing money to cover the rent or providing a guarantee of employment to relatives seeking to immigrate—are of insufficient importance to fulfill that objective. A second constraint stems from the physical environment of the immigrant garment firm: far from being a self-enclosed entity, it sits amid a host of other garment firms. Consequently, while traditional obligations may inhibit collective or individual protest, workers can easily exit from the situation. "If they want to leave," commented a large factory owner with over twenty years in the trade, "they will. There is no stopping them." Employers' comments, corroborated by key informants, indicated that exiting from unsatisfactory work situations is what immigrant workers customarily do: "Garment workers in Chinatown move around so much that it's expected that hometown acquaintances do too."

A final weakness of paternalism is that its ideological, or perhaps moral

underpinnings, are undercut by the way of life that the immigrants encounter in the United States and gradually adopt. Patron-client relationships are common to the cultures from which both Chinese and Dominican immigrants come. But the environment that the immigrants encounter in New York rewards more competitive and individualistic modes of action, and it is in this direction that the value orientations of immigrants seem to evolve. The owners' most common explanation for the transiency and lack of attachment to the firm was that the immigrant workers had learned to look out for their own:

The U.S. is a material world. Wherever there is a good salary, people will go there, no matter how close we are.

They will go take another job even when you need them the most. In the U.S. people are realistic. If they can earn more at other factories, they will leave you.

When you need them the most, the workers always leave you. You have workers with experience, and when someone else offers them a better job, they just leave. Those who come to this country are just interested in dollars.

Moreover, the interviews suggested that the owners, too, were less inclined to adopt a paternalistic role by virtue of their own adjustment to the New York situation. For example, one Dominican owner reported:

What I have I earned through my own merit and sacrifice. And that's how it has to be with my workers. It doesn't matter whether they are family or not. For example, I had problems with my brother. I brought him over from Santo Domingo, and I put him to work with me. After a little while he asked me for a raise of fifty percent. I didn't give him the raise, so he left. Here you can only get a raise on merit.

A Hong Kong Comparison. One relevant bench mark from which to evaluate these findings is the literature on small firms in Hong Kong, the point of origin for most of the Chinese owners and a place where the small sector (50 workers or less) accounted for 91 percent of all manufacturing establishments and 40 percent of all manufacturing employment as of 1977.[4] Like the immigrant capitalists in New York's garment industry, Hong Kong's small manufacturers operate in highly competitive and unstable markets. In such an environment the turnover rate is naturally high—according to one source, 35,000 new firms are started and 25,000 firms go under each year. To some extent, the high death rate is due to the severity of competitive

pressures, but to some extent it also reflects the instrumentality of small factory owners, who set up a factory to make a particular product and then shut it down when the item is no longer in demand.[5]

Family labor is an important component of Hong Kong's small sector, but with only 5 percent of its work force consisting of unpaid family help, most small firms depend on the outside market. One study, which surveyed 415 small firms, found that almost half of the sample establishments employed relatives but that the majority were working at the managerial level or in supervisory jobs. Moreover, 67 percent of the establishments using relatives paid full pay to the relatives as if they were ordinary workers.[6] Another study of small firms in an industrial estate in Hong Kong found employment of relatives equally prevalent. But, when queried about their hiring preferences, the owners "almost universally answered that 'being a relative' is not the determinant factor, but rather because they are 'trustworthy,' 'capable,' and 'responsible.'"[7] The small firm thus remains tied to the kinship system, though more for reasons of economic rationality than for obligations of a traditional kind. However, the relationship to nonkin workers is based almost entirely on the cash nexus. As England notes in a study of industrial relations in Hong Kong:

[Apart from the hardcore of technical and family workers] all other labor is treated as hirelings to be taken on or disposed of as orders fluctuate. In their turn, the majority of these workers have little loyalty to any firm or industry and move frequently to better paying jobs.[8]

The Role of Ethnic Networks: A Reassessment

The argument developed in Chapter 2 attributed a dual function to the connections that link the immigrant firm to the broader community. First, these networks would act as a conduit for information, whereby immigrant employers can learn about the salient characteristics of their workers, and thus reduce the uncertainty associated with hiring and training. Second, they would provide the basis for constructing a set of shared understandings about obligations and responsibilities binding immigrant owner and immigrant worker.

The interviews, however, suggest a modification: namely, that ethnic relationships are maintained but transformed under the impact of economic change. While the immigrant business is organized around ethnic connec-

tions and preexisting relationships, those relationships take on a different, rationalized meaning within the context of the firm. The normative pattern common to the more traditional environments from which the immigrants come is to value kin and kinlike relationships in and of themselves. To the extent that those relationships are sustained in the immigrant factory, it is for a novel purpose: that of advancing the goals of the firm. Thus, immigrant owners tend to hire new arrivals or unskilled relatives of their employees, in part out of a sense of traditional obligation, in part because greater trust inheres in the relationships between immigrant owner and co-ethnic employee. But this predilection is bounded by considerations of economic rationality: kin or friends will be preferred when conditions allow, and not only out of custom, but because more dependable workers are thereby obtained. Similarly, the fact that many immigrant owners adopt the role of broker, acting as intermediaries who help their workers adapt to the new environment, is a carryover of preexisting patterns of patron-client relationships. Yet again, the role of broker fulfills the economic function of maintaining a contented, and hence productive, work force, and it is facilitated because immigrant employees and owners work under conditions that encourage more informal patterns of interaction.

Furthermore, the severity of the competitive environment makes it difficult to fulfill traditional expectations: thus, a firm may take on kin and other workers because custom so obliges, but if the business goes under, as so many do, then it is each to his or her own. And since the immigrant worker's job is not protected from these external threats, there is strong inducement for workers to seek out a better opportunity in some other firm. For these reasons, the assumption common to both owner and worker is that each is out to maximize individual economic gain: the owner's concern is with efficiency and productivity; the worker's is with higher wages and stable employment. What appear to be at work in the immigrant garment factory are relationships of "limited liability": an engagement based primarily on self-interest and subject to termination when it no longer fulfills that principal end.

[8]

Who Gets to Be a Boss?

New York's garment industry, as we have seen, has once again become an immigrant industry; in large measure, this latest change in the industry's complexion is due to the influx of newcomers from Asia and Latin America. Among these newcomers, two groups stand out: the Chinese and the Dominicans. Both were present in the industry in 1970, but in relatively small numbers. (Chinese accounted for 2.4 percent of the industry's employment in 1970; Dominicans, for 4.3 percent.) Over the course of the 1970s, both groups' contingents greatly increased. By 1980 the Chinese made up just over a tenth (10.6 percent) of all workers in New York's garment industry; Dominicans constituted a virtually equal share (9.0 percent).

But if the two groups are almost evenly represented among the needle trades' proletariat, the Chinese have come to dominate the ranks of the industry's new garment capitalists. Tabulations from the 5 percent Public Use Sample of the 1980 Census of Population show that the Chinese accounted for 7.8 percent of the self-employed in the garment industry in 1980, whereas Dominicans accounted for only 2.1 percent. My own survey did not succeed in producing an estimate of the size of these two immigrant enclaves in the garment industry, but what I learned about the characteristics of Chinese and Dominican firms and their owners confirmed the image of Chinese predominance.

First, the Chinese firms were considerably larger and longer established; whereas the average Chinese firm employed 47.2 workers and had been in business for 5.7 years, longevity averaged 3.6 years among the Dominicans, with the average firm containing only 19 workers. Second, the Chinese owners reported a better level of performance than did their Dominican counterparts: two thirds of the 63 Chinese owners surveyed said that business was either stable or growing, as against only one third for the 32 Dominicans. Third, the Chinese were more likely to have developed a plan

for business expansion and to report future planned commitment to business activity. Thus, when asked about plans to build up the business, only 1 Dominican owner reported plans to become a manufacturer; 12 said that they had no plans; and the remaining 19 planned to just improve on what they had been doing: "do a lot of work," " take whatever work I can get," "get to know more manufacturers," and so on. To be sure, almost half of the Chinese owners were passive about building up their businesses (31 reported no plans to build up the business). The remaining 32, however, reported ambitious plans for expansion and improvement, including buying machinery, improving productivity ("using more machines to replace people so labor costs would be less"), moving into higher-quality lines, opening additional factories, and becoming manufacturers. Similar differences emerged in response when owners were queried about their plans 10 years hence: whereas 24 of the Chinese owners said that they expected to still be active in the garment industry or in some other business, only 3 of the Dominican owners indicated similar plans. Finally, most Dominican owners saw the Chinese as their principal competitive threat, whereas the Chinese owners were, with one exception, concerned with competition from other Chinese-owned factories:

The Chinese make clothing more cheaply. They work twenty-four hours a day; they exploit their employees; and they don't pay taxes.

The Chinese are killing the business for us. They are taking all the work and doing it cheaper than we.

These disparities among Chinese and Dominicans in the garment industry conform to the pattern that these two groups have established in other areas of economic life as well. The census reports that in 1980 self-employment rates for Chinese nationwide were four times the level attained by Dominicans. Why is it, then, that Chinese are more likely to succeed in business activity than Dominicans? And what accounts for the fact that the Chinese, and not the Dominicans, have been the main successors to the Italians and Jews as the garment industry's prime source of entrepreneurs?

In Chapter 2 I developed several explanations for ethnic differences in self-employment rates among immigrant groups; let us briefly review those explanations before considering the cases at hand. One possibility is that the Chinese begin with a stronger aptitude for business than do the Dominicans, perhaps because they are more intense in the desire for indepen-

dence, perhaps because they are more predisposed toward the risk-taking required for setting up a small business. Another possibility is that the Chinese are better equipped than the Dominicans to go into business when they arrive in New York—by virtue of prior experience in business or by virtue of greater exposure to the competitive environment of an industrial economy. In addition to these various types of "human capital," the two groups might differ in terms of their access to the types of informal ethnic resources needed in organizing the small immigrant business: most importantly, the Chinese may have a higher level of solidarity. Whatever the role that these premigration experiences play in spurring entrepreneurial behavior, the circumstances of migration may be of equal importance, though as I noted in Chapter 2, the literature is contradictory about the implications of settlement type for entrepreneurial behavior.

The Spirit of Immigrant Capitalism

If the Chinese and not the Dominicans have been the main inheritors of petty proprietorship in the garment industry, the answer may lie in the Chinese' orientation to economic life. Just such an explanation was adduced by Weber for the role that Calvinists, with their concern for discipline, self-control, and measured expenditure of time and energy, played in the early development of capitalism. For Max Weber the spirit of capitalism was the "attitude which seeks profit rationally and systematically."[1] But the late twentieth century is a world where the rational and systematic pursuit of profit has become universal; hence, the spirit responsible for impelling immigrants into business is necessarily distinctive. The literature suggests two possibilities. One is that immigrants differ, not so much in their approach to economic life, but in the intensity of their desire for independent business ownership. Thus, Kessner has described the aspirations that led Russian-Jewish immigrants into small business positions, upon their arrival in New York at the turn of the century, in the following way:

Russian Jews were driven by a demon, seeking the security that had constantly eluded them in Europe. If "ruthless underconsumption" could help one become a "sweater," a contractor, or a shopkeeper, it seemed a small price to pay for self-employment. Because of their past they did not trust outsiders, whom they considered fickle and untrustworthy. They placed great emphasis on independence, on being a *balabos far sich* [being one's own boss].[2]

The alternative is the possibility suggested in Chapter 2: that immigrants resemble natives in aspirations but differ in opportunities; while not initially disposed toward risk-taking and independent enterprise, immigrants fall back on an entrepreneurial mode of behavior because they find themselves excluded from the normal lines of career advancement.

My interviews were designed to examine the economic orientation of immigrant business owners and to determine, insofar as was possible, whether they evinced a preference for business and, if so, to seek out whence that preference came. The queries began at a general level, asking open-ended questions about the typical immigrant's chances and about the best way that an immigrant had of getting ahead. I also attempted to look directly at the possible sources of small business appeal. First I tried to see whether business ownership was a response to blocked aspirations, inquiring whether working for a large corporation was the better way to get ahead, or if small business was preferable, on the ground that jobs in large corporations weren't available. Next I tried to assess risk orientation and the intensity of immigrants' desire for independence by asking owners to compare the advantages of getting a check every week from an employer as opposed to being one's own boss.

The Dominicans. To begin, let us consider how the owners responded to the question about the chances for the typical immigrant in New York. Virtually all the Dominican owners took an expansive view. Taken as an ensemble, their responses added up to a vision of opportunity awaiting the individual risk-taker. The idea that "they don't close the doors to anybody here" and that consequently "the opportunities here are equal for everybody" was the dominant theme of the interviews. One owner, speaking in this vein, said that "there are plenty of opportunities, if you take advantage of them," and this point of view was expressed in one form or another by many of the owners:

The only opportunity is to work. Those who don't get ahead, don't want to work. Those who want to work can get ahead. In this country, working leads to success.

People here want to see hard work and honesty. As long as you do the work there are no problems and plenty of chances to get ahead.

I began with nothing. It's true that I work like an animal. But now I have a factory— where we employ more than twenty people and do a tremendous business—and I also own a gas station.

To be sure, some owners pointed to obstacles, but these were usually related to some missing individual quality, as in the case of one owner who said, "We have plenty of opportunities, but we don't know how to take advantage of them." Only a very small number agreed with the owner who claimed that "There are not as many opportunities for us as for others."

When asked about the best way of getting ahead in New York, not one Dominican owner mentioned salaried employment. Rather, the common sentiment was that "If you open your own business, you have more opportunities." Some owners did suggest that small business was not suited for everyone, but if so, this was mainly a matter of personal abilities or character. As one owner put it: "It depends on the person. If you have the ability, open your own business." Moreover, the Dominicans' assessment of the trade-off between working for a large corporation and running one's own business was consistent with their perception of opportunities for mobility. Virtually all the owners signaled a preference for having one's own business, usually for reasons of independence and for its promise of greater financial rewards. As one owner noted: "Working for a big corporation is limited. To have your own business is risky but without limits on profits or on how far you can get." Furthermore, the Dominican owners evinced little interest in the security of salaried employment, frequently emphasizing the advantages of self-employment in quite emphatic and explicit terms:

They are cowards [those who prefer a salary]. You have to take a risk to be your own boss.

It's twenty times better to be your own boss. No one checks you, and you have more opportunities to earn money.

It's good that those who can set up their own business do so. Those who work for others are slaves.

I don't want anybody to tell me what to do. If you have a mind, you don't need anybody to tell you what to do.

He who works for someone else is going to be a slave forever.

There are people who prefer a check—but they don't want responsibility: if you're an owner, you have to have responsibility, dedication, sacrifice. Many people don't want to sacrifice; they just want to make a clean living.

Despite the evident appeals of being one's own boss, only a minority of the owners indicated that the thrust for independence—"to be my own boss and

not depend on anyone else," as one owner said—was the principal reason for starting on their own. For the largest group of owners, setting up a business was simply the best way available of getting ahead when the alternative was continued work in low-paying, dead-end factory or service jobs:

I came here from Santo Domingo to work in a company and to learn the profession that I now have—that of patternmaker. I thought that the only way to have something and save money was to work on your own and use your own experience. My philosophy is, if you know pleating, do that, if you know how to cook, open a restaurant.

As far as I'm concerned, if you stay working as an employee, all you'll ever get is enough to eat and sleep. You can't go far enough.

I had worked for someone else as a manager of a record store. I saw that I was wasting my time, not going anywhere, not doing anything for myself. I decided to take a chance. I wanted to have something of my own. I can work as many hours as I have to. I'm not afraid of work.

But, as happens when one goes from more abstract issues to more concrete ones, the owners' responses further suggested that their motivation for starting out on their own was also predicated on their assessment of the possibilities. Thus, for many of these immigrant owners, setting up a garment business was an appropriate way of getting ahead, because they knew the industry, could assess the possibilities it offered, and had the skills needed to run a small garment firm:

Why did I go into business? In my case there were two factors. I had the experience and I knew the work. And I also wasn't making enough money as an employee.

I decided to go into business because where I was working I had all the responsibility and I wasn't being paid what I deserved. Plus, this was also a business that didn't require a lot of investment.

The Chinese. The Chinese offered a more critical assessment of the chances for the typical immigrant, and their view of the opportunities available was marked by considerably less optimism. The dominant group thought that the chances of getting ahead were poor; whereas some difficulty was ascribed to language and inadequate capital, complaints about discrimination, virtually unmentioned among the Hispanics, were voiced frequently:

The chances are very poor; I would say, really, almost none at all. Especially for the immigrant; I would say no chances at all.

Very tough; it's very hard to get ahead.

If no education and capital the chances are fifty-fifty. Otherwise there is a good chance.

Compared to Americans, it is harder. There's the language problem plus the racial problem.

No matter what kind of job it is, the Chinese have to work twice as hard as the Americans in order to get ahead in the U.S.

To some extent, this pessimism was tempered by the owners' assessment of the prospects for the second generation. One owner, for example, pointed out that "mid-age immigrants have language problems, and therefore their chances are less good. But the younger generations have very good chances of getting ahead." This view that younger, educated Chinese would do better in the race to get ahead was quite widely shared, yet interestingly, the future of the second generation went unmentioned among the Hispanics.

While pessimistic about their chances for getting ahead, only a minority of Chinese owners agreed that "business is the best [way of getting ahead] because it allows you to go as far as you can." Being a factory owner was certainly a step ahead of being a waiter or a sewing-machine operator, but many owners acknowledged that the immigrant garment capitalist was also hemmed in by the inherent constraints of the ethnic economy:

People working in the garment factories and the restaurants will never get ahead in the U.S. We have low status. Plus, the Jews occupy most of the garment business.

Most owners thought that mobility would come only with education, which in turn could unlock access to those "good jobs in American corporations with more chances to get promotion," and "a steady income," where "one would not have to worry about anything":

Get a higher education so that you can get a job in an American corporation. In the U.S., if you want to achieve a high status, you have to understand the American way of working; and working for American firms you know more Americans and have a better chance of getting ahead.

Education is very important in America because you can raise your status. In order to compete with Americans, we must have the knowledge to represent ourselves.

A minority of business owners saw politics and other activities that would organize the Chinese community as still preferable routes of mobility; again, it is interesting that this possibility went unmentioned among the Hispanics.

The owners' ambivalence about business as a means of getting ahead was further expressed when they were asked to assess the independence and control offered by ownership against the security and possibly even greater gains afforded by salaried employment. Not surprisingly, those owners who saw business as the best way of getting ahead also emphasized the advantages of ownership over salaried employment:

If you own your own business you can get ahead. If you work for someone else, the best that you can do is work as executive manager, but you still end up working for other people and you depend on other people.

Working for a big corporation is not the best way to get ahead because you are controlled by others and you need a long time to move up the ranks.

By contrast, those owners less optimistic about the chances in business tended to emphasize the benefits of working for others:

For those who get tired of getting a paycheck every week and have decided to go into business, once they start out on their own they'll learn about all the headaches and responsibilities involved. I'd rather get a check every week now.

I would work for a big corporation because I've owned a business and I know the difficulties involved.

Yet these owners' responses indicated that few thought they had the option of working in a large, stable firm; while this was a preferred alternative for almost half, the problem was that most owners lacked the needed linguistic and technical skills. "When you don't have the required education, of course you should open your own business," one factory owner pointed out. "But if you are a college graduate, then you look for a job with a large corporation." "While education is the best way to get ahead," noted one new garment capitalist, "that depends on the family background. But I came from a poor family, with no money to go to school." Thus, if business seemed less promising when compared with the opportunities opening up for the second generation, it still offered the immigrants a way of escaping the ethnic economy of garment factories and restaurants, with its constricted opportunities and highly regimented jobs:

I like to be my own boss. This way I don't have to take any commands from someone, and instead I give out orders now. I like this way better.

Education is better than business, but business is better than working for someone else: this way you can make profits.

I couldn't find enough money for my family in my last job, and since I couldn't find a better job, I decided to open this factory. This is the best way for me to earn more money.

Thus, for the Chinese, the impetus to entrepreneurship stemmed from their aspirations for social mobility that were blocked by lack of appropriate skills. While most owners agreed that "to really get ahead, the best thing is to . . . get ahead in a big American corporation," they also acknowledged that "you have to be well educated if you want to work outside the community." Hence, the limiting factor was that "for immigrants, it's either the restaurant business or the garment business"; and despite the fact that life "will be more stable if you're working for someone else, for someone like me, who can only get a low-paid check because of the educational background, it's better to take a chance to open your own business." As several owners put it: "I had no choice: that's why I went into business."

Thus, the two groups of immigrant owners differed significantly, in both perception of opportunity and preference for self-employment. The Hispanic owners had the more optimistic assessment of their chances in the United States and also evinced a strong predisposition toward business; the Chinese found the situation more constraining overall and opted for business out of expediency. These disparities have several implications for the theoretical issues discussed at the beginning of this chapter. First, the relationship between the immigrant business owners and the attitudes ascribed to them is inconsistent with theories that ascribe a group's success in business to a cultural or psychological propensity toward entrepreneurship. One set of business owners evinces many of the classic attitudes associated with the self-employed: a strong desire for independence and a correspondingly low aversion to risk. By contrast, the other set expresses a preference for salaried employment and appears inclined to take the entrepreneurial path only as a last recourse in the face of other obstacles. Thus, if we take Kessner's argument at its face value, Russian Jews became garment capitalists in 1900 because for them business was a way of life. But, for the Chinese immigrants who are replacing Jews in the garment industry in the

1980s, business is a way of making a living when life provides few other chances.

The second possibility is that immigrants turn to petty enterprise, not in search of independence, but in response to disadvantage. But if this is the case, how then does one account for the differences in perception and aspirations among Chinese and Dominicans? After all, both share the disadvantages of foreign birth, lack of English-language facility, and cultural and physical features that distinguish them from the native population. The problem with imputing entrepreneurial behavior to a reaction against disadvantage is that goals and obstacles are defined in an a priori way. What is left out is the actor's point of view and the factors that might condition his or her perspective. This implies that Dominicans and Chinese might share a common situation—immigrants segregated at the low end of the labor market with few outlets for upward mobility other than business—but would still define that situation quite distinctively, should they also differ in background and aspirations.

Now consider the characteristics of the owners and the communities in which they originate. Although research on New York's Dominican population indicates that most have come from urban centers, most of the owners interviewed were originally from the rural areas in the northern part of the Dominican Republic. On average, they received 9.9 years of schooling; 12 of the 32 owners had obtained a high school education or more. Not all the owners had worked prior to moving to the United States, but of those with work experience, most had been involved in activities of a blue-collar or trading nature. Once arrived in New York, most owners had made a livelihood as garment workers, and the movement from worker to owner was often protracted, lasting on average 14 years.

Seen in this light, one better understands the optimistic lens through which the Hispanic owners viewed their position in society. Relative to the depressed conditions in the rural areas from which they came, the opportunities in New York were indeed expansive. Of equal importance, these are opportunities of which natives are unlikely to avail themselves, as some of the Dominican owners pointed out when queried about the chances for getting ahead:

Yes, there are many opportunities. Hispanics have a greater desire to work. We come from countries where one appreciates the dollar.

This country gives us more opportunities than our own.

There are plenty of opportunities in New York because the Americans don't like to do this type of work.

Similarly, Dominicans' position in the social structure explains the specific attraction of business ownership. First of all, their previous jobs were low status, regimented, often prone to a high level of insecurity; hence, the push to start up one's own business and the powerful appeal of independence, as noted above. Second, ownership represents significant mobility, given the occupational position of the Dominican community, in which less than 5.3 percent were employed in professional or managerial jobs as of 1980. From this flows a third factor: that Dominicans' depressed position isolates them from the broader social hierarchy and thus mitigates against a perception of relative deprivation.

To the influence of social structure must be added the reinforcing effects of the circumstances of migration. "I want to return, like every Dominican," pointed out one owner. Indeed, more than half of the Dominicans came with the intention of returning home, and after a stay in the United States that has averaged almost 17 years, more than half still planned to return at some future time. Altogether, 21 of the 32 Dominican owners said that they saw themselves as temporary immigrants at one point or another. This unsettled, almost transient nature of the owners' status strengthens their orientation toward their homeland. Insofar as the immigrants think of themselves as temporary, what counts is how far they have gone toward fulfilling their initial goal of buying more land or accumulating capital for some other investment project. A quarter of the Dominican owners said that they expected to open a business in the Dominican Republic within the next 10 years, and some spoke of these plans in quite specific terms. Even if there is no specific project in mind, the intention or, more accurately, the dream of return means that the immigrant is likely to assess his or her achievement in light of the standards back home. "We always say that we come here until we make enough money to go back," explained one owner when queried about his settlement plans. "As for me," noted another owner, "I hope to live in both places."

For the Chinese owners, however, the mix of opportunities and constraints took on a considerably different form. Their position prior to migration more closely approximated their status in American society. The vast majority came from Hong Kong, where many had been involved in industrial or commercial pursuits. Those owners with prior work experience were split

between those who had previously been employed in blue-collar positions (mainly in the garment industry) and those who had worked in white-collar jobs or had run their own business. Of those who had not worked before moving to the United States, most had been enrolled in school. On average, the owners had obtained 11.5 years of schooling; 32 of the 63 owners had at least a high school education.

These background factors should help explain why the Chinese were so much less optimistic than the Hispanics in assessing their chances of getting ahead. First, their social position in New York involved a continuation of a preexisting social role. Second, those owners with higher levels of education faced the prospect of a decline in social status, at least in the short run. Furthermore, reference-group considerations, which are linked to the social structure of the broader Chinese community, diminish the appeal of business ownership, making it an activity that immigrants do not so much seek out but accept for lack of anything better. Despite the importance of the ethnic economy, with its key industries of restaurants, garments, petty retailing, and laundries, one sixth (16.8 percent) of New York's Chinese immigrants reported working as professionals or managers in 1980. Moreover, almost a tenth of all employed Chinese immigrants had a college education, whereas only 1.5 percent of the Dominicans had gone as far. Thus, while ownership may represent a step up from being a waiter or a sewing-machine operator, what the owners' comments indicate is that its social standing is relatively depressed precisely because so many Chinese are launched on white-collar careers. Differences between Chinese and Hispanics in their responses to the question about the best ways of getting ahead are particularly interesting in this respect. As I have noted, many of the Chinese saw education and the professions as the best ways of getting ahead (not surprisingly, they often linked the two). Yet, by contrast, virtually none of the Dominicans mentioned these options as viable routes to success. Moreover, the Chinese' pessimism about prospects for success was often tempered by comments about the brighter prospects facing the younger, more Americanized generations.

Just as important as the owners' assessment of their standing relative to their own group was their assessment relative to the broader society that they had recently joined; in this respect, the circumstance of their migration was a crucial influence. The great majority of Chinese owners migrated as permanent residents, and after an average 15 years' residence, a still larger number planned to remain in the United States on a permanent basis. Thus,

whereas an indeterminate settlement status worked to deflect the Dominican owners from competition for higher-level positions, permanence had the opposite effect among the Chinese—extending their ambitions to the jobs and rewards held by the native population and also heightening their sensitivity to their exclusion from those opportunities.

The interviews found that the perception of relative disadvantage was greatest among the younger, more educated owners—in other words, those who most resembled the native population. It was these owners who saw themselves in conflict with the native population. The same group was also most likely to advocate collective responses to the problem of disadvantage, as in the following suggestive comment: "If we want to get ahead we should be like the Jews: we should unite and stick together." Of course, such collective responses do not necessarily conflict with the pursuit of individual business opportunity: it is precisely the younger Chinese garment-factory owners that have been in the forefront of conflict with the garment workers' union and with the manufacturers' association.

Immigrant enterprise in the garment industry is thus an adaptation to the circumstances that the newcomers encountered upon their migration to New York. But the two groups, Dominicans and Chinese, have adapted in different ways and for different reasons. For the first group, business exercises the same appeal as it does to the American factory worker: for the Dominicans it is an escape hatch from the regimentation of factory work and its limited opportunities for economic advancement. For the Chinese, the attraction of business lies in the chance to compensate for a situation in which they are disadvantaged relative to the style, standard, and way of making a living to which they aspire—that of the American middle class.

The Sources of Business Success

As I argued above, the spirit of immigrant capitalism in the garment industry is not an import but rather an adaptation to the environment that Chinese and Dominican immigrants encountered in New York. However well disposed a group may be to pursue business opportunities, its success will depend on more than a propensity to start up on its own. In this section I will discuss the factors that condition Chinese and Dominicans for business activity and the resources that they can draw on in organizing their own concerns.

The rate at which immigrants set up their own businesses and then suc-

ceed depends in part on how well equipped they were for business activity at the time of migration. Direct involvement in business prior to emigration will certainly facilitate the newcomer's starting out on his or her own again after becoming a resident in a new land. Among the immigrant owners whom I interviewed, such involvement was considerably more common among the Chinese than among the Dominicans. However, the effect of prior business experience on the aggregate self-employment rate will largely depend on its distribution among the pool of prospective Dominican and Chinese entrepreneurs—not just among those immigrants who are already in business. Unfortunately, there is no way of knowing the percentage of Chinese and Dominican immigrants who were self-employed prior to their arrival in the United States.

Still a more important condition of entrepreneurial growth is the ability to learn how to run a business of one's own. That ability, in turn, is likely to hinge on several attributes, whose importance has been underlined by Mars and Ward in their discussion of ethnic business development in Britain: concepts of time and resource allocation that encourage deferred gratification, experience of the possibility of achieved roles and the legitimacy of competitive achievement, and experience of the use of money. The interviews provide information, albeit indirectly, about some of these attributes.[3] The importance attributed by the Chinese to education; the frequency with which they spoke of the prospects for the younger generation; and their predilection (however ambivalently expressed) for employment in large organizations—all suggest that business-relevant attributes are present among the Chinese garment capitalists more than among their Dominican counterparts.

There are also other, more general attributes that will hasten the acquisition of business skills: one is prior exposure to a competitive economy; the second is education. On these indicators, as I have already noted, the Chinese garment-factory owners do better than the Dominican garment capitalists. More importantly, the same pattern appears to hold for the broader populations from which these entrepreneurs stem, thus increasing the pool of Chinese immigrants who might realistically aspire to ownership. Comparisons of Hong Kong and Taiwan with the Dominican Republic show higher levels of urbanization, of employment in nonagricultural pursuits, and of literacy among the Chinese than among the Dominicans. Moreover, levels of prior professional and managerial experience were far higher among those Chinese immigrating to the United States between 1970 and 1979 than

among those Dominicans who arrived during the same period, as can be seen from Table 8.1. Similarly, Dominicans in New York have a considerable educational deficit when compared with their Chinese neighbors; though the difference among those immigrants employed in the garment industry is not as great, the Chinese still have a preponderance of newcomers with an educational background that is relevant to business success.

While the Chinese and the Dominicans may thus differ in the skills they bring with them, the diverging circumstances of their migration will affect the rate at which they accumulate skills after arriving in New York. The differences in settlement plans between Chinese and Dominican owners appear to reflect the overall orientations of their respective communities. While the Chinese community, by all accounts, is a settlement of permanent immigrants, Hendricks has noted that:

few individuals arrive from Santo Domingo with the idea of permanent settlement in New York . . . most arrive with the idea of remaining only long enough to accumulate, through hard work and thrift, enough capital to return home and buy land, build a house, or set themselves up in business.[4]

Table 8.1 Occupational Background of Chinese and Dominican Immigrants to the United States, 1970–1979

	Dominicans		Chinese	
	Number	%	Number	%
All immigrants	139,006	100.0	230,021	100.0
Occ. indicated	51,466	37.0	93,885	40.8
Prof., tech. and kind.	3,225	2.3	34,372	14.9
Mgrs. and admin.	2,679	1.9	12,796	5.6
Sales	676	0.5	2,522	1.1
Clerical	3,191	2.3	10,099	4.4
Craft	6,850	5.0	4,597	2.0
Operatives	13,251	9.5	8,903	3.9
Laborers	5,403	3.9	3,485	1.5
Farmers	607	0.4	232	0.1
Farm laborers	5,091	3.7	2,140	0.9
Service workers	4,056	2.9	13,259	5.8
Pri. hsehold wrs.	6,380	4.6	1,427	0.6

Source: U.S. Department of Justice, Immigration and Naturalization Service, *Statistical Yearbook of the Immigration and Naturalization Service*, annual editions. (Occupational data are given only for those immigrants reporting prior occupation.)

Considerably fewer Dominicans seem ready to abandon their homeland, as indicated by the very large disparity in naturalization rates for the two communities. In 1980, when 50.5 percent of the United States foreign-born population were naturalized, 50.3 percent of immigrants from China were citizens, as were 38.3 percent of those Chinese who had come to the United States from Hong Kong; by contrast, only 25.5 percent of Dominicans residing in the United States had become naturalized citizens.[5] Moreover, a substantial portion of the Dominican population consists of people who are necessarily oriented toward a short-term stay; by this I am referring to the large, though indeterminate, number of nonimmigrants who arrive on tourist visas and remain beyond the length of their alloted stay. Of course, no one knows how many people arriving on tourist visas opt for longer stays, but one indicator of the potential is the number of people arriving on tourist visas and their ratio relative to the number of permanent, legal immigrants. As Table 8.2 shows, Dominicans arriving in New York City on tourist visas outnumbered their compatriots who landed in New York City as legal immigrants during seven of the ten years between 1970 and 1979. By contrast, only in 1977 and 1978 did visitors from China outnumber their compatriots who chose to immigrate to New York.

Table 8.2 Number of Legal Immigrants to New York City and Temporary Visitors Admitted at New York City Airports, Chinese and Dominicans, 1970–1979

Years	Dominicans			Chinese		
	Legal Immigs.	Visitors	Legals/ Visitors	Legal Immigs.	Visitors	Legals/ Visitors
1970	7,131	12,418	0.57	3,658	2,698	1.35
1971	8,217	9,002	0.91	3,856	3,116	1.23
1972	6,970	6,867	1.01	5,279	3,442	1.53
1973	9,577	9,394	1.01	5,210	3,429	1.52
1974	10,795	12,378	0.87	4,958	4,147	1.20
1975	9,778	13,304	0.73	5,233	3,511	1.50
1976	8,505	13,098	0.65	5,102	3,640	1.40
1977	8,400	14,054	0.60	4,034	4,506	0.90
1978	13,227	17,065	0.78	4,922	5,210	0.94
1979	11,898	11,341	1.05	6,112	4,030	1.52
1970–79	94,498	118,921	0.79	48,364	37,729	1.28

Source: U.S. Department of Justice, Immigration and Naturalization Service, *Statistical Yearbooks*, annual editions.

My concern here is for the consequence of this difference in settlement patterns for entrepreneurial outcomes. One such implication has already been discussed: that permanent immigrants are more likely to feel excluded from opportunities for advancement and simultaneously to aspire to higher-level positions. Moreover, the situational pressures confronting the temporary migrant are likely to impede the pursuit of business opportunity. To begin with, the "bird of passage" is oriented toward those economic activities that will hasten the day of return rather than toward acquiring those skills that are needed to get ahead in New York. In the early stages, temporary migrants may be so preoccupied with making money that they become isolated socially and find themselves so consumed by working that they lack the time with friends and kin needed to make contacts and acquire needed skills. As Hendricks notes:

It is during this initial period that an immigrant most often holds several jobs at once . . . It was during this period, many informants told me, that they got jobs in *el campo* [the countryside], in New Jersey or Long Island; suburban restaurants and clubs paid for overtime work and in some cases even furnished living quarters. Even for those who remained in the city, the time consumed by holding down two or more jobs left scarcely any time for socializing with family or friends.[6]

Though the immigrants' commitment to New York tends to deepen over time, some newcomers retain the dream of returning to their native country with intensity. For these immigrants, spending for present consumption and saving for future accumulation remain a pole of tension. As Pessar has noted, the saying "five dollars wasted today means five more years of postponement of the return to the Dominican Republic" is a common refrain among Dominicans in New York.[7] Starting a business means taking a risk with one's hard-earned capital; the more serious the temporary migrant is, the more committed to return, the less likely he or she is to take the chance and start out on one's own. Moreover, the *cadena*, the chain that links many Dominican immigrants to kin who stayed home, exercises a further constraint on risk taking and expending any surplus saved from one's hard-earned wages. Because many Dominican newcomers see themselves as temporary migrants, they move in a chain: first a husband or other adult arrives; then other members of the family who are old enough to be employed follow. As a result, relatives back home continue to be dependent on migrants for remittances. Studies of sending communities in the Dominican Republic show that the migrants' remittances play a very significant role in sustaining the local economies.[8] Of course, the tremendous growth of New York's Domin-

ican population since 1965 indicates that many immigrants do settle down. But often the process is slow and imperceptible. The goal of returning is simply postponed, not abandoned, and consequently migrants may not be as deliberate as settlers in acquiring the relevant skills that are needed to get ahead. As several of the Dominican owners told me, "I want to go back to Santo Domingo, but I can't right now."

But however important the owner's human capital, and whatever the factors that condition the acquisition of needed business knowhow, the commercial success of the ethnic business owner is also likely to depend on a willingness to work long and hard. Perhaps the Chinese owners do better because they are more disciplined than their Dominican counterparts. The evidence from the survey, however, is that when effort is measured in terms of hours and days worked, little difference distinguishes Dominican from Chinese garment capitalists: the former report working 51.4 hours and 5.5 days a week; the latter indicate that their work week averages 51.8 hours and 5.8 days.

Another possibility is that the difference lies, not in the effort of the owners, but in the quality of the labor force on which the two groups of owners can draw. This hypothesis, suggested by the high productivity and efficiency for which the labor force in Hong Kong and Taiwan is known, is that the Chinese immigrant population exhibits a stronger orientation to work and a greater commitment to labor-force activities. Though mixed, the evidence on this question suggests that this virtue is more or less evenly distributed between the two populations. In fact, tabulations from the 5 percent Public Use Microdata Sample of the 1980 Census of Population indicate that Dominicans employed in the garment industry average slightly longer hours and more weeks worked than their counterparts among the Chinese. However, the Chinese do come out ahead in the proportion of the adult population engaged in paid labor. In 1980, 81.1 percent of Chinese males and 63.5 percent of Chinese women were in the labor force, whereas the comparable indicators for Dominican men and women were 75.4 percent and 45.6 percent, respectively.

Ethnic solidarity is also likely to be an important influence on business success. Both Chinese and Dominican firms were highly encapsulated within their respective communities, though the Dominican firms showed a greater tendency to recruit from the broader Hispanic immigrant labor force. But other points of divergence suggest that these informal organizational resources may be more developed among the Chinese. One indicator is the

percentage of firms in which family was employed: on this count, the Dominicans, with 18 out of 32 firms employing relatives, came out ahead of the Chinese, among whom only 29 out of 63 firms employed relatives. On the other hand, the ratio of family members to employees in firms that employed relatives was almost twice as high among Chinese (3.33:1) as among the Dominicans (1.72:1). A more important disparity, however, emerged when owners were queried about their own employment experience. Both groups of immigrant owners were asked whether their previous employers were Americans or members of their own group; the subsequent query asked about the owners' preference for working for one group or the other. As one would expect, given the larger size of the Chinese immigrant economy, a considerably higher percentage of Chinese owners had been previously employed by their co-ethnics than was the case for their Dominican counterparts. But not anticipated was the difference in employment preferences: the Chinese indicated a predilection for members of their own group; the Dominicans opted for employment under North Americans:

(Would you prefer to work for a Hispanic or a North American?)

Not for an Hispanic because they don't work or pay you well. The Jews pay you for the work that you do.

North Americans: they know more about the laws and they pay you better. They exploit you less.

With Hispanics, because we understand one another better. However, it's actually better with North Americans, because they are more conscientious.

How, then, does one account for these differences in ethnic solidarity among the Chinese and Dominican owners? And what might their import be? One possible explanation, which remains somewhat hypothetical, would link the disparities to the initial patterns of entry and incorporation into the garment industry's labor force. As we saw in Chapter 4, the Dominicans came into the garment industry as replacements for Puerto Ricans, and the Dominicans were recruited into firms that had already adjusted to other Hispanic employees. Since those firms offered better earnings possibilities and better conditions than did the existing Hispanic competitors—and we can note that the quotes from the Dominicans above indicate that their preference for employment in nonethnic firms was grounded in strictly eco-

nomic considerations—a pattern may have developed whereby Dominican firms operated as ports of entry for newcomers who picked up rudimentary sewing skills and then went on to work in nonimmigrant factories. Some confirmation of this is provided by Sherrie Grasmuck's research on legal and undocumented Dominican workers in New York. She shows that undocumented immigrants were more likely than their legal counterparts to work for Dominican or other Hispanic employers; since these undocumented immigrants often succeed in legalizing their status, the immigrant firms may simply serve as way stations for the newest arrivals.[9]

By contrast, the Chinese immigrants were funneled into the small Chinatown garment industry that slowly grew from 8 shops in 1960 to 102 shops in 1970 (see Table 4.5) without much notice from the industry at large. Thus, the Chinese employers had access to a more or less captive labor force while the immigrant sector was in its formative stages. Since then, native employers have become cognizant of the large Chinese presence in the garment industry. Though Chinese workers are viewed favorably, and native employers ascribe to them a higher level of discipline and productivity than they find in the general labor force, none of the Jewish or Italian employers surveyed employed Chinese workers. Nonetheless, many of the white ethnic employers with whom I have spoken had sought to recruit Chinese workers at one time or another; yet, virtually none had ever succeeded in doing so. One reason for this may be a tendency toward self-segregation, which is rooted in Chinese culture, and the emphasis that it has traditionally placed on a sense of distinctiveness in relationship to the West and to non-Chinese people.

Thus, in the competition to replace Jews and Italians as the petty proprietors in New York's garment industry, advantage goes to the Chinese. The source of their competitive edge, though, has little to do with a cultural predisposition toward business. In fact, the Chinese view business and the prospect of entrepreneurial careers less favorably than do their Dominican counterparts. And to the extent that we can measure the two groups' endowment of the good puritan virtues of hard work and discipline, the Chinese seem to work no harder than the newcomers who have arrived from the Dominican Republic. Rather, the source of Chinese advantage stems from a multiplicity of reinforcing factors. The Chinese begin with more of the general attributes needed for the acquisition of business skills. Furthermore, most of them arrive as permanent settlers, whereas a large proportion of the Dominicans come as temporary migrants. The difference in the circumstance of migration serves to heighten aspirations among the Chinese

while burdening the Dominicans with obligations and reducing their propensity for risk-taking behavior. The Chinese also have better access to the ethnic labor force, in part for historical reasons, and in part because culture breeds a preference for self-segregation. Finally, the Chinese benefit from the principle of cumulative advantage. Better equipped to start with, the Chinese outdo their Dominican counterparts. But since the two groups are direct competitors, the Chinese' competitive edge also sets a limit on the Dominicans' potential for growth.

[9]

Through the Eye of the Needle

At the end, as at the beginning of this book, it is tempting to recite the story of New York's latest immigrant garment capitalists as a panegyric to the newcomers' determination, hard work, and grit. Only the hard-bitten cynic would try to gainsay the importance of the immigrants' drive to get ahead, especially in an industry like garments, where the death rate of new firms should daunt even the most risk-prone of prospective entrepreneurs. But, if the newest immigrants have pushed their way to ownership, the argument of this book is that they have done so under conditions that kept the eye of the needle open.

New York's garment industry has proved favorable terrain for the new immigrant capitalists. The city's industry is diminished in size—due to changing patterns of consumption; to the growth of large apparel companies that spin off their operations to distant, lower-cost locations; and to a rising tide of clothing imported from low-labor-cost countries that has grabbed an increasing share of the market. But as shown in Chapters 3 and 4, these changes have also introduced considerable rigidity to an industry where flexibility is at a premium. While reductions in cost can be obtained by producing in Hong Kong or South Korea, doing so also means anticipating consumer wants by as much as a year. The large apparel company, while well suited for making staple goods, is too cumbersome an entity to respond efficiently to sudden and unanticipated fluctuations. Hence, problems arise when consumers' tastes shift unpredictably or when overall needs change. Because apparel is a product very much subject to the vagaries of fashion change and the volatility of consumer spending, there is a role for a spot market that specializes in making up fashion items and overruns on more standardized goods and for the small facilities that are best suited to producing small quantities of short-lived fashions. That spot market is preeminently located in New York City for two reasons: the importance of proximity

to its concentration of designers and merchandisers; and the effects of the new immigration on the relative costs of making garments in New York and on the supply of potential garment capitalists.

Thus, there is a segment of the apparel industry where bigness is not better; because this environment proved supportive of small, new entities, it is here that immigrant firms grew up. One crucial factor was that New York's garment industry provided built-in market mechanisms that lowered the barriers to entry and maximized the importance of immigrants' informal resources. Immigrants seeking to go into business faced low capital and technological thresholds. They could supplement their own capital with readily available loans from machinery dealers; and the division of labor between manufacturer and immigrant contractor spared them the costs of purchasing raw materials, sheltered them from the risks of accumulating inventory, and also increased the level and rapidity of cash flow. Furthermore, producing the style-oriented items in which New York's garment industry specialized kept the traditional technology in place. Not only did this lower entry barriers; it also meant that new immigrants could avail themselves of the traditional paths of movement from employee to owner—just as earlier generations of immigrant and ethnic garment capitalists had done. Finally, there was an ample supply of cheap, available factory space in which immigrant owners could house their firms; during the 1970s, the time when the immigrant garment sector developed, the quantity of this space increased and its cost declined.

While garments was an industry easily permeated by immigrant owners, it is unlikely that these neophytes would have done as well were it not for the fact that the industry's traditional sources of entrepreneurs—Jewish and Italian immigrants and their descendants—had largely dried up. Like other small business lines, garments is an industry where firms are created and turn over at a very high rate. But for most of the industry's history in New York, there was also an ample supply of Jewish and Italian sewing-machine operators, cutters, salesmen, and patternmakers eager to step up and start up a business on their own. The changing social structure of these two groups has altered patterns of recruitment: both are now largely middle class, and while a predilection for self-employment persists, especially among Jews, it is more likely to take the form of the independent professional. Thus, while there remain many Jewish- and Italian-owned firms in the contracting lines where new immigrants have become prevalent, only a negligible proportion consists of new start-ups: most are long-established firms, run by aging owners whose children have chosen other pursuits.

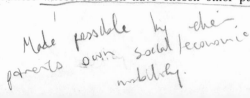

Consequently, ethnic succession has created a space for new immigrant owners whose investment calculus is shaped by a very different assessment of the available opportunities. In contrast to the older ethnic business owners, who tend to be risk-averse, immigrant garment capitalists are quick to exploit fashion changes. However uncertain these fashion trends may be, they offer a chance to build up business. Most of these new immigrant entities actually fail; and on average, the immigrants' failure rate is higher than that of their older ethnic competitors. But the crucial factor is that the remaining Jewish- and Italian-owned firms turn over at a high rate as well. Since these two groups provide scant replacements for failing entrepreneurs, there are ample vacancies for immigrants seeking to start out on their own; and as we have seen, the immigrants' search for opportunity through business has kept the rate of new-firm formation high.

Once in business, the immigrants can draw on informal resources through their connections with the broader immigrant communities from which they stem. These resources provide a source of limited advantage in competition with the older ethnic firms. The mobilization of kinship and ethnic ties plays an important role in the organization of immigrant firms: most firms surveyed were owned by relatives or by partners of the same ethnic group. Whereas the size of immigrant garment firms made it necessary to recruit outsiders, immigrants' concerns were tightly encapsulated in their own communities and chiefly hired workers of common ethnicity. By contrast, the older ethnic firms relied on market mechanisms to obtain labor. Owing to ethnic succession in the labor force, this meant hiring black and Hispanic immigrants or natives. These differences in recruitment patterns in turn had ramifications for skill training and conflict between management and labor. Network hiring on the part of immigrant firms bred the level of trust needed for instruction in skills; it also promoted a paternalistic relationship between immigrant owners and their employees, though this was bounded by the imperatives of efficiency. Nonimmigrant firms, by contrast, were more dependent on skilled labor than immigrant concerns, yet little skill training took place. Rather than a limited paternalism, antagonism and distance were characteristic of the employment relationship.

Immigrant Enterprise in a Changing Environment

The window of opportunity that opened up for neophyte garment capitalists in the 1970s and early 1980s is currently narrowing under stress. Their future prosperity hinges on the changes in this environment and the

extent to which the immigrant entrepreneurs can maintain a viable market niche under altered conditions. The most important factor is probably the maintenance of a continued flow of newcomers, without which New York's entire garment complex will find itself short of labor. In broad form, the immigrant system that was put into place in 1965 and, in turn, renewed large-scale immigration to New York, is unlikely to change. By all accounts, the levels of legal immigration attained during the 1970s can be expected to continue. However, changes in the complex criteria by which immigrants are selected have been included repeatedly in the immigration bills that have been considered by Congress in each of the past three congressional sessions. Thus far, no bill has been passed, but changes in the composition of the immigrant flows remain a possibility: should new criteria favor an increase in the number of higher-skilled immigrants, the number of newcomers gravitating toward the garment industry will undoubtedly decline.[1]

A second and much darker cloud on the horizon is the threat of international competition. Import penetration levels have risen steadily over the past twenty years, as we saw in Chapter 3. Particularly sharp rises were recorded between 1980 and 1984. As a result, total employment in the nation's garment industry has been sent tumbling, and New York's garment industry has not escaped this downward trend. Thanks to its role as a spot market, New York has held its own relative to the rest of the domestic industry. Since the quota system in apparel encourages retailers to import goods with a longer lead time in advance of sales, it is unlikely that the industry can make do without a source capable of supplying short-term, unpredictable needs. Nonetheless, consumers do make a trade-off between price and fashion, and should import levels continue to rise as they have, consumers are likely to opt for somewhat less fashionable foreign-made goods than for New York's more expensive, if also more stylish clothes. Thus, the crucial factor is the evolving system of trade regulation. The congressional drive to cut back on imports is stronger than ever before, as shown in Chapter 3, but whether the flow of imports will actually be curbed is very much subject to doubt.

Whether the external environment remains supportive or not, New York's immigrant garment capitalists must in any case contend with severe internal pressures. New York's immigrant garment industry, as we have seen, emerged at at time when economic crisis was emptying much of the manufacturing space in the city's central business district. For Hispanic owners, this development opened up cheap factory space in the garment center where con-

tracting shops could be operated in close proximity to manufacturers—a matter of particular importance in an immigrant specialization like pleating, where individual pleating firms work for many customers, each of which depends on rapid deliveries. For the Chinese immigrant garment sector, the effects of the economic downturn proved still more beneficial because it freed up space in an area that lay within the chief concentration of the local Chinese population and thus maximized the supply of available labor.

Over the course of the 1980s, the availability of space decreased, in part because New York's economy enjoyed a vigorous revival and in part because public economic development efforts threatened to displace industrial users. — Gian tion Both developments greatly affected the garment center. Because it offered lower-cost space than did other central business district areas, commercial firms flocked to the garment center, bidding up rents to a plateau that manufacturing firms could never afford. Second, local governments chose to sponsor two massive development projects on the borders of the garment center—a convention center on the west and a large office complex on Forty-second Street on the north—and both projects encouraged the influx of higher-paying users into the area.[2]

The market for industrial space also changed in Chinatown. By the mid-1980s rents were considerably higher and vacancies were much scarcer than was the case a decade earlier. In addition, Chinatown's stock of loft space became attractive to other users—businesses and cultural organizations serving the burgeoning Chinese community, as well as non-Chinese gentrifiers using loft space for residential purposes. As of 1981 residential dwellers took up one fifth of the loft space in Chinatown; since their presence also signaled that this previously depressed manufacturing district could attract an upper-income clientele, large-scale real estate developers began to show interest in the area.[3]

The changing real estate situation has altered the prospects for immigrant businesses in several respects. First, as the demand for loft space has intensified, rents have escalated, moving from $1.00 to $2.00 a square foot in the mid-1970s to $5.00 to $8.00 as of 1985. Second, the inflow of commercial tenants, especially in the garment center, has made landlords less willing to make long-term commitments to industrial users. In one sense, this has facilitated new start-ups, especially when landlords have sought to rent premises on a month-to-month basis. On the other hand, month-to-month rent is a destabilizing influence, discouraging any permanent investment in plant or equipment. Finally, because vacancy rates have dropped, it

has become more difficult and more expensive to start up a new firm. In Chinatown the dwindling supply of additional industrial space has put a premium on the existing loft spaces; increasingly, new owners must pay "key money" in order to obtain a new loft.

Over the long term the transformation of the central business district from manufacturing to commercial and residential uses poses a major threat to the viability of the immigrant garment sector. The stock of industrial space has been steadily dwindling ever since New York's economic revival began in the mid-1970s, and the economics of industrial real estate are such that manufacturing cannot compete with its rival uses. Management and labor have organized to stabilize the stock of loft space available to immigrant firms, but this effort has registered only modest success.

One possible line of response to the changes in both the external and the internal environment is for immigrant owners to seek out a new, more protected market niche. As shown in Chapter 5, and summarized again above, making cheap yet fashion-sensitive items was the point of entry for most immigrant businesses because the technology of garment production in these lines was simple, easy to master, and inexpensive to obtain. But whether immigrant firms can continue to survive in these lines much longer is uncertain, since these are also the categories most sensitive to import penetration.

An alternative is to move into more sophisticated lines: doing this would involve making higher-priced, higher-fashion products where the profit margins are correspondingly greater and where proximity to New York's designing facilities is of particular advantage. Indeed, many of the Chinese owners are currently in pursuit of this more protected market niche. The consensus among the larger, more established immigrant firms is that they have to produce higher-quality fashions in order to expand the market for their product. The example that many of the immigrant owners are trying to emulate is that of a young Chinese immigrant, John Lam:

At age 17, John Lam immigrated to New York from Hong Kong with the rest of his family and began work in a small contract sewing shop learning to evaluate and set prices for a budget-line of women's sportswear. Two years later, with $10,000 from family and personal savings, he bought his first shop at 52 East Broadway employing about 30 people . . . Lam began to reorganize his shops from producing standard goods to specializing in higher skilled sewing jobs, gradually improving the skill of his work force and the quality of his garments. Within four years he bought the building at 52 East Broadway, with four floors totaling 10,000 square feet, and he increased his work force to 120. By then he had graduated to the industry's better

priced sportswear lines where the margins weren't as tight and he could afford to invest the time to train his seamstresses in more difficult work. He brought in supervisors from Hong Kong shops to help manage his burgeoning enterprises. He invested in more efficient machinery and specialized equipment, graduating to the industry's top-of-the-line garments. Today, Lam has 12 garment shops, employs over 1,000 people, and pulls in $30 million plus in annual revenues for producing high quality goods for Liz Claiborne and other top labels.[4]

To succeed in this high-fashion/high-price strategy, as the example above suggests, the immigrant owners will need to alter their technological arrangements, both in order to lower costs and to improve quality. John Lam is not the only garment capitalist to seek growth through technological change, and many immigrant firms have begun to plow back profits into the business, investing in new equipment with laborsaving devices. The trend toward more sophisticated technology is particularly noticeable among the Chinese owners. As I noted in Chapter 8, most of the Chinese owners interviewed planned to improve their competitive position through new investments in plant and equipment. Some of the Chinese owners have also organized delegations to visit the national apparel industry equipment show, which is held in Atlanta, Georgia, each year, and have also set up equipment exhibitions in Chinatown itself.

If the growth of the ethnic economy has set the stage for a shift to a more viable, more profitable market position, this new stage also promises to alter employment conditions. The new forms of production being adopted by immigrant owners threaten to displace unproductive workers, increase supervision, and rigidify work rules and employment practices. Thus, the need to rationalize operations may further heighten the tension between the limited paternalism characteristic of the immigrant firm and its drive for efficiency. As one observer pointed out, the introduction of new machinery in several factories made workers "very worried about being made 'extinct.'"[5] As one Chinatown newspaper noted, in commenting on this trend:

Under the impact of modernization and concentration, Chinatown's former family-style management is disappearing. Under these circumstances, who will take care of the children, young people, and old people and immigrants who cannot be accommodated in the garment shops?[6]

Over the near term, however, we can expect that New York's immigrant garment industry will continue to grow. The simple process by which new immigrants replace older ethnics whose firms naturally go under will con-

tinue to provide immigrant neophytes with additional opportunities. Moreover, the situation of the immigrant population is such as to furnish a continuing supply of potential entrepreneurs. A large proportion of New York's Chinese and Hispanic immigrants lack the skills needed to move into the ever growing white-collar sector; this should continue to generate new cohorts of neophyte capitalists willing to risk their capital in order to escape confinement to menial and regimented factory or service jobs. The growth record of the immigrant garment industry itself is likely to provide a further spur to business formation. Immigrants, like other business owners, learn through imitation. The fact that some newcomers have succeeded in business encourages other, less adventurous members of a group to follow suit. As one Chinese factory owner put it: "My boss was making money, so I decided to go into business for myself."

However, the chief source of uncertainty in predicting the future of New York's immigrant garment industry does not lie in the immigrants themselves. Rather, it is found in the broader environment, which may no longer be as supportive as it has been in the past. What we know is that the drive that led immigrants to seek their fortune in a new country will keep them pushing to get ahead. But whether the immigrants will continue to get ahead as garment capitalists largely depends on whether the eye of the needle can still be threaded. The answer to that question is a matter largely beyond the newcomers' control.

Good Quote!

Appendix A

Classification of Apparel Industries

The purpose of this appendix is to give a full description of the various industries that make up the "Women's and Children's Apparel Industry." Chapters 3 and 4 were primarily focused on nine so-called four-digit apparel industries, as defined in the *Standard Industrial Classification Manual*, issued by the Executive Office of the President, Office of Management and Budget. The text, however, mainly referred to the broader three-digit industries in which the smaller four-digit industries are classified. For example, the three-digit women's outerwear industry (SIC 233) contains the four-digit blouse industry. Below are listed the relevant three- and four-digit industries, with their official titles and with descriptions, where informative.

SIC 233   Women's Outerwear (full title: Women's, Misses', and Juniors' Outerwear). This three-digit group includes blouses, dresses, coats, suits, and the miscellaneous category, "other outerwear." Since the latter includes those clothes marketed as sportswear, the term "sportswear" is used in the text to refer to the other outerwear industry.

SIC 2331   Blouses (full title: Women's, Misses', and Juniors' Blouses, Waists, and Shirts).

SIC 2335   Dresses (full title: Women's, Misses', and Juniors' Dresses).

SIC 2337   Coats and Suits (full title: Women's, Misses', and Juniors' Suits, Skirts, and Coats). Establishments primarily engaged in manufacturing women's, misses', and juniors' suits, skirts, and coats except for raincoats. Establishments primarily engaged in manufacturing fur garments are classified in Industry 2371, raincoats in Industry 2385, and knitting mills primarily engaged in manufacturing knit outerwear in Industry 2253.

SIC 2339 Other Outerwear or Sportswear (full title: Women's, Misses', and Juniors' Outerwear, Not Elsewhere Classified). Establishments engaged primarily in manufacturing women's, misses', and juniors' outerwear, not elsewhere classified, such as athletic clothing, bathing suits, untailored jackets, slacks, and shorts, cut and sewed from purchased woven or knitted fabric.

SIC 234 Undergarments (full title: Women's, Misses', Children's, and Infant's Undergarments).

SIC 2341 Women's and Children's Underwear (full title: Women's, Misses', Children's, and Infant's Underwear and Nightwear).

SIC 2342 Brassieres (full title: Brassieres and Allied Garments).

SIC 236 Children's Outerwear (full title: Girls', Children's, and Infants' Outerwear).

SIC 2361 Girls', Children's, and Infant's Dresses, Blouses, Waists, and Shirts: includes girls', children's, and infants' dresses and blouses.

SIC 2363 Girls', Children's, and Infants' Coats and Suits.

SIC 2359 Girls' Children's, and Infants' Outerwear, Not Elsewhere Classified. Includes such products as girls', children's, and infants' bathrobes, swimwear, robes, playsuits, shorts, skirts, and slacks.

Appendix B

Survey Procedure

Chapters 5 through 8 are primarily based on interviews with 136 contractors, of whom 63 were Chinese, 41 were white ethnic (Jewish or Italian), and 32 were Dominican. Many garment contractors, as noted in the book, are small and evanescent; this is particularly true for the immigrant firms with which I have been mainly concerned. What this means is that many garment contractors, especially those that are immigrant-owned, are never detected by the otherwise comprehensive industrial directories published by various commercial firms. Moreover, for my purposes, the industrial directories suffered from an additional liability: they made no distinction between contractors and manufacturers; instead they listed firms of both types under the appropriate industrial specialization (for example, blouses or coats, etc).

Consequently, I generated my sample from a variety of different sources. Because the vast majority of firms in the garment center and in the rest of Manhattan are manufacturers I combined a list of all unionized contractors in the garment center, which was provided to me by the International Ladies' Garment Workers' Union, with a listing of all contracting firms located in the Bronx, Brooklyn, and Queens (where contractors are prevalent). This latter list was compiled from Macrae's *State Industrial Directory*, Dalton's *New York Metropolitan Directory*, and George D. Hall's *New York Manufacturer Directory*. Because I knew from previous research and contacts that virtually all of the unionized firms in the garment center were owned by Jews or Italians and because the directories usually listed the proprietor's name, which made it possible to screen out Hispanic or Chinese names, these sources effectively limited the sampling universe to nonimmigrant firms. Combined together these sources produced a total of 1,000 firms; I then selected firms on a random basis. Interviews were conducted in person or over the phone, depending on the preference of the owner. I conducted about two thirds of the interviews; the rest were conducted by a research assistant.

The sample of Chinese firms was generated from a list, provided me by the International Ladies' Garment Workers' Union, of all Chinese contractors in

Chinatown. This list, which included 480 factories, arranged shops by address. The interviewers, all native Chinese speakers, were instructed to visit every fourth shop.

Since the Dominican firms are the smallest and shortest-lived, these firms were the most difficult to sample. In the course of my dissertation research in 1981 I had learned that Corona, a neighborhood in Queens, Washington Heights, an area in northern Manhattan, Sunset Park in South Brooklyn, and certain buildings in the garment center, contained concentrations of Dominican firms. At the time, I developed a listing of firms in these three clusters through street censuses and use of special reverse telephone books which organize phone subscribers by address. I rechecked and updated this list in 1983 and 1984 through similar techniques and generated a sample of 50 firms. Native-Dominican research assistants then conducted on-site interviews with 32 owners.

Appendix C

Questionnaire for Immigrant Firms

Clothing Industry Survey

NAME OF FIRM: _____

ADDRESS: _____

TELEPHONE: _____

INTERVIEWEE: _____

INTERVIEWER: _____

DATE: _____

First I would like to ask you some general questions about your business and then I would like to ask you some questions about your experience as a garment factory owner.

1. Could you tell me a little bit about your business? For example, how long have you been in business? What products are you making here? How many people do you employ?

    Years in business:_____

    Product:_____

    Number employed:_____

2. Could you now tell me a little bit about yourself? For example, what was your last job before going into business?

    Last job:_____

3. (If last job was in garment industry): For how long have you worked in the garment industry? What different jobs have you had during that period?

    Years in garment industry:_____

    Different jobs:_____

Did you have any supervisory experience on any of your jobs?

Yes _____ No _____ (If yes): What type of supervisory job did you have?

4. (If last job was not in garment industry): Since you didn't previously work in the garment industry, why did you decide to open a garment factory?

---

5. Did you work for a Chinese/Hispanic boss or for an American boss on your last job? _____ Have you ever worked for an American boss? _____ Did you/would you prefer working for an American or a Chinese/Hispanic employer? _____ Chinese/Hispanic _____ American

Why did you/would you prefer a Chinese/Hispanic/American boss?_____

---

6. What do you think is the best way for Chinese/Hispanic immigrants to get ahead in the United States?_____

---

7. (If business): Why is business the best way to get ahead?_____

---

8. (If other): Why do you think that _____ is a better way to get ahead than business?_____

---

9. Why did you decide to go into business for yourself?_____

---

10. Were any of your friends in business before you opened your factory? Yes _____ No _____ (If yes): What did they think about the idea of going into business?_____

---

11. What do you think the chances are for the typical Chinese/Hispanic living here in New York City who wants to get ahead?_____

---

12. Now I'd like to ask your opinion: Some people prefer working for someone else, because that way they know they get a check every week. Other people don't like to work for someone else because they want to be their own boss. How do you feel about this?_____

---

13. I'd like to ask your opinion once again: Some people think that the best way for Chinese/Hispanics to get ahead is by getting a job with a big corporation. Other people say that you can't get a job with a big corporation so the best way to get ahead is to open your own business. What do you think?___

---

14. (For Chinese employers only): Now I'd like to ask you some questions about the people who work for you. From what part of China do most of your workers come?

Part of China with most workers_____

What percentage of workers are from that part of China?_____

From what other parts of China do your workers come?_____

15. (For Hispanic employers only): Now I'd like to ask you some questions about the people who work for you. From what country do the majority of your workers come?

Country from which the majority of workers come_____

About what percentage of the workers are from this country?_____

From what other countries do your workers come?_____

16. Now I'd like to ask your opinion again: Some owners say that they prefer to hire workers from their part of China/from their own country because they're more responsible. Other owners say that it's not a good idea because these people take advantage of the relationship. What do you think?_____

17. How do you mainly recruit workers? _____ word of mouth/recommendations? _____ ads? _____ walk-ins off the street? _____ agencies?
18. Why do you recruit workers that way?_____

19. Sometimes a worker comes and asks the owner to hire her relative or her friend. What do you usually do when that happens?_____

(If hires/doesn't hire): Why?_____

20. Do you hire unskilled workers or workers with very little experience? _____ Yes _____ No
(If no): Why not?_____

(If yes): Many owners don't like to hire unskilled workers because they learn how to do the work in your shop and then they leave you to go work somewhere else. What do you think?_____

21. Are any of your relatives employed in the factory?_____
22. (If yes): How many?_____

What do they do in the factory?_____

Do they do the same jobs as the other workers?_____

_____

How many hours do they work?_____

23. Some owners say that in the garment business you need relatives working for you in order to succeed. Other owners think relatives aren't needed. What do you think?_____

_____

24. Is there anybody working with you whom you knew in your hometown? _____ (If yes): How many people from your hometown are working in the shop?_____

25. I would like to ask your opinion again: Some owners say that they try to help their workers out with problems. Other owners say that they don't like to get involved. What do you think?_____

_____

26. (If helps out with problems): Could you give me some examples of how you help your workers?_____

_____

27. Some owners say that compatriots and hometown acquaintances will go take another job, even when you need them the most. Other people say that these workers stay with you longer than anyone else. What is your experience?_____

_____

28. What happens when work gets slow? Do you lay people off? Do you share the work or what?_____

_____

29. How long has the average worker been with you?_____

30. Why do people usually leave?_____

31. Is there anything that you do to keep your best workers from going to work somewhere else?_____

_____

32. Who are your competitors?_____

33. What are your advantages and disadvantages in competing with them?

_____

_____

34. How does the future look for this business? Is it growing, stable, or getting worse?_____

_____

35. Are you doing anything to build up the business?_____

_____

36. What do you hope to be doing 10 years from now?_____

_____

37. Do you own the business yourself or do you have a partner?
_____ partner _____ no partner
(If partner): Is your partner a relative, or hometown friend, or from the same part of China as you?_____

_____

38. (If partner): How do you and your partner divide the work?_____

_____

_____

39. How many hours a week do you work?_____
40. How many days a week do you work?_____
41. Is your firm union or nonunion?_____
42. (If union): Which union is it?_____
43. (If union): What are relations like with the union? Has the union changed your relationship with the workers?_____

_____

44. (If nonunion): Why do you think that the union has never succeeded in organizing your company?_____

_____

45. What do you think the government can do to help Chinese/Hispanic business owners in the garment industry?_____

_____

46. Do you think that the Chinese/Hispanic community can do anything to help Chinese/Hispanic business owners?_____

_____

47. Is there anything that you do to develop a good relationship with your workers?_____

_____

_____

48. (If Chinese): Do you celebrate the Chinese New Year in your shop?
_____ Yes _____ No (If yes): What do you do to celebrate the Chinese New Year?_____

49. From what country/part of China do you come?_____

50. In what town or city were you born?_____

51. What was your last job in China/your home country?_____

52. When did you come to the United States?_____

53. How many years of education have you received?_____

54. What would you like your children to do when they grow up?_____

55. When you came to New York did you come with the idea of staying permanently or did you hope to stay temporarily and then go back to China/your home country?_____

56. And now, do you plan to stay in the United States permanently or do you hope to go back to China/your home country?_____

57. How old are you?_____

58. What was your father's main occupation?_____

59. How much money did you need to start up the business?_____

60. How difficult was it to get the money needed to start up the business? Was it:
_____ easy _____ difficult _____ somewhat difficult

61. Did anybody help you to raise the money needed to start up the business? For example, did you get help from:
_____ friends _____ relatives _____ a family association _____ savings _____ other sources (please specify)

62. How much do you pay your workers per hour?_____

63. Do you pay your workers in check or in cash?_____

Appendix D

Questionnaire for Ethnic (Jewish and Italian) Factory Owners

Clothing Industry Survey

NAME OF FIRM: ————————————————————————

ADDRESS: ———————————————————————————

TELEPHONE: ——————————————————————————

INTERVIEWEE: ————————————————————————

INTERVIEWER: ————————————————————————

DATE: ————————————————————————————

1. For how long have you been in business? What products are you making here? How many people do you employ?

Years in business:——————————————————————

Product:————————————————————————————

Number employed:————————————————————————

2. What is the average age of your workers?————————————

3. What is the average seniority?————————————————

4. How do you mainly recruit workers? ———— agencies ———— union ————word of mouth/recommendations ———— ads ———— walk-ins ———— unemployment service

5. Why do you recruit workers that way?————————————

————————————————————————————————————

————————————————————————————————————

6. What happens if a worker comes and asks you to hire a relative or friend? Do you prefer to hire this way or not? And why?

What happens and why:————————————————————

————————————————————————————————————

7. How common is this type of hiring as a source of new labor? Would you say that it's very common, somewhat common, not common at all?

———— very common ———— somewhat common ———— not common at all

8. What are the skill requirements for the jobs that you offer? Do you hire mainly skilled workers, semiskilled, or unskilled? _____ mainly skilled _____ mainly semiskilled _____ mainly unskilled

9. Why do the jobs require such (high/low) levels of skill?_____

_____

_____

10. What are the main ethnic groups that work in the factory?
percent: _____ Hispanic _____ Italian _____ black _____ Asian _____ other

11. (If owner employs Hispanics): Do you know where the Hispanics come from? Are they mainly Puerto Rican, Dominican, or what? _____ Puerto Rican _____ Dominican _____ other

12. Has the ethnic composition of the work force changed over the past 10 to 15 years? If so, how and why?_____

_____

_____

13. Are there any American black workers employed in the factory? _____ Yes _____ No (If no): Were they employed at some earlier time? And why aren't there any blacks left?_____

_____

_____

14. (If work force contains white ethnics and other ethnic groups): How do you think the various ethnic groups differ in terms of skill, interest, commitment, attendance, etc.?_____

_____

_____

15. (If work force only contains nonwhites): How would you rate the workers in terms of skill and commitment to the job?
a. Would you say that their skill level is high, low, or medium? _____ high _____ low _____ medium
b. And how about their commitment to the jobs? Would you say that this is high, low, or medium? _____ high _____ low _____ medium
c. Why do you say that the workers are (high/low/medium) in their commitment to the job? Could you give me some examples of this?_____

_____

_____

_____

16. How would you rate the supply of labor? Would you say that it's ample or sufficient or in shortage? _____ ample _____ sufficient _____ shortage

17. (If shortage): Why do you think that there is a shortage?_____

_____

_____

18. (If shortage): When did the shortage begin to be felt?_____

19. How much turnover is there? And why does it occur?_____

20. Is there anything that you can do to reduce the amount of turnover?___

21. Is absenteeism a problem? _____ Yes _____ No (If yes): How does it affect the operation of your firm?_____

22. How would you characterize your relationship with the workers? Is it very good, very bad, good, bad, so-so? _____ very good _____ very bad _____ good _____ bad _____ so-so

23. What do you do/what could you do to create a good relationship with the workers?_____

24. Is the shop a full-garment or a section-work shop?_____

Now I'd like to ask some questions about your own experience as a businessperson and your thoughts about being a businessperson in the garment industry.

25. What was your last job before opening your business?_____

26. Why did you decide to go into business for yourself?_____

27. Now I'd like to ask your opinion: Imagine that a young person, aged 20–25, told you that his goal was to get ahead in American society and asked your advice. What would you think would be the best way of getting ahead?

(If response is general, e.g., "work hard and be aggressive," then ask): Do you think that there is a particular field or occupation that provides the best way of getting ahead?_____

28. In comparison to that way, how would you rate having a garment shop?

29. I'd like to ask your opinion again: Some people prefer working for someone else, because that way they know they get a check every week. Other people don't like to work for someone else, because they want to be their own boss. How do you feel about this?_____

_____

30. Are your children active in the business? _____ Yes _____ No

31. Why are your children active/not active in the business?_____

_____

32. How does the future look for this business? Is it growing, stable, or getting worse?_____

33. Do you own the business or do you have a partner? _____ single owner-ship _____ partner

34. (If partner): Is your partner a relative? _____ Yes _____ No

35. How many hours a week do you work?_____

36. How many days a week do you work?_____

Now I'd like to ask you five personal questions and then I'll end the interview.

37. Where were you born?_____

(If foreign-born): When did you come to the United States?_____

_____

38. How many years of education did you receive?_____

39. What was your father's main occupation?_____

40. How old are you?_____

41. What is your ethnicity?_____

Notes

Chapter 1

1. This is a highly stylized summary of a complex phenomenon. For sophisticated accounts that develop an argument much along these lines, see W. R. Boehning, "The Economic Effects of the Employment of Foreign Workers with Special Reference to the Labor Markets of Western Europe's Post-Industrial Countries," in W. R. Boehning and Denis Maillat, *The Effects of the Employment of Foreign Workers* (Paris: Organization for Economic Cooperation and Development [hereafter OECD], 1974), and Michael Piore, *Birds of Passage* (Cambridge: Cambridge University Press, 1979).
2. "Hispanic Immigrants: Soon the Biggest Minority," *Time*, October 16, 1978.
3. Ivan Light, "Asian Enterprise in America: Chinese, Japanese and Koreans in Small Business," in Scott Cummings, ed., *Self-Help in Urban America: Patterns of Minority Business Enterprise* (Port Washington, N.Y.: Kennikat, 1980); Raymond Russell, *Sharing Ownership in the Workplace* (Albany, N.Y.: SUNY Press, 1985), pp. 120–135; David R. Koos, "South Asians in the Garment Industry: A Preliminary Study," *South Asia Bulletin* no. 1 (1982): 59–67.
4. Illsoo Kim, *The New Urban Immigrants: Korean Immigrants in New York City* (Princeton: Princeton University Press, 1981), Lisa Belkin, "For the City's Korean Greengrocers, Culture Often Clashes with the Law," *New York Times*, September 30, 1984, p. 25; Thomas Bailey, "Labor Market Competition and Economic Mobility in Low-Wage Employment: A Case Study of Immigrants in the Restaurant Industry" (Ph.D. diss. MIT, 1983); John Greenwald, "Finding Niches in a New Land," *Time*, July 8, 1985, p. 73.
5. "Indian Immigrants Prosper as Owners of Motels," *New York Times*, June 22, 1985; Greenwald, "Finding Niches"; Ivan Light, "Immigrant Entrepreneurs in America: Koreans in Los Angeles," in Nathan Glazer, ed., *Clamor at the Gates* (San Francisco: ICS Press, 1985).
6. James Watson, "The Chinese: Hong Kong Villagers in the British Catering Trade," pp. 181–213 in James Watson, ed., *Between Two Cultures: Migrants and Minorities in Britain* (Oxford: Basil Blackwell, 1977); David Mullins, "Asian Retailing in Croyden," *New Community* 7 (1979):403–5; Jeremy Boissevain and Hanneke Grotenberg, "Culture, Structure, and Ethnic Enterprise: The Surinamese of Amsterdam," unpublished paper, University of Amsterdam, 1985.
7. L. J. Tap, "Turkish Entrepreneurs in the Amsterdam Clothing Industry," unpublished paper presented at the workshop on Minorities in the Clothing Trade, Research Unit on Ethnic Relations, Birmingham, 1983; Sarah Ladbury, "Choice, Chance, or No Alternative? Turkish Cypriots in Business in London," pp. 105–25 in Robin Ward and Richard Jenkins, *Ethnic Communities in Business: Strategies for Economic Survival* (Cambridge: Cambridge University Press, 1984); Roger Leigh and David North, "The Clothing Industry in the West Midlands: Structure, Problems, and Policies," paper prepared for the Economic Development Unit, West Midlands County Council, England, 1983; Victor Nee and Brett de Bary Nee, *Longtime Californ'* (New York: Pantheon, 1973); Peggy Li, Buck Wong, and Fong Kwan, *The Garment Industry in Los Angeles' Chinatown, 1973–74*, working paper of the

UCLA Asian Studies Center, 1975; Light, "Immigrant Entrepreneurs," p. 166; Madeline J. Haug, "Miami's Garment Industry and Its Workers," pp. 173–91, in I. H. Simpson and R. Simpson, eds., *Research in the Sociology of Work*, vol. 2 (Greenwich, Conn.: JAI Press, 1983); Greenwald, "Finding Niches."

8. See U.S. Department of Commerce and Labor, Bureau of the Census, *Twelfth Census of the United States, Special Reports, Occupations* (Washington, D.C.: Government Printing Office, 1904).

9. Self-employment rates for immigrants and natives in New York City calculated from the Public Use Microdata Sample of the 1980 Census of Population.

10. Max Weber, *The Protestant Ethic and the Spirit of Capitalism* (New York: Scribner's, 1958).

11. Nathan Glazer, "Social Characteristics of American Jews," *American Jewish Yearbook*, vol. 55 (New York: American Jewish Committee, 1955), pp. 3–43.

12. William Petersen, *Japanese Americans: Oppression and Success* (New York: Random House, 1971).

13. Ivan Light, *Ethnic Enterprise in America* (Berkeley: University of California Press, 1972).

14. Aubrey Bonnett, *Institutional Adaptation of West-Indian Immigrants to America: An Analysis of Rotating Credit Associations* (Washington, D.C.: University Press of America, 1981); Michel Laguerre, *Haitian Odyssey: Haitians in New York City* (Ithaca, N.Y.: Cornell University Press, 1984); Kwang Chung Kim and Won Moo Hurh, "The Formation and Maintenance of Korean Small Business in the Chicago Minority Area," unpublished manuscript, Department of Sociology and Anthropology, Western Illinois University, 1984.

15. Kim, *The New Urban Immigrants*, pp. 281–304.

16. Werner Cahnman, "Socio-Economic Causes of Anti-Semitism," *Social Problems* 5 (1957):27.

17. Light, *Ethnic Enterprise in America*; John Modell, *The Economics and Politics of Racial Accommodation* (Urbana, Ill.: University of Illinois Press, 1977).

18. This interpretation leans on the material presented by Stanford Lyman; see his *Chinese-Americans* (New York: Random House, 1974) and *Asians in North America* (Santa Barbara: ABC–Clio Press, 1977). In addition, it should be pointed out that elite dominance was related to the migration process itself. Emigration from China was organized by wealthy kinsmen or fellow villagers who lent funds for transportation; control over the indebted emigrants facilitated their organization into elite-dominated economic organizations.

In work written subsequent to *Ethnic Enterprise in America*, Light has himself given greater emphasis to social control factors. For example, in a 1975 article, coauthored with Charles C. Wong, Light noted that "the dependence of Chinatowns upon the tourist industry has exerted a strong brake on abrupt change. The conservative force is economic rather than cultural in origin. [Dependence on the tourist industry is the] industrial foundation for the self-sufficiency and hard work which have, in the past, been too glibly attributed to the cultural endowment of Chinese-Americans." ("Protest or Work: Dilemmas of the Tourist Industry in American Chinatowns," *American Journal of Sociology* 80 [1975]:1345.)

19. On competition among the Koreans, Philip K. Y. Young's "Family Labor, Sacrifice, and Competition: Korean Greengrocers in New York City," *Amerasia* 10 (1983):53–71, is particularly informative. Young reports that "the real source of competition for the individual store owner is not from supermarkets or grocery stores but from other Korean-owned produce stores located close by" (p. 67).

20. John Armstrong, "Mobilized and Proletarian Diasporas," *American Political Science Review* 70 (1976):396. See also Walter Zenner, "Middleman Minority Theories: A Critical Review," in Roy S. Bryce-Laporte, ed., *Sourcebook on the New Immigration* (New Brunswick, N.J.: Transaction Books, 1980).

21. Edna Bonacich, "A Theory of Middleman Minorities," *American Sociological Review* 38 (1973):583–94; Edna Bonacich, "Middleman Minorities and Advanced Capitalism," *Ethnic Groups* 2 (1980):211–20; Edna Bonacich and John Modell, *The Economic Basis of Ethnic Solidarity* (Berkeley: University of California Press, 1980).

22. Bonacich and Modell, *The Economic Basis*, pp. 61, 251.

23. Bonacich and Modell, ibid., p. 19.

24. For one attempt to account for changing host society responses, see Calvin Goldscheider and Alan Zuckerman, *The Transformation of the Jews* (Chicago: Chicago University Press, 1985), esp. chap. 9.

25. Goldscheider and Zuckerman, ibid., summarize a great deal of valuable material; see pp. 16–18, 46–47, 87–90, 95–98, 162–63. On the characteristics of the Russian-Jewish immigrants and their distinctiveness from the broader population from which they stemmed, see Thomas Kessner, *The Golden Door: Italian and Jewish Immigrant Mobility in New York City, 1880–1915* (New York: Oxford University Press, 1977).

26. Self-employment rates for immigrants are presented in Robert Higgs, "Participation of Blacks and Immigrants in the American Merchant Class, 1890–1910: Some Demographic Relations," *Explorations in Economic History* 13 (1976):162. On differences in return migration, see Kessner, *The Golden Door*, p. 30.

27. For Jews in the department store trade in Germany, see Salo Baron et al., *The Economic History of the Jews* (New York: Schocken, 1975), p. 237; Ezra Mendelson, *Class Struggle in the Pale* (Cambridge: Cambridge University Press, 1970) provides an excellent discussion of Jewish employment practices and patterns in Poland.

28. Although this interpretation is drawn from the material presented by Modell (*Economics and Politics*, pp. 25–27, 94–112), the argument about the importance of market structure is barely hinted at and nowhere made explicit. Modell does comment that the rapid rise in land prices promoted small-scale farming. But he never brings out the implications of land speculation for investment patterns and entrepreneurial mobility paths. His discussion of the speculative nature of California agriculture as a whole suggests that the particular Japanese orientation toward farming was not qualitatively different, but simply a variation on a common theme (*Economics and Politics*, p. 106). Yet in *The Economic Basis*, Bonacich and Modell simply note that "some economic niches were available and the immigrants were able to take advantage of them" (p. 61). Although no causal weighting is given to any of the independent variables (context, culture, and antagonism), the five lines devoted to these "economic niches" suggest that market factors occupy little importance in the overall scheme. Indeed, in their concluding remarks, Bonacich and Modell review (and largely dismiss) the conventional contextual factors (p. 252) without once mentioning the opportunities inherent in the economic structure.

29. Data calculated from *The State of Small Business: A Report of the President* (Washington, D.C.: Government Printing Office, 1984), Table 1.30, pp. 65–66.

30. Ibid., p. 382.

31. Piore, *Birds of Passage*.

32. F. M. Scherer, *Industrial Market Structure and Economic Performance*, 2d ed. (Boston: Houghton Mifflin, 1980), pp. 86–150.

33. Arthur Stinchcombe, "Social Structure and the Invention of Organizational Forms," in Tom Burns, ed., *Industrial Man* (Penguin: Harmondsworth, England, 1969), pp. 161–63; Howard Aldrich, *Environments and Organizations* (Englewood Cliffs, N.J.: Prentice-Hall, 1979).

Chapter 2

1. For the original formulation of the special-consumer-tastes argument, see Robert Kinzer and Edward Sagarin, *The Negro in American Business: The Conflict between Separatism and Integration* (New York: Greenburg, 1950); for a recent, quantitative assessment of the effects of culturally based tastes on business opportunities for immigrants and minorities, see Howard Aldrich et al., "Ethnic Residential Concentration and the Protected Market Hypothesis," *Social Forces* 63, no. 4 (June 1985):996–1009.

2. Glenn Hendricks, *The Dominican Diaspora* (New York: Teachers College Press, 1974), pp. 123–24.

3. Ibid., p. 124.

4. Howard Aldrich, "Ecological Succession in Racially Changing Neighborhoods: A Review of the Literature," *Urban Affairs Quarterly* 10 (1975):327–48; Howard Aldrich and Albert Reiss, Jr., "Continuities in the Study of Ecological Succession: Changes in the Race Composition of Neighborhoods and their Businesses," *American Journal of Sociology* 81 (1976):846–66; Howard Aldrich, John Cater, Trevor Jones, and Dave McEvoy, "From Periphery to Peripheral: The South Asian Petite Bourgeoisie in England," in I. H. Simpson and R. Simpson, eds., *Research in the Sociology of Work*, vol. 2 (Greenwich, Conn.: JAI Press, 1982).

5. Deborah Dash Moore, *At Home in America* (New York: Columbia University Press, 1981); Betty Liu Ebron, "Chinese-American Developers Poised to Smash Old Barriers," *Crain's New York Business*, September 9, 1985; Kirk Johnson, "Asians Galvanize Sales Activity in Flushing," *New York Times*, July 25, 1984, section 8, p. 1.

6. Theodore Saloutos, *The Greeks in the United States* (Cambridge: Harvard University Press, 1964).

7. Carmenza Gallo, "The Construction Industry in New York: Black and Immigrant Entrepreneurs," working paper, Conservation of Human Resources, Columbia University, 1983.

8. Marcia Freedman and Josef Korazim, "Self-Employment and the Decision to Emigrate: Israelis in New York City," *Contemporary Jewry*, vol. 7 (forthcoming); Raymond Russell, "Ethnic and Occupational Cultures in the New Taxi Cooperatives of Los Angeles," paper presented at the 77th Annual Meeting of the American Sociological Association, San Francisco, September 8–10, 1982.

9. Gorman Gilbert, "Operating Costs for Medallion Taxicabs in New York City," report prepared for the Mayor's Committee on Taxicab Regulatory Issues, New York City, October 1981; Edward G. Rogoff, "Regulation of the New York City Taxicab Industry," *City Almanac* vol. 15 (1980):1–9, 17–19.

10. E. A. G. Robinson, *The Structure of Competitive Industry* (Cambridge: Cambridge University Press, 1931); William Shepherd, *The Economics of Industrial Organization* (Englewood Cliffs, N.J.: Prentice-Hall, 1979).

11. Michael Piore, "The Technological Foundations of Dualism and Discontinuity," in Suzanne Berger and Michael Piore, *Dualism and Discontinuity in Industrial Society* (Cambridge: Cambridge University Press, 1980).

12. Gallo, "The Construction Industry."

13. This analysis is based on a case study of the grocery store industry prepared as part of a report on youth employment for the New York City Office of Economic Development (Thomas Bailey and Roger Waldinger, "Youth and Jobs in Post-Industrial New York" [New York, 1984]). For a similar analysis of the effects of population heterogeneity on market size and large-firm shares in the grocery store industry, see Paul Cournoyer, "The New England

Retail Grocery Industry," working paper 1121–80, Sloan School of Management, MIT, Cambridge, Mass., 1980.

14. Quoted in Russell, *Sharing Ownership in the Workplace*, p. 126.

15. Gallo, "The Construction Industry"; Bailey, "Labor Market Competition."

16. Data on establishment size and capital investment are calculated from the 1977 Census of Manufactures.

17. Data on specialization ratios are drawn from the 1982 Census of Manufactures.

18. For a similar argument based on research conducted in the U.K., see Aldrich, Cater, Jones, and McEvoy, "From Periphery to Peripheral." This work has been very helpful in my own thinking on the process and implications of ethnic succession. Aldrich et al., however, were principally concerned with the effects of residential succession on business opportunities for immigrant shopkeepers; they concluded that as neighborhoods shifted from white to Asian, the proportion of white storekeepers declined and the proportion of Asian storekeepers increased.

19. Data calculated from U.S. Department of Commerce, Bureau of the Census, *1970 Census of Population: National Origin and Language* (Washington, D.C.: Government Printing Office, 1973), PC(2)–1A, Table 16.

20. For the historical background, see Kessner, *The Golden Door*, and Moses Rischin, *The Promised City* (Cambridge: Harvard University Press, 1962); on the persistence of corporate discrimination against Jews, see the studies summarized in Nathan Glazer and Daniel Moynihan, *Beyond the Melting Pot*, 2d ed. (Cambridge: MIT Press, 1969), pp. 147–49.

21. Steven M. Cohen, *American Modernity and Jewish Identity* (New York: Tavistock, 1983), p. 21.

22. Ibid., pp. 86–87.

23. Data calculated by me from the 1981 New York Area Jewish Population Survey. I am grateful to my colleague, Paul Ritterband, for making the survey available to me.

24. Calvin Goldscheider and Frances Kobrin, "Ethnic Continuity and the Process of Self-Employment," *Ethnicity* 7 (1980):262.

25. Chemical Bank, *Small Business Speaks: The Chemical Bank Report* (New York: Chemical Bank, 1983), pp. 23–24, 38–39, 78–79.

26. New York Interface Development Project, "Proposal for a Pilot Employee Ownership Project," unpublished manuscript, 1982, p. 2; the citation summarizes the information reported in studies of five New York City industries (electric and electronic equipment, fabricated metals, plastics, machine trades, and banking) and six industrial neighborhoods (Jamaica, Woodside, Staten Island, Greenpoint/Williamsburg, East Williamsburgh/North Bushwick, Sunset Park, Long Island City) all conducted by the Interface organization for the city of New York.

27. David Birch, "Who Creates Jobs?" *The Public Interest* 65 (1981):7; Catherine Armington and Marjorie Odle, "Small Business—How Many Jobs?" *The Brookings Review* 1 (Winter 1982):17.

28. Kim, *The New Urban Immigrants*, p. 111.

29. New York City, City Planning Commission, *City Assistance for Small Manufacturers*, report prepared by the City Planning Commission, 1982; Young, "Family, Labor, Sacrifice, and Competition," p. 70.

30. Roger Waldinger, "The Occupational and Economic Integration of the New Immigrants," *Law and Contemporary Problems* 45 (1982):197–222.

31. Bailey, "Labor Market Competition."

32. C. Wright Mills, *White Collar: The American Middle Classes* (New York: Oxford, 1958).

33. Ellen Auster and Howard Aldrich, "Small Business Vulnerability, Ethnic Enclaves and Ethnic Enterprise," in Ward and Jenkins, *Ethnic Communities*, p. 44.

34. Barry Chiswick, "Immigrants and Immigration Policy," in William Fellner, ed., *Contemporary Economic Problems* (Washington, D.C.: American Enterprise Institute, 1978).

35. Piore, *Birds of Passage*.

36. This point is made by Gerald Mars and Robin Ward, "Ethnic Business Development in Britain: Opportunities and Resources," in Ward and Jenkins, *Ethnic Communities*, pp. 17–18.

37. See, for example, J. S. MacDonald and L. D. MacDonald, "Chain Migration, Ethnic Neighborhood Formation, and Social Networks," in Charles Tilly, ed., *An Urban World* (Boston: Little, Brown, 1974), and Charles Tilly and Harold Brown, "On Uprooting, Kinship, and the Auspices of Migration," in Tilly, *An Urban World*.

38. Orme W. Phelps, "A Structural Model of the U.S. Labor Market," *Industrial and Labor Relations Review* 10 (1957):406.

39. In addition to Phelps, see Peter Doeringer and Michael Piore, *Internal Labor Markets and Manpower Analysis*, (Lexington, Mass.: Heath, 1971).

40. Michael Piore, "An Economic Approach," in Piore and Berger, *Dualism and Discontinuity*, p. 18.

41. Thomas Bailey, "A Case Study of Immigrants in the Restaurant Industry," *Industrial Relations* 24, no. 2 (1985):205–21.

42. A. Michael Spence, *Market Signalling* (Cambridge: Harvard University Press, 1974), pp. 2–3.

43. Doeringer and Piore, *Internal Labor Markets*; Richard Lester, *Hiring Practices and Labor Competition*, Industrial Relations Section, Princeton University, Research Report 88, 1954.

44. Thomas Bailey and Roger Waldinger, "Youth and Jobs in Post-Industrial New York," p. 55; also Roger Waldinger and Thomas Bailey, "The Youth Employment Problem in the World City," *Social Policy* (1985), pp. 55–8.

45. Elliot Liebow, *Tally's Corner* (Boston: Little, Brown, 1967); see also Michael Piore, "On-the-Job Training in a Dual Labor Market," in Arnold R. Weber, et al., eds., *Public-Private Manpower Policies* (Madison, Wis.: Industrial Relations Research Association, 1969).

46. Kim, *The New Urban Immigrants*, p. 112.

47. Hendricks, *Dominican Diaspora*, p. 31; Bernard Wong, *A Chinese-American Community* (Singapore: Chopmen, 1979).

48. Bailey, "Immigrants in the Restaurant Industry."

49. Doeringer and Piore, *Internal Labor Markets*; Richard C. Edwards, *Contested Terrain* (New York: Basic Books, 1979).

50. See Geoffrey K. Ingham, *Size of Industrial Organization and Worker Behavior* (Cambridge: Cambridge University Press, 1970), and references cited therein.

51. Doeringer and Piore, *Internal Labor Markets*, pp. 17–27; William F. Whyte et al., *Money and Motivation* (New York: Harper, 1955).

52. Gerald Suttles, *The Social Order of the Slum* (Chicago: Chicago University Press, 1968); Thomas Kochman, *Black and White Styles in Conflict* (Chicago: Chicago University Press, 1983).

53. Wong, *A Chinese-American Community*, p. 103.

54. Harry Herman, "Dishwashers and Proprietors: Macedonians in Toronto's Restaurant Trade," in Sandra Wallman, ed., *Ethnicity at Work* (London: Macmillan, 1979).

55. Data on characteristics of Greeks, Koreans, and Chinese calculated from, U.S. Bureau of the Census, 1980 Census of Population, I, Part D, Table 255.

56. Cf. Kessner, *The Golden Door*; Goldscheider and Zuckerman, *The Transformation of the Jews*.

57. Interview with Gary Kugler, Associated Fur Merchants of New York, February 1983. For an analysis of the fur industry and its labor requirements, see Roger Waldinger and Thomas Bailey, "Displacement Pressures on Manhattan Manufacturing Industries and Job Retention Strategies," Report No. 2, prepared for the New York City Office of Economic Development, 1983.
58. Piore, *Birds of Passage*, pp. 57–68.
59. Ibid., Chapter 3, esp. pp. 55–68.
60. Young, "Family Labor," pp. 64–65.
61. Bonacich, "A Theory of Middleman Minorities"; Bonacich and Modell, *The Economic Basis*.
62. Robin Ward, "Minority Settlement and the Local Community," in Bryan Roberts, Ruth Finnegan, and Duncan Gallie, eds., *New Approaches to Economic Life* (Manchester: Manchester University Press, 1985), pp. 189–209.
63. Kessner, *The Golden Door*, p. 167.
64. Employment rates for West Indians calculated from the Public Use Microdata sample of the 1980 Census of Population.
65. Bailey, "Immigrants in the Restaurant Industry."

Chapter 3

1. The data in this paragraph come from Leo Wolman, "Garment Industries," *Encyclopedia of the Social Sciences*, 1st ed. (New York: Macmillan, 1930–33), p. 577. The following section is indebted to a number of studies, mainly historical, that have traced the development of New York's needle trades. Mabel Willet, *The Employment of Women in the Clothing Trade* (New York: Columbia University Press, 1902), and Jesse E. Pope, *The Clothing Industry of New York* (Columbia, Mo.: University of Missouri, 1905), are the early works; though still worth consulting, their focus is primarily on the then larger men's clothing industry. Two government studies, U.S. Senate, *Report on Conditions of Women and Child Wage-Earners in the United States*, vol. 2: *Men's Ready-Made Clothing* (Washington, D.C.: Government Printing Office, 1911), and U.S. Immigration Commission, *Immigrants in Industries*, vol. 11, 6: "Clothing Manufacturing" (Washington, D.C.: Government Printing Office, 1911), are also valuable. Louis Lorwin, *The Women's Garment Workers' Union* (New York: Huebsch, 1924), while still the authoritative history of the International Ladies' Garment Workers' Union, is a compendium of information about the development of the women's apparel industry. In the 1920s and then again in the 1950s, the Regional Plan Association sponsored two large-scale studies of the New York economy, both of which produced additional contributions to the literature on the clothing industry: Benjamin Selekman et al., *The Clothing and Textile Industries in New York and Its Environs* (New York: Regional Plan Association, 1925); Roy Helfgott, "Women's and Children's Apparel," in Max Hall, ed., *Made in New York* (Cambridge: Harvard University Press, 1959). Helfgott's study, though obviously dated, proved an invaluable reference tool in the writing of this chapter and the next. I have given more extended treatment to the early history of the New York garment industry, with implications for trade unionism, in "Another Look at the International Ladies' Garment Workers' Union: Women, Industry Structure, and Collective Action," in Ruth Milkman, ed., *Women, Work and Protest* (London: Routledge and Kegan Paul, 1985), pp. 86–110; this article contains additional references to the historical literature.
2. Data on Jewish and Italian migration to New York are from Kessner, *The Golden Door*, pp. 14–20.
3. Waldinger, "Another Look," pp. 89–94.

4. In addition to the sources cited in note 1, above, see also Moses Rischin, *The Promised City: New York's Jews, 1880–1914* (Cambridge: Harvard University Press, 1962), pp. 61–75, 180, 182–83; and Irving Howe, *World of Our Fathers* (New York: Harcourt Brace Jovanovich, 1976), pp. 77–84, 154–59.

5. Rischin, *The Promised City*, p. 63.

6. Edward Ewing Pratt, *Industrial Causes of Congestion in New York City* (New York: Columbia University Press, 1911).

7. On Jews and Italians before World War I, see Kessner, *The Golden Door*; the statistics on the employment characteristics of second-generation Jews in 1925 are from Thomas Kessner, "New Yorkers in Prosperity and Depression: A Preliminary Reconnaissance," in Diane Ravitch and Ronald K. Goodenow, *Educating an Urban People* (New York: Teachers College Press, 1981), pp. 94–100. Deborah Dash Moore, *At Home in America*, (New York: Columbia University Press, 1980).

8. On the demand-side changes of the 1920s, see Waldinger, "Another Look," pp. 101–3, and the literature cited therein.

9. Robert Lynd and Helen Merrill Lynd, *Middletown: A Study in Modern American Culture* (New York: Harcourt, Brace and World, 1956), pp. 159–67.

10. "Cloak and Suit," *Fortune* 1, no. 5 (June 1930), pp. 98–99.

11. Data for employment in 1909 and 1919 are from the Census of Manufactures; the figure for 1939 is from Helfgott, "Women's and Children's Apparel," p. 68.

12. See tables on operating ratios in the Census of Manufactures reports on the various clothing industries.

13. On the ILGWU's organizing activities of the 1930s, see Irving Bernstein, *The Turbulent Years* (Boston: Houghton Mifflin, 1969), pp. 84–85; Joel Seidman, *The Needle Trades* (New York: Farrar and Rinehart, 1942); Benjamin Stolberg, *Tailor's Progress* (New York: Doubleday, 1944).

14. Helfgott, "Women's and Children's Apparel," pp. 83–89.

15. U.S. Bureau of Labor Statistics, *Earnings and Employment for States and Areas, 1938–1980*, Bulletin 1370–15, 1981.

16. "Apparel's Last Stand," *Business Week*, May 14, 1979, p. 61.

17. This section draws on John Brooks's article on Levi Strauss, "A Friendly Product," *New Yorker*, November 12, 1979, pp. 58–94. The 1983 data are from Moody's Industrials.

18. Lisa Anderson, "Leslie Fay: A Tough Company in a Tough Market," *Women's Wear Daily*, July 12, 1977, p. 6.

19. "The Garment Trade Learns Sophisticated Selling," *Business Week*, September 22, 1973, p. 66.

20. Stanley Ginsburg, "Farewell to the Ice–Cream Suit (Palm Beach)," *Forbes*, October 13, 1980, pp. 205–6.

21. Louis Kraar, "Palm Beach Inc.'s Lucrative Labels," *Fortune*, January 15, 1979, pp. 104–7.

22. Sandra Salmans, "Jonathan Logan Comes Back," *New York Times*, March 26, 1982.

23. See Helfgott, "Women's and Children's Apparel," pp. 42–46.

24. This transformation is analyzed in Barry Bluestone et al., *The Retail Revolution* (Cambridge, Mass.: Auburn House, 1981). Establishment data are from the 1977 Census of Retail Trade.

25. "Leslie Fay Unit Taking Aim at Volume Market," *Women's Wear Daily*, December 10, 1975, p. 1.

26. Bluestone et al., *The Retail Revolution*, pp. 115–16.

27. OECD, *Textile and Clothing Industries: Structural Problems and Policies in OECD Countries* (Paris: OECD, 1983).

28. Kurt Salmon Associates, *Marketing Strategies for U.S. Apparel Producers to Compete More Effectively with Imports* (Atlanta: Georgia Institute of Technology, 1980), p. 53.
29. For an analysis of the relationship between product characteristics, firm size, and the location of industrial activity, with particular reference to New York, see Robert J. Lichtenberg, *One-tenth of a Nation* (Cambridge, Mass.: Harvard University Press, 1960). Generalizing from the findings of the New York Metropolitan Regional Study, of which he was director, Raymond Vernon developed the notion of the "product cycle" and applied it to changing patterns of international trade in "International Investment and International Trade in the Product Cycle," *Quarterly Journal of Economics*, 80, no. 2 (1966):190–208. For a recent review of the literature on the causes of industrial concentration and dispersion, see Allen J. Scott, "Locational Patterns and Dynamics of Industrial Activity in the Modern Metropolis," *Urban Studies* 19, no. 12 (1982):111–42.
30. This point is noted by Lichtenberg, *One-Tenth of a Nation*.
31. On the ILGWU's organizing efforts, see Harry Crone's interesting official history, *Thirty Northeast: A Short History of the Northeast Department* (New York: International Ladies' Garment Workers' Union, 1970). Wage data for the 1950s are from Helfgott, "Women's and Children's Apparel," p. 85; data for 1982 are calculated from Bureau of Labor Statistics, *Employment and Earnings for States and Areas, 1938–1982*, Bulletin 1370–17.
32. Data from tables kindly supplied me by the ILGWU Research Department.
33. U.S. Department of Commerce, *Major Shippers of Man-Made Fibers, Textiles, and Cotton*, 1984.
34. See OECD, *Textile and Clothing Industries*, and National Research Council, *The Competitive Status of the U.S. Fibers, Textiles, and Apparel Complex* (Washington, D.C.: National Academy Press, 1983).
35. Cited in G. P. F. Steed, "International Location and Comparative Advantage: The Clothing Industries and Developing Countries," pp. 265–303 in F. E. I. Hamilton and G. J. R. Linge, eds., *Spatial Analysis and the Industrial Environment, Volume II: International Industrial Systems* (London: Wiley, 1981), p. 279.
36. Barry Bluestone and Bennett Harrison, *The Deindustrialization of America* (New York: Basic Books, 1982), p. 115.
37. National Research Council, *Competitive Status*; Steed, "International Location"; G. P. F. Steed "Global Industrial Systems—A Case Study of the Clothing Industry," *Geoforum* 9, (1978) pp. 35–47.
38. Steed, "Global Industrial Systems," p. 44.
39. Z. A. Silberston, *The Multi-Fibre Arrangement and the UK Economy* (London: HMSO, 1984), p. 12.
40. Steed, "International Location"; Stewart F. Richards, "Industrial Activity in the Periphery: Hong Kong," in Hamilton and Linge, *Spatial Analysis*; Angus Hone, "Multinational Corporations and Their Multinational Buying Groups: Their Impact on the Growth of Asia's Exports of Manufactures—Myths and Realities," *World Development* 2, no. 2 (1974): 145–49; Keith Hopkins, ed., *Hong Kong: The Industrial Colony* (Hong Kong: Oxford University Press, 1971); David Lethbridge, ed., *The Business Environment in Hong Kong*, 2d ed. (Hong Kong: Oxford University Press, 1984); Theodore Geiger and Frances Geiger, *Tales of Two City-States: The Development and Progress of Hong Kong and Singapore* (Washington, D.C.: National Planning Association, 1973).
41. Geiger and Geiger, *Tales of Two City-States*, p. 73.
42. Steed, "International Location," pp. 301–2; National Research Council, *The Competitive Status*, p. 63.

43. David Morawetz, *Why the Emperor's Clothes Are Not Made in Colombia*, World Bank working paper, no. 368, January 1980, p. 102.

44. Related party data are from Joseph Grunwald and Kenneth Flamm, *The Global Factory: Foreign Assembly in International Trade* (Washington, D.C.: Brookings Institution, 1985), pp. 22–23. Whereas related party imports accounted for 62.6 percent of the textile products (mainly clothing) imported from Mexico in 1979, the share of related party imports in total textile product imports from Hong Kong, Taiwan, and South Korea was 2.7 percent, 1.3 percent, and 7.6 percent, respectively. Data on patterns of foreign investment in Hong Kong underscore the relative unimportance of direct foreign investment in the export-oriented clothing sector: in 1981 foreign-owned plants accounted for only 5.0 percent of employment in Hong Kong's textile and garment industries (C. L. Hung, "Foreign Investments," in Lethbridge, *The Business Environment in Hong Kong*, p. 194).

45. Grunwald and Flamm, *The Global Factory*; Sol C. Chaikin, "The Needed Repeal of Item 807.00 of the Tariff Schedules of the United States," testimony presented to the Subcommittee on Trade, Committee on Ways and Means, U.S. House of Representatives, March 25, 1976; Michael Sharpston, "International Subcontracting," *Oxford Economic Papers* 21, no. 1 (1975):94–136.

46. Data from tables were kindly supplied to me by the International Ladies' Garment Workers' Union, Research Department.

47. Grunwald and Flamm, *The Global Factory*, p. 18.

48. Ibid., pp. 137–180; Maria Patricia Fernandez-Kelly, *For We Are Sold, I and My People: Women and Industry on Mexico's Frontier* (Albany, N.Y.: SUNY Press, 1983); North American Congress on Latin America, "Hit and Run: U.S. Runaway Shops on the Mexican Border," *NACLA's Latin America and Empire Report*, vol. 9, no. 5 (August 1975).

49. Grunwald and Flamm, *The Global Factory*, p. 166.

50. Fernandez-Kelly, *For We Are Sold*, pp. 34, 104.

51. Grunwald and Flamm, *The Global Factory*, pp. 180–206.

52. James Summerour, "The Island Option," *Apparel Industry Magazine*, January 1985.

53. Manuel Gaetan, "Sourcing in the Caribbean Basin," and Mary Scannapieco, "Sourcing Competitively," *Bobbin*, February 1985; Standard and Poor's *Industry Surveys*, "Textiles, Apparel, and Home Furnishings" (1984), p. T85.

54. Steed, "International Location" and "Global Industrial Systems"; Silberston, "The Multi-Fibre Arrangement"; Geoffrey Edwards, "Four Sectors: Textiles, Man-Made Fibers, Shipbuilding, Aircraft," pp. 85–122 in John Pinder, ed., *National Industrial Strategies and the World Economy* (Totowa, N.J.: Allenheld, Osmun, 1982); Vinok K. Aggarwal with Stephen Haggard, "The Politics of Protectionism in the U.S. Textile and Apparel Industries," in John Zysman and Laura Tyson, eds., *American Industry in International Competition: Government Policies and Corporate Strategies* (Ithaca, N.Y.: Cornell University Press, 1983), pp. 249–312.

55. "Commerce Department Imposes Monthly Limits to Restrict Sudden Surges," *New York Times*, December 26, 1984, p. D7.

56. The text of the proposed "Textile and Apparel Trade Enforcement Act of 1985" appears in the *Congressional Record* 131, no. 31 (March 19, 1985), pp. 3079–82; testimony in favor of the bill, by ILGWU President Sol C. Chaikin, offers the industry's point of view (Testimony before the Subcommittee on International Trade, Committee on Finance, U.S. Senate, July 15, 1985).

57. Steed, "International Location"; Chaikin testimony, 1985.

58. "Apparel Import Curbs Force Retailers in U.S. to Shift Their Tactics," *Wall Street Journal*, August 8, 1984, p. 1.

59. "Conditions in the Women's Garment Industry," Research Department, International Ladies' Garment Workers' Union, June 24, 1985, p. 9.

60. Calculated from U.S. Census of Manufactures, 1963 and 1977.

61. Data on capital investment from 1982 *Census of Manufactures Industry Series*, Table 1a, Historical Statistics for the Industry, 1982 and earlier years, reports for relevant apparel industries. Dollars adjusted according to the Commerce Department's Producer Price Index. On the lack of progress toward automation, see American Apparel Manufacturers Association, *Using the Computer in Apparel Manufacturing*, Report of the Technical Advisory Committee (Arlington, Va.: American Apparel Manufacturers Association, 1980.)

62. "Levi Strauss Legs it Towards Automation," *Business Week*, July 21, 1971; "Apparel's Last Stand," *Business Week*, May 14, 1979; "Cutting Room Equipment," *Bobbin*, January, 1980; "Cutting Costs in the Cutting Room," *Bobbin*, January, 1980; U.S. Bureau of Labor Statistics, *Technological Change and Its Labor Impact in Five Industries*, Bulletin No. 1969 (Washington, D.C.: G.P.O., 1977) pp. 1–5.

63. OECD, *Textile and Clothing Industries*, p. 22; Joseph Gerber, "Apparel Manufacturing Looks to Technology in the 1990's," *Knitting Times Yearbook* (1982).

64. OCED, *Textile and Clothing Industries;* "Microprocessors Called Key to Future," *Women's Wear Daily*, July 23, 1982.

65. "Apparel's Last Stand," *Business Week*, May 14, 1979; *Moody's Industrial Manual*.

66. Roger W. Schmenner, *Making Business Location Decisions* (Englewood Cliffs, Prentice-Hall, 1982), p. 121.

67. Glenn McLaughlin and Stefan Robock, *Why Industry Moves South*, National Planning Association, Committee of the South, Report No. 3, 1949, pp. 71–73.

68. Schmenner, *Making Business Location Decisions*, p. 123.

69. Ibid., p. 157.

70. Unionization rates from U.S. Bureau of Labor Statistics, *Handbook of Labor Statistics*, Bulletin of Labor Statistics, Bulletin 2070, 1980; data on garment industry employment from, U.S. Bureau of Labor Statistics, *Earnings and Employment for States and Areas, 1938–1980*.

71. *ILGWU* membership censuses, 1973, 1982.

72. "Kellwood Little Rock Plant, Another Import Victim," *Justice* (March 1984). I am grateful to Cyd Weldon of the ILGWU for digging through the *Justice* file on Kellwood and finding this citation and other relevant material.

73. On the problems of organizing southern garment workers, see "Capital's Flight: The Apparel Industry Moves South," *NACLA's Latin American and Empire Report*, V. 9, no. 3 (March 1977).

Chapter 4

1. Standard and Poor's *Industry Surveys*, 1981, p. A108.

2. Kraar, "Palm Beach Inc.'s Lucrative Labels," p. 106.

3. "It's Back to the Kitchen for General Mills," *Business Week*, February 11, 1985; Bill Saporito, "When Business Got So Good It Got Dangerous," *Fortune*, April 2, 1984.

4. "Warnaco: Returning to Profits After Cutting Back," *Business Week*, August 28, 1978; "Warnaco: To Dream the Impossible Dream," *Clothes*, January 15, 1977; "Warnaco: Prospering by Slimming and Donning Big-Name Labels," *Business Week*, June 18, 1982.

5. "The Garment Trade Learns Sophisticated Selling," *Business Week*, September, 1973.

6. Sandra Salmans, "Jonathan Logan's Comeback" *New York Times*, March 20, 1982; "Butte

Knits Pins Future on Fall II," *Women's Wear Daily*, January 22, 1981; "Jonathan Logan to Close 3 Plants, Sees 3rd Period Loss," *Wall Street Journal*, September 10, 1981.

7. "Warnaco," *Business Week*, 1978.

8. Susan Alai, "How Brooks Found Itself in Rough Water," *Women's Wear Daily*, January 20, 1982.

9. Thomas Peters and Robert Waterman, Jr., *In Search of Excellence* (New York: Harper and Row, 1982).

10. Levi Strauss chairman quoted in *Wall Street Journal*, January 31, 1985, p. 4; for further discussion of Levi's problems, see *Business Week*, "Levi Strauss: A Touch of Fashion — and a Dash of Humility," October 24, 1983; "A Kick in the Pants for Levi's," *Business Week*, June 11, 1984.

11. John Quirt, "Levi Strauss Is Stretching Its Wardrobe," *Fortune*, November 10, 1979, p. 87.

12. Peter Vanderwicken, "When Levi Strauss Burst Its Britches," *Fortune*, April 1974.

13. Quirt, "Levi Strauss Is Stretching Its Wardrobe," p. 89.

14. "It's Back to Basics for Levi's," *Business Week*, March 8, 1982; "Levi's Pins Hopes on Two Chains' Deals," *Women's Wear Daily*, April 8, 1982.

15. *Wall Street Journal*, January 31, 1985.

16. "Apparel Import Curbs," *Wall Street Journal*, August 8, 1984.

17. Isadore Barmash, "Depression Takes Hold on 7th Avenue," *New York Times*, February 9, 1974; "Women's Apparel: Cautious for Fall," *Business Week*, June 6, 1976; Deborah Yaeger and Stanley Slom, "Apparel Retailers, Bruised by Sales-Slump This Summer, Order Cautiously for Fall," *Wall Street Journal*, August 12, 1976; Deborah Yeager, "Apparel Makers Face Consolidation as Stores Stiffen Delivery Terms," *Wall Street Journal*, February 2, 1978.

18. Ann M. Morrison, "The Upshot of Off-Price," *Fortune*, June 13, 1983, p. 124.

19. For further consideration of the concept of external economies and its application to the garment industry, the research produced by the New York Metropolitan Region Study is still worth consulting. See Helfgott, "Women's and Children's Apparel"; Lichtenberg, *One-Tenth of a Nation;* Edgar Hoover and Raymond Vernon, *Anatomy of a Metropolis* (New York: Doubleday, 1959). Allen Scott, "Locational Patterns and Dynamics of Industrial Activity," offers a valuable review and updating.

20. Jay Cohen "What's Wrong with American Contractors," *Bobbin*, April 1983, p. 84.

21. Elsa Chaney, "Columbian Migration to the United States" Washington D.C.: Interdisciplinary Communications Program, *Occasional Papers*, Nancie Gonzalez, "Peasants' Progress: Dominicans in New York," *Carribean Studies*, vol. 10 (1970); Hendricks, *Dominican Diaspora*, p. 76.

22. Stuart Catell, *Health, Welfare and Social Organization in Chinatown*, (New York City, Community Service Society of New York, 1962); Chinatown Study Group, *Chinatown Report: 1969* (New York: Columbia University East Asian Studies Center), p. 52.

23. Piore, *Birds of Passage*, pp. 35–43.

24. Benjamin Selekman, *The Clothing and Textile Industries of New York*, pp. 24–25, 58–60.

25. Irving Howe, *A Margin of Hope* (San Diego: Harcourt Brace Jovanovich, 1982).

26. Herbert Northrup, *Organized Labor and the Negro* (New York: Harper and Bros., 1944), p. 121.

27. Irving R. Stuart, "A Study of Factors Associated with Intergroup Conflict in the Ladies' Garment Industry in New York City" (Ph.D. dis., New York University, 1951), p. 133.

28. Roy B. Helfgott, "Puerto Rican Integration in the Skirt Industry in New York City," in Aaron Antonovsky and Louis Levine, eds., *Discrimination and Low Incomes*, New York State Interdepartmental Committee on Low Incomes (Albany, N.Y., 1959), p. 254.

29. Martin Segal, *Wages in the Metropolis* (Cambridge: Harvard University Press, 1960).
30. Richard Leone, *The Location of Manufacturing Activity in the New York Metropolitan Area* (New York: National Bureau of Economic Research, 1975).
31. Herbert Koshetz, "A Major Labor Shortage Squeezing New York Garment Center," *New York Times*, August 10, 1969.
32. Elaine G. Wrong, *The Negro in the Apparel Industry* (Philadelphia: Industrial Research Unit, Wharton School, 1974).
33. Miriam Ostow and Charles Brecher, "Work and Welfare," in Eli Ginzberg, ed., *New York Is Alive and Well* (New York: McGraw-Hill, 1973); Elizabeth Durbin, "The Vicious Circle of Welfare: Problems of the Female-Headed Household in New York City," in Cynthia B. Lloyd, ed., *Sex, Discrimination and the Division of Labor* (New York: Columbia University Press, 1975).
34. Wrong, *The Negro in the Apparel Industry*, p. 63.
35. Ibid., pp. 97–100.
36. Hendricks, *Dominican Diaspora*, pp. 75–76.
37. Ibid., p. 75.
38. Loraine Dixon and Miles Storper, *Trends in the Characteristics of AFDC Families in New York City: 1969–1979* (New York: City of New York, Human Resources Administration, 1981), pp. 17–18; A.J. Jaffe et al., *The Changing Demography of Spanish Americans* (New York: Academic Press, 1980), pp. 236–238; Emmanuel Tobier, "Foreign Immigration," in Charles Brecher and Raymond Horton, eds., *Setting Municipal Priorities* (New York: Russell Sage Foundation, 1982), p. 175.
39. "Apparel Labor Markets Shrinking, Shifting, *Southern Garment Manufacturer*, May 2, 1974; William D. Toal, "The Southeast's Cutting Up and Needle Trades," *Monthly Review*, V. 58, no. 12, Federal Reserve Bank of Atlanta, 1973.
40. "Apparel's Next Problem: Poor Worker Attitudes," *Industry Week*, June 26, 1978, p. 102; "Hire Workers Who Won't Quit," *Bobbin*, December 1979; "The Bleeding Ulcer-Turnover," *Bobbin*, November 1979; "Levi Strauss: Concerned About People," *Bobbin*, October 1979.
41. American Apparel Manufacturers Association, *Using the Computer in Apparel Manufacturing*, Report of the Technical Advisory Committee (Arlington, Va.: American Apparel Manufacturers Association, 1980).

Chapter 5

1. Rischin, *The Promised City*, pp. 67, 245.
2. Glazer and Moynihan, *Beyond the Melting Pot*, p. 150.
3. Chester Rapkin, *The South Houston Industrial Area: A Study of the Economic Significance of Firms, the Physical Quality of Buildings and the Real Estate Market in an Old Loft Section of Lower Manhattan*, prepared for the City of New York, City Planning Commission–Department of City Planning, February 1963, pp. 47–62.
4. Sharon Zukin, *Loft Living* (Baltimore: Johns Hopkins University Press, 1982), p. 37.

Chapter 6

1. Light, *Ethnic Enterprise in America*; Lyman, *Asian-Americans*.
2. Hendricks, *Dominican Diaspora*, pp. 113–114.
3. Edward A. Gargan, "The New Chinatown: Community in Change," *New York Times*, December 28, 29, 1981.

4. Emmanuel Tobier, *The Industrial Space Market in Manhattan*, unpublished manuscript, New York University, Graduate School of Public Administration, 1980. See also Hoover and Vernon, *Anatomy of a Metropolis*, pp. 29–30.

5. Rapkin, *The South Houston Industrial Area*, pp. 245–56.

6. Stinchcombe, "Social Structure and the Invention of Organizational Forms," p. 162.

7. Gallo, "The Construction Industry," p. 26.

8. Pnina Werbner, "Business on Trust: Pakistani Entrepreneurship in the Manchester Garment Trade," in Ward and Jenkins, *Ethnic Communities in Business*, p. 169.

9. Light, *Ethnic Enterprise in America*; Bonacich and Modell, *The Economic Basis of Ethnic Solidarity*.

Chapter 7

1. Wong, *A Chinese-American Community*, p. 97.

2. Howard Newby, "Paternalism and Capitalism," in Richard Scase, ed., *Industrial Society: Class, Cleavage, and Control* (New York: St. Martin's, 1977), p. 69.

3. Lewis Coser, *Greedy Institutions* (New York: Free Press, 1974).

4. Victor Fung-Shuen Sit et al., *Small-Scale Industry in a Laissez-Faire Economy*, Centre of Asian Studies, University of Hong Kong, 1979; cited in Lisa Peattie, "Small Enterprises in the Development Process" unpublished manuscript, Department of Urban Studies and Planning, MIT, Cambridge, Mass., 1983. I am grateful to Lisa Peattie for suggesting the Hong Kong comparision and for bringing this material to my attention.

5. Jon Woronoff, *Hong Kong: Capitalist Paradise* (Hong Kong: Heinemann Asia, 1980), p.115.

6. Sit et al., *Small-Scale Industry*, pp. 354–55.

7. Ambrose Y. C. King and Peter J. L. Man, "The Role of the Small Factory in Economic Development," Unpublished manuscript, Social Research Centre, The Chinese University of Hong Kong, June 1974, p. 40. See also the discussion in Lethbridge and Sek-Hong, "The Business Environment and Employment," in Lethbridge, *The Business Environment in Hong Kong*, pp. 73–77.

8. Joe England, "Industrial Relations in Hong Kong," in Keith Hopkins, ed., *Hong Kong: The Industrial Economy* (Hong Kong: Oxford University Press, 1971), p. 224.

Chapter 8

1. Weber, *The Protestant Ethic and the Spirit of Capitalism*, p. 64.

2. Kessner, *The Golden Door*, pp. 171–2.

3. Mars and Ward, "Ethnic Business Development in Britain," in Ward and Jenkins, *Ethnic Communities in Business*, pp. 11–12.

4. Hendricks, *Dominican Diaspora*, p. 84.

5. "Country of Birth of Foreign Born Persons in the United States by Sex, Citizenship, and Year of Immigration, 1980," in U.S. Department of Commerce, *News*, October 17, 1984.

6. Hendricks, *Dominican Diaspora*, p. 87.

7. Patricia R. Pessar, "Kinship Relations of Production in the Migration Process: The Case of Dominican Emigration to the United States," Center for Latin American and Carribean Studies, New York University, Occasional Paper 32, (1982), p. 27.

8. Patricia R. Pessar, "The Role of Households in International Migration and the Case of the U.S.-Bound Migration from the Dominican Republic," *International Migration Review*, 16,

no. 2 (1982): 342–365; Sherri Grasmuck, "The Impact of Emigration on Development: Three Sending Communities in the Dominican Republic," Center for Latin American and Caribbean Studies, New York University, Occasional Paper 33, (1982).

9. Sherri Grasmuck, "Immigration, Ethnic Stratification and Native Working Class Discipline: Comparisons of Documented and Undocumented Dominicans," *International Migration Review* 18, no. 3 (1985), p. 709. On the tendency for undocumented Dominican immigrants to legalize their status over time, Glauco Perez's survey of 246 Dominican immigrants living in the Washington Heights area of Manhattan, conducted in 1978, is informative. Of these 246, 104 were "one-time" illegals. Perez found that the majority of these "one-time" illegals succeeded in regularizing their immigration status and furthermore that this objective was their number one priority. (Glauco Perez, "Dominican Illegals in New York: Preliminary Findings," paper presented at the Center for Inter-American Affairs, New York University, 1981.)

Chapter 9

1. For a discussion of the recent attempts to reform immigration policy, see the articles in Glazer, ed., *Clamor at the Gates*.

2. On the impact of these changes on the garment industry, see Roger Waldinger, *The Impact of the 42nd Street Redevelopment Project on the Garment Industry*, report prepared for the Federation of Apparel Manufacturers, 1984.

3. These trends are documented in Abeles, Schwartz, Haeckel, and Silverblatt, *The Chinatown Garment Industry* (New York, 1983), chap. 6.

4. Bobby Minter, "Chinatown Overtakes Seventh Avenue," *City Business*, 1985.

5. "The Trend for the Garment Factories Is to Increase Supervision," *Pei Mei Daily*, November 10, 1982; thanks to Muzaffar Chishti, research director of Local 23–25, for providing me with translations of this and other articles from the Chinatown press.

6. "Questions of Chinatown's Modernization," *Pei Mei Daily*, November 10, 1982.

Index

D1201632